# God Matters

'A must-read for Year 12 and 13 Philosophy of Religion students and their teachers, which will also be of great value for Undergraduate students . . .'

*Dr Paul Rout OFM, Lecturer in the Philosophy of Religion,*
*University of London*

'Once again Peter and Charlotte Vardy have done what so many teachers find so difficult - communicated complex philosophical and theological ideas with clarity, ease and a good deal of humour.'

*Catrina Young, Deputy Headmistress, The Dixie Grammar School*

'It certainly made me think and I recommend this book to those people that are seeking a better understanding of the mysteries of life.'

*Diana Parsk, Chairman of the Banstead 5 Churches and RE teacher at*
*St Bede's Ecumenical School, Redhill*

'Exactly what I was hoping to find for my students to encourage and stimulate learning in this intellectually rigorous and demanding subject.'

*Christien Bembridge, Head of Religious Studies and Philosophy,*
*St Peter's School, York*

'The Vardys are gifted communicators and many have benefited from their excellent conferences. Now they have transferred their high standard of scholarship into this book and, as ever, all ideas are presented with clarity and precision. In a sea of introductory books, this is a very welcome development . . . God Matters will prove to be the "go to" book for both the seasoned teacher and the enquiring young philosopher.'

*Tim Madeley, Assistant Vice Principal and Director of VI Form,*
*Carmel College, Darlington*

'This book is the embodiment of the authors; engaging and intellectually stimulating!'

*Gerard McNulty, Religious Education Coordinator,*
*Mount Carmel College, Hobart, Tasmania*

'A perfect springboard from which to launch an essential journey to contemplate truth.'

*Janet Thomson, Vice Principal & Head of RE,*
*Harvey Grammar School, Folkestone*

'*God Matters* is an excellent and thoroughly readable updated discussion of the arguments concerning the existence of God and the challenges to that belief. Abrahamic religious perspectives and relevant inputs from such authors as C. S. Lewis, Iris Murdoch and Dostoyevsky also enrich the debates. I would have really enjoyed reading such a work when I was an undergraduate and I'm sure it will be thoroughly appreciated by both sixth formers and undergraduate students of this subject area. Well done the Vardys once again!'

*Dr Vaughan Salisbury, Director of ITET Secondary Education,*
*University of Wales Trinity Saint David*

# God Matters

Peter and Charlotte Vardy

scm press

© Charlotte Vardy and Peter Vardy 2013

Published in 2013 by SCM Press
Editorial office
3rd Floor Invicta House
108–114 Golden Lane
London EC1Y 0TG

SCM Press is an imprint of Hymns Ancient & Modern Ltd
(a registered charity)
13A Hellesdon Park Road
Norwich NR6 5DR, UK

www.scmpress.co.uk

British Library Cataloguing in Publication data
A catalogue record for this book is available
from the British Library

978-0-334-04392-8

Typeset by Manila Typesetting
Printed and bound in Great Britain by
CPI Group (UK) Ltd, Croydon CR0 4YY

# Contents

# To Thora

*Doubt isn't the opposite of faith;
it is an element of faith.*

# Introduction

# Why Does God Matter?

Whether or not you believe in God, you must believe this: when we as a species abandon our trust in a power greater than us, we abandon our sense of accountability . . . Religion is flawed, but only because man is flawed.

(Dan Brown, *Angels and Demons*)

In 2004 Richard Dawkins proposed that 'religion is the root of all evil', following this up by sponsoring billboards on London buses advertising that 'there is probably no God, so wake up and enjoy life'. He caught the mood of the times. Between 2001 and 2011 a startling decline in religion took place. In the United Kingdom, the percentage of people claiming to be Christians fell from 72 to 59, while the numbers claiming no religion rose by 4 million.[1] When census data was released, there was another wave of calls for religion to be removed from school curricula and for its influence in other areas of public life to be reassessed.

For increasing numbers of people religion has become something sinister, and talk of God has become irrelevant, even obscene. Aeroplanes flying into tower blocks, mothers blowing themselves up on shopping streets, child abuse being systematically concealed – it is not difficult to understand why, for many people, religion has become identified with what is primitive, irrational, regressive and brutal in humanity, rather than with what is essentially good.

Growing awareness of the inadequacy of religion should make God matter more, not less. 'Religion' is not the same as God. Religion is a human-created phenomenon which seeks to express, capture and

---

1 http://www.bbc.co.uk/news/uk-20677321.

sometimes control the idea of God, but the reality of God is greater than any religion.

What is God if not what is supreme, perfect and beyond the limitation of human understanding – the origin of all things, Truth itself? Karl Rahner described God as 'Holy Mystery'; God is the ultimate Mystery that lies beneath all reality. No thinking person really thinks that God is humanlike, bearded and sitting on a cloud. God is the essence of reality, its alpha and omega, the cause of things being this way and not otherwise.

Jesus said 'I am the way, the truth and the life' (John 14.6). God can be another way of saying 'objective truth', contemplating God a way of reflecting on the implications of reality existing independently of how we human beings see things, realizing that humans are not the measure of all things and that beneath the changing world lies an unchanging, transcendent and perfect reality.

Religion may begin in our common understanding of the truth, it may support our common search for the truth, but it is not itself the truth. God is not a human being, nor are human beings God. God is Other, that than which nothing greater can be conceived, neither something nor nothing – outside and beyond normal categories and even language.

Religion at its true sense should stand against human arrogance and human ignorance, against relativism in all its forms and for divine truth. Just because of that, religion should rejoice in being a journey not a destination. As Nils Bohr is said to have remarked of quantum science, 'anyone who claims to have understood it has not!', the same could be said of the objects of religion, of truth and of God. By definition any person who proudly claims to possess the truth and to have understood God cannot have done so. Far from finding membership of a religion a secure place where one can delegate thinking to others, as Confucius taught, everyone 'should study as though there is not enough time and still feel fear of missing the point'.[2]

The word 'religion' derives from the Latin for 'to bind together'. Religious beliefs, traditions and practices are designed to hold

---

2  Analects 8.17.

communities and cultures together, to inspire, motivate and to control. Sadly, the value of the unity offered by religion often makes it seem more important than truth. The value of religion makes people more likely to defend unity, to stand up for 'us' against 'them', rather than to exert themselves for the truthful purpose of religion, which lies beyond itself in contemplating God.

As Coleridge reminds us, 'he who begins by loving Christianity better than Truth, will proceed by loving his own sect or Church better than Christianity, and will end by loving himself better than all . . .'[3] This wisdom applies equally to other faiths and goes some way to explain the route from religion to the evils of recent years. When evil is done in the name of God it is in truth rooted in pride, greed, envy or sloth, in self-love, the very essence of human vice and the manifest denial of truth. Also, as W. K. Clifford (1845–79) observed, 'there is only one thing in the world more wicked than the desire to command and that is the will to obey . . .'[4]

While putting religion first, ahead of love for truth, leads to evil, so too does bundling religion (along with any thought for God or objective truth) into the background. Silent resignation of thought and responsibility, passive acceptance of authority and tradition (calling it quaint or picturesque), polite refusals to discuss or engage with matters of truth and reality; all of these allow evil to take hold. Dismissing religion as if it were a comfort blanket, the crux of the needy soul or even a hedged bet has actually caused religion itself to foster extremism.

If fundamentalism is dangerous, leading to a dogmatic assertion of a single narrow view of truth and a rejection of all others, then 'liberalism' can lead to irrelevance and to seeing religion to be characterized as apathetic, marching under the questionable banner 'unity in diversity' while focusing on hatching, matching and dispatching, coffee mornings and admissions policies in schools – rather than any important quest for truth. In effect, some liberals may ignore the

---

3   Notebooks, IV, 5026; *Aids to Reflection: Moral and Religious Aphorisms*, London: William Pickering, 1839, pp. 106–7.

4   *Lectures and Essays*, Cambridge: Cambridge University Press, [1879] 2011, p. 35.

purpose of religion as much as fundamentalists. As the Holocaust survivor Elie Wiesel observed, 'indifference, to me, is the root of all evil', and it may be fair to say that the very word 'liberal' has been tarnished by association with indifference, with behaving as if central questions of truth and God do not matter.

Nevertheless Liberalism, at least as John Stuart Mill conceived it, and for the avoidance of confusion here with a capital 'L', is the love of truth. 'Know the truth and the truth shall set you free.' Liberal religion should be the love of God in its purest human expression – men and women actively seeking the truth, shoulder to shoulder as equals, supporting but never coercing each other. The Anglican Lambeth Conference in 1930 said that Anglicanism should be committed to 'a fearless love of truth' and this should characterize all religion.

If God exists, then love of God must come before all other allegiances – it was this that the Hebrew scriptures recognized in their condemnation of idolatry. It will leave us in what Kierkegaard called a state of 'fear and trembling', on shifting sands, knowing our own inadequacy in the face of the enormity of the task at hand; yet to relegate truth can be to live in relation to a lie and renders any happiness or achievement utterly hollow and transitory.

Discussion and the active doubt that follows it are an essential part of religion, if they are to function as more than a conservative power-structure. Doubt is usually a symptom of depth in understanding and belief rather than of a shallow want of care. As Archbishop Leighton wrote, 'Never be afraid to doubt, if you only have the disposition to believe, and doubt in order that you may end in believing the Truth.'[5]

There can be no discussion where only one view is utterable and no true belief where the alternatives have not been considered. Like good science, liberal religion should encourage and facilitate debate, embrace uncertainty and change and welcome genuine advances as they come. It should not be static nor bend with the whim of fashion. Pope John Paul II recognized the vital importance of using philosophy to engage with relativism and postmodernism in his 1998

---

5 Richard Holmes, *Coleridge, Darker Reflections*, San Francisco: Harper Perennial, 2005, p. 538.

encyclical *Fides et Ratio* – faith should never be afraid of philosophy; reason should illuminate faith, not undermine it.

Awareness that science is always incomplete, always a partial view of what is true is important, otherwise science itself can lead human beings towards nihilism or callousness, assuming that it has all the answers. Understanding of human transience, insignificance, and powerlessness will, in isolation, lead people to despair and stand in the way of achieving their potential. Understanding of natural selection, how in nature only the fittest survive, can when taken in isolation lead people to discriminate against the weak and also lead to a denial of meaning and value. This is not to denigrate the importance of science, but to claim that science may not have all the answers.

The philosophy of religion encourages and enables 'recurrence to the highest philosophy'; it represents liberal religion at its best. It offers the rare opportunity to engage with the question of God, to search for truth and to seek to 'know thyself'. It is important to discuss and debate with intellectual rigour but always with a heart that is open and fully engaged. The philosophy of religion is not easy or polite, offers little enough comfort let alone any sense of final achievement, but in being concerned with the truth it satisfies the whole person in a way that other partial disciplines cannot.[6] It may not provide final answers, but it is an essential road on the way to understanding.

---

6  http://www.youtube.com/watch?v=1IAhDGYlpqY is worth a watch. It would provide a useful starting point for a discussion of these issues.

# PART ONE

# Calling Things by Their Proper Names

To know when you know something,
and to know when you don't know,
that is knowledge . . .

(Confucius Analects 2.17)

# I

# Faith and Reason

I do not feel obliged to believe that the same God who has endowed us with sense, reason, and intellect has intended us to forgo their use.

(Galileo Galilei, *Letter to the Grand Duchess Christina*)

Today, the common perception is that faith and reason are in opposition.

The polarization of religion and science led to a shift in how people understand the nature of faith. Whereas in the past faith was understood as an intellectual response to any study of the universe and atheism seen as a mark of ignorance, following Darwin there seemed less and less need to posit a divine designer. Atheism is sometimes seen today as the mark of the informed mind, and faith is portrayed in terms of weakness, stemming from a need for simple answers as well as a search for comfort and a basic fear of facing the truth.

As scientists uncovered more about how the universe operates the creative role of God grew smaller; God was pushed into the gaps in human knowledge. Religious texts had to be reinterpreted to account for longer timescales, ice ages, the existence of other hominid species and dinosaurs. This raised huge questions. If God's role and nature seemed to change according to the state of human knowledge, could that suggest that God is dependent on us, rather than we on God? If 'revealed' wisdom falls short at precisely the same point as the state of human knowledge, could that imply that religious texts and traditions owe more to human authors than to divine inspiration?

## The Tide Turns

In 1841 German writer Ludwig Feuerbach (1804–72) wrote a book called *The Essence of Christianity*. Feuerbach was a 'Young Hegelian', one of a group of radical thinkers inspired by the writings of Georg Hegel (1770–1831).

Hegel suggested that human history is dynamic, that ideas and society move forward through a process of dialectic. The dominant philosophy is challenged by a new theory and, over time and out of the tension between the two, a new synthesis develops, which then becomes the dominant philosophy. Hegel's model was exciting, partly because it suggested that things constantly change and progress, and partly because it suggested that there could be more than one way of seeing the world, that 'truth' to some extent depends on the world-view which dominates at the time. Young philosophers saw in Hegel's ideas hope that society could and would progress, that their radical ideas could challenge established orthodoxy and contribute to human advancement.

In the mid nineteenth century Christianity dominated all life in Europe. In most cases, the Church held the keys to education and employment; it exerted a powerful influence on all governments, their laws and policies. Although many of the horror stories of actual repression are untrue, in some cases the Church seemed to stand in the way of scientific progress; it was slow to accept new ideas and continued to invest in areas of study which seemed archaic and irrelevant. By Hegel's own theory, it was natural that some 'Young Hegelians' would challenge the Church and propose radical, new ways of looking at and running the world. It was also natural that they should be inspired by scientific materialism, which offered a world-view diametrically opposed to that held by Christians.

Ludwig Feuerbach claimed to be 'a natural philosopher in the domain of the mind'.[1] He was a materialist and tried to apply

---

1 *The Essence of Christianity*, Preface to the 2nd edn, London: Cosimo, 2005, p. 5.

scientific method to his study of society, history and philosophy. Starting with a definition of existence which limited what could be known to that which could be experienced, Feuerbach examined Christianity and concluded that '[r]eligion is the dream of the human mind'.[2] He explained how religion had developed and changed over time and he noted that doctrines and structures seem to adapt in order to fulfil societal needs.

For example, in the power vacuum after the decline of the Roman Empire the Church grew into a provider of governance. God was portrayed as emperor–judge and there was a great emphasis on teachings about heaven and hell. In a world with little infrastructure, no police service and few courts, Christianity transformed from a minority faith which encouraged believers to stand against social norms into a state religion which gradually assumed the functions of government.

As Feuerbach saw it, religion was a form of social control. In order to maximize its effectiveness, he argued that people were being encouraged to accept nonsensical things on the basis of authority, to suspend their critical faculties. He wrote that 'in these days illusion only is sacred, truth profane . . . Religion has disappeared and it has been substituted, even amongst Protestants, with the appearance of Religion – the Church – in order at least that "the Faith" might be imparted to the ignorant and indiscriminating multitude.'[3]

Feuerbach went on to argue that it is not just the Church which seems to respond to social needs and wants; the personal concepts of God held by different people often fulfil their needs and desires. Thus, a person without a strong father-figure sees God in this role, as authoritarian, while another person who lacks affection in their

---

2 Ibid., p. 10.

3 Feuerbach's ideas went on to shape the views of Karl Marx, another radical German writer, who famously claimed that 'man makes religion, religion does not make man' and concluded that '[r]eligion is the sigh of the oppressed creature, the heart of a heartless world, and the soul of soulless conditions. It is the opium of the people'. Karl Marx, http://www.marxists.org/archive/marx/works/1843/critique-hpr/intro.htm.

upbringing sees a God of love and forgiveness. For Feuerbach, faith in God is a form of subconscious wish-fulfilment.

It follows that analysing people's concepts of God can tell us much about their psychology and about the characteristics of their society, but it is difficult to escape the implication that the object of faith, God, has no independent existence. If God is simply a projection, a product of deep-seated imagination, then faith is not credible and not compatible with reason.

Sigmund Freud (1856–1939) was influenced by Feuerbach when he described faith in these terms. The child experiences the father as the source of fear and guilt, yet the child wants unconditional love from a father so creates an idealized image in God.

The disturbed psyche projects images so that they appear to be outside of the mind. All human beings long for an unconditional, loving father figure who can accept them as they are and forgive all the dark sides of their character, so the religious idea of God is a projection of the human imagination and is the means whereby humans cope with the lack of love and the lack of meaning in the world.[4]

Religion is a neurosis, albeit an attractive one; wishful thinking cannot create something that does not exist:

It would be very nice if there were a God who created the world and was a benevolent providence, and if there were a moral order in the universe and an after-life; but it is a very striking fact that all this is exactly as we are bound to wish it to be.[5]

Feuerbach's work influenced others too. *The Essence of Christianity* was translated into English in 1853 by Marian Evans

---

4 *Totem and Taboo: Resemblances Between the Mental Lives of Savages and Neurotics*, London: Ark Paperbacks, [1913] 1983.
5 *The Future of an Illusion*, London: Hogarth, [1927] 1978 (http://free-ebooks.net/ebook/The-future-of-illusion/html/20).

(1819–80), who wrote novels under the name George Eliot.[6] While Evans was working on the text, the poet Matthew Arnold was writing the famous poem 'Dover Beach' which reflects the devastating effect that ideas like those of Feuerbach had on British intellectuals in the 1850s. He wrote:

> The Sea of Faith
> Was once, too, at the full, and round earth's shore
> Lay like the folds of a bright girdle furled.
> But now I only hear
> Its melancholy, long, withdrawing roar,
> Retreating, to the breath
> Of the night-wind, down the vast edges drear
> And naked shingles of the world.[7]

The development of Biblical Criticism led some Protestants, like Marian Evans, to lose their faith altogether – but it led others to cling to it in the face of rational objections. Reason and scholarship started to seem like the enemy of faith and religion. Many focused on personal experiences of God, on feelings and emotions rather than on verifiable fact or argument.

In the second half of the nineteenth century rational, bright and open neo-classical churches went out of fashion; neo-gothic swept in, embracing shadows and symbolism. The Gothic revival went further than bricks and mortar, making a case for 'a return to the faith and the social structures of the Middle Ages'. Faced with the fruits of scientific research, mass industrialization, urban migration, child labour, poverty, ignorance, crime and social breakdown, people

---

6 Evans started her life as a devout Christian, but after translating the work of Feuerbach and other young Hegelians from German into English, lost her faith and struggled to re-order her life in the knowledge that God probably did not exist. She came to London and made contact with others in the same position; among them the scientist Herbert Spencer and the philosopher John Stuart Mill.

7 http://www.victorianweb.org/authors/arnold/writings/doverbeach.html.

hankered after a golden age, before factories and the threat of famine. Christians saw in the Gospels a message of anti-materialism, simplicity and socialism which could help restore the world.

Whether in the works of novelists like Elizabeth Gaskell, designers like William Morris or the Pre-Raphaelite artists, suspicion of 'progress' and a longing for people to re-engage with tradition, embrace myth and emotion and be suspicious of calculating reason is plain to see. The Church had never been so popular; it offered the possibility of blocking out the real world and nourishing the parts of humanity which modern life ignored – imagination, spirituality, beauty.

Nevertheless, the human horrors which led on from industrialization, graphically described by Karl Marx and Friedrich Engels, led to worse horrors on the Western Front of the First World War, in the gas chambers of Auschwitz and in the streets of Hiroshima.

The Church failed to change and rearticulate its essential message in a way that could seem relevant. Christianity, at its best, appeals because it engages with the truth and with all it is and could be to be human. It does not defer to authority, get hung up in power structures, belittle, ignore or exclude people. It is not obsessed with sex, however much it may seem to be today, and cares little for tradition and appearances. Jesus stood for what is good in humanity – for honesty, bravery, generosity, forgiveness, love – and against lies and injustice, cowardice and apathy, selfishness of all sorts. When people have turned to the Christian faith it is because they see it offering this sort of better life, not just an alternative political power structure to submit to. This is why some forms of Islam are so popular and make it the fastest growing world religion. When religion offers a message of equality, justice and truth, people flock to become part of it – but when it starts to prize unity and power over truth and justice, they disengage.

In the twentieth century, it became more and more difficult to reconcile faith in an all-powerful and loving creator-God with the realities of life in an obviously imperfect world. Religion has offered little to make it any easier. Theology has become an obscure discipline; theologians write papers which will only ever be read by other theologians. The philosophy of religion has become a backwater, seldom considered even by academic philosophers. How can this be? Theology used to be the queen of the sciences, the capstone of education, providing the opportunity to ask the big questions about truth, origins and meaning. It has in all too many cases become relegated to being a sub-branch of the sociology department.

Because of this, in the face of glaring questions about how a good and powerful God could allow injustice, how the scriptures can be reconciled with modern science and how people can just keep on believing, apparently in spite of the evidence rather than because of it, it might seem as if one might be justified in accepting Dawkins' characterization of faith as 'anti-intellectual'.

To do so would, however, ignore the fact that there have always been different types of faith. Broadly speaking, there are five different approaches to defining faith:

- *Propositional faith*: Faith is based on evidence and/or argument. It depends upon propositions and may be destroyed if its basis is destroyed.
- *Non-propositional faith*: Faith is not based on evidence or argument but may be enriched or explored through either.
- *Fideism*: Faith is independent of reason, perhaps hostile to it and definitely superior to it in providing a complete account of the world.
- *Voluntarism*: Belief is under our control, directly or indirectly. It is rational to will oneself to believe, at least to put oneself in a position whereby faith may develop, because doing so will yield positive results.
- *Non-voluntarism*: Faith is not a matter of choice – God chooses some to believe and others not to, and we are not necessarily in a position to understand why.

## Propositional Faith

'Propositional faith' identifies faith with justified belief or knowledge. Faith that God exists may be compared with belief that evolution through natural selection occurs. Evidence (propositions) supports a conclusion, theory or explanation; if the evidence changes, the conclusion will be *falsified* and the theory may have to change. Most, though not all, proponents of propositional faith use natural theology (arguments for God which start with observations of the natural world) to provide the propositions on which faith depends.

The traditional definition of faith is best articulated by Thomas Aquinas (1215–74), who wrote that 'from the perspective of the one believing . . . the object of faith is something composite in the form of a proposition'.[8] Aquinas' five 'ways' provide natural, rational grounds for belief in God. For Aquinas, the world is moved, caused, contingent, and this suggests that God is unmoved, uncaused and fully actual and so *must* be understood in terms of omnipotence and omnibenevolence, at least as Aquinas interprets them.

It follows that although *natural theology* provides strong evidence to support belief, that evidence and the faith it supports is always subject to challenge. Arguably, propositional faith is not as strong as other forms of faith. Indeed, some would say that it is not really faith at all. Even Aquinas admitted that reason and natural theology cannot take us all the way to God. For Aquinas, it is as if faith is a destination city served by two railway lines. The fast line, reason, stops just short of the city and leaves passengers to walk the final stage of the journey. The slow line, revelation, takes ages, is tortuous and prone to breaking down, but delivers passengers into the city centre.

Today the mainstream Roman Catholic Church has a positive approach to natural theology and propositional faith. The anti-modernist oath promulgated by Pope Pius X required Catholics to affirm that

God, the origin and end of all things, can be known with certainty by the natural light of reason from the created world (cf. Rom. 1.20), that is, from the visible works of creation, as a cause from its effects, and that, therefore, his existence can also be demonstrated . . .[9]

---

8 *Summa Theologica*, 2a2ae, 1, 2.

9 1910, text available at http://www.papalencyclicals.net/Pius10/p10moath. htm.

Pope John Paul II's encyclical *Fides et Ratio* (1998) also affirms that reason is necessary for faith. He wrote:

> Faith and reason are like two wings on which the human spirit rises to the contemplation of truth; and God has placed in the human heart a desire to know the truth – in a word, to know himself – so that, by knowing and loving God, men and women may also come to the fullness of truth about themselves.[10]

## Non-Propositional Faith

C. S. Lewis wrote of faith:

> I am not asking anyone to accept Christianity if his best reasoning tells him that the weight of the evidence is against it. That is not the point at which Faith comes in. But supposing a man's reason once decides that the weight of the evidence is for it . . . There will come a moment when there is bad news, or he is in trouble, or is living among a lot of other people who do not believe it, and all at once his emotions will rise up and carry out a sort of blitz on his belief . . . I am not talking of moments at which any real new reasons against Christianity turn up. Those have to be faced and that is a different matter. I am talking about moments where a mere mood rises up against it. Now Faith, in the sense in which I am here using the word, is the art of holding on to things your reason has once accepted, in spite of your changing moods. For moods will change, whatever view your reason takes. I know that by experience . . . That is why Faith is such a necessary virtue: unless you teach your moods 'where they get off', you can never be either a sound Christian or even a sound atheist, but just a creature dithering to and fro, with its beliefs really dependent on

---

10 http://www.vatican.va/holy_father/john_paul_ii/encyclicals/documents/hf_jp-ii_enc_15101998_fides-et-ratio_en.html.

the weather and the state of its digestion. Consequently one must train the habit of Faith.[11]

For Lewis, it is clear that faith is more than just an intellectual decision; it involves a commitment so that belief in God can survive the buffeting which life will bring.

The Welsh philosopher H. H. Price (1899–1984) distinguished between *believing in* something and *believing that* something. To *believe that* is propositional, the result of argument and so potentially falsified. It is an intellectual decision. To *believe in*, however, is an attitude which requires that one's whole being changes. To believe that God exists is a matter of the intellect, to believe in God means to trust one's life to God. For Price, *believing in* is what religious faith is really about – it cannot be reduced to believing that, whatever atheist philosophers seem to argue.

Søren Kierkegaard (1813–55) maintained a non-propositional definition of faith. Kierkegaard wrote:

> I do not believe . . . that God exists, but I know it; whereas I believe that God has existed . . . even from the Greek point of view, the eternal truth by being for an existing person, becomes an object of faith and a paradox.[12]

Faith is the individual's reaction to the paradox of Christianity expressed in the claim that Jesus is both fully human and also fully God. Since essential truth is far beyond our comprehension, it appears to us in the form of a paradox which can either be accepted or rejected. 'Paradox' is not the same as a logical contradiction – it is where two claims appear to be in tension and this tension cannot be resolved by the human mind. Since, for Kierkegaard, we cannot know the nature of God, the claim that Jesus is both God and man is

---

11 Chapter 11 in Book III (*Christian Behaviour*) of C. S. Lewis, *Mere Christianity*, London: Collins, 1955, p. 121.

12 *Philosophical Fragments*, trans. Hong & Hong, Princeton: Princeton University Press, 1985, p. 222.

a paradox and not a contradiction as, in a contradiction, both terms have to be understood and known.

It is more likely that the human mind is limited than that the truth is limited by what the human mind can conceive. Kierkegaard would not have us believe the impossible or the contradictory, because faith is necessarily puzzling and uncertain,

> when faith requires that he relinquish his understanding, then to have faith becomes just as difficult for the most intelligent person as it is for the person of the most limited intelligence, or it presumably becomes even more difficult for the former.[13]

Kierkegaard is often identified with the idea that faith requires irrational trust. Like in *Indiana Jones and the Last Crusade*,[14] faith is not real unless it requires one to put one's weight on nothing, expecting it to hold. For Kierkegaard,

> there is no gradual accumulation of sensory data or rational proofs for God's existence or for the resurrection of Christ, etc. One performs a willed act of faith despite fear, doubt, and sin. The leap is not out of thoughtlessness, but out of volition.

The so-called 'leap of faith' is not simply a suspension of one's critical faculties becoming certain of something beyond reason. For Kierkegaard, faith is the acceptance of the necessity of doubt and struggle with reality, a giving up of any hope of certainty but a commitment to stake one's life on one's belief. Existential engagement is crucial – as Kierkegaard said: 'As you have lived, so have you believed.'

In his book *Dynamics of Faith*[15] Paul Tillich (1886–1965) explored the nature of faith. Faith involves a risk or wager, existential courage. It involves the certain acceptance of uncertainty, which can be

---

13 'Concluding Unscientific Postscript', ibid., p. 377.
14 Steven Spielberg, 1989.
15 New York: Harper & Row, 1957.

overwhelming and lead us to live in what Kierkegaard called a state of 'fear and trembling'. Nevertheless, for Tillich God is nothing short of 'the ground of our being'. It may be difficult to accept and live in relationship with God, but God concerns us ultimately and ignoring God is like ignoring reality itself.

For neither Kierkegaard nor Tillich is faith a comfortable state or an easy option!

## Fideism

Alvin Plantinga (b. 1932) defined fideism as 'exclusive or basic reliance upon faith alone, accompanied by a consequent disparagement of reason and utilized especially in the pursuit of philosophical or religious truth'. He went on to define a fideist as someone who 'urges reliance on faith rather than reason, in matters philosophical and religious' and who 'may go on to disparage and denigrate reason'.[16] Reason and philosophy, therefore, are dismissed as groundings for faith – reason operates within faith and does not provide a basis for faith.

Traditionally the fideist position was associated with the writings of Tertullian, a lawyer from Carthage who converted to Christianity sometime around the year 197. Tertullian asked the famous questions 'What does Athens have to do with Jerusalem? What have heretics to do with Christians?'[17] For Tertullian, the Christian faith and pagan philosophy were polar opposites. The truth of Christianity had been revealed through the life of Christ and the scripture which recorded it. To use pagan philosophy to find God's message risked distorting it. Famously, Tertullian wrote that

> [t]he Son of God was crucified: I am not ashamed – because it is shameful. The Son of God died: It is immediately credible – because

---

16 Alvin Plantinga, 'Reason and Belief in God', in Alvin Plantinga and Nicholas Wolterstorff (eds), *Faith and Rationality: Reason and Belief in God*, Notre Dame: University of Notre Dame Press, 1983. p. 87.

17 *De Praescriptione Haereticorum* 7.9.

it is silly. He was buried, and rose again: It is certain – because it is impossible.[18]

The last phrase is sometimes translated as 'It is certain because it is impossible' in the sense that 'I believe because it is impossible!', yet it is important to appreciate that Tertullian's meaning is misrepresented by this.

Elsewhere in his writings, Tertullian observed that

> reason is a property of God's, since there is nothing which God, the creator of all things, has not foreseen, arranged and determined by reason; moreover, there is nothing He does not wish to be investigated and understood by reason . . .[19]

There are 340 passages in Tertullian where the word *ratio* appears, making it one of the most frequently used nouns in his work, so it is fair to say that he did not dismiss reason altogether. In fact, Tertullian utilized those elements of Greek philosophy and logic that he believed to be compatible with Christian belief; his faith was not based on rational argument, but he was not averse to using it in order to explore or defend that faith. When he does speak of the absurdity of Christian belief, Tertullian is referring to the unlikelihood that any human mind could conceive of God's plan.

Some Christians have interpreted Tertullian as meaning that faith is only really faith if its object is irrational, even absurd. The incarnation, miracles, the resurrection – they all run counter to reason, yet unless a Christian believes that they happened then many would question their faith. However, modern scholarship has largely abandoned the idea that Tertullian was the father of fideism. Eric Osborn wrote, 'Not only did he never say "credo quia absurdum", but he never meant anything like it and never abandoned the claims of Athens upon Jerusalem.' He went on to explain that the context of the famous quotation is an argument with Marcion, who was held

---

18 *De Carne Christi* 5.4.
19 *De Paenitentia* 1.2.

to be a heretic, and who believed in the resurrection but did not believe that Christ had a real body, and that the flesh was shameful. Tertullian pointed out that Christ himself said that worldly wisdom was not to be trusted on such things, so if Marcion was following it, he must be in the wrong. Tertullian, Osborn concluded, was a most improbable fideist.[20]

Another commonly used example of a fideist approach to faith is Martin Luther (1483–1546). Luther wrote

> How, then should we be able to comprehend or understand the secret counsels of God's majesty, or search them out with our human sense, reason, or understanding? Should we then admire our own wisdom? I, for my part, admit myself a fool . . .[21]

Indeed, he taught that 'All the articles of our Christian faith, which God has revealed to us in His Word, are in presence of reason sheerly impossible, absurd, and false . . .'[22] continuing that 'Reason is the greatest enemy that faith has.'[23] Yet even Luther conceded that reason can be used to enhance faith, if not to create it. He also wrote, 'so it is with human reason, which strives not against faith, when enlightened, but rather furthers and advances it'.[24]

## Voluntarism

In his *Pensées*, Blaise Pascal (1623–62) described a reason to believe which might convince an atheist. He wrote:

---

20 Eric Osborn, *Tertullian: First Theologian of the West*, New York: Cambridge University Press, 1997, pp. 27–30.

21 *The Table Talk Or Familiar Discourse of Martin Luther*, trans. Hazlitt, London: G. Bell and Sons, 1902, p. 28.

22 Quoted in Will Durant, *The Reformation: A History of European Civilization from Wyclif to Calvin, 1300–1564*, New York: Simon & Schuster, 1957, p. 370.

23 *The Table Talk Or Familiar Discourse of Martin Luther*, trans. Hazlitt, p. 164.

24 Ibid., p. 144.

If there is a God, He is infinitely incomprehensible . . . This being so . . . Who then will blame Christians for not being able to give a reason for their belief . . . Let us then examine this point, and say, 'God is, or He is not.' But to which side shall we incline? Reason can decide nothing here . . . What will you wager . . . according to reason, you can defend neither of the propositions . . . but you must wager. It is not optional. You are embarked. Which will you choose then . . . Let us weigh the gain and the loss in wagering that God is. Let us estimate these two chances. If you gain, you gain all; if you lose, you lose nothing. Wager, then, without hesitation that He is . . . there is here an infinity of an infinitely happy life to gain, a chance of gain against a finite number of chances of loss, and what you stake is finite . . . there is no time to hesitate, you must give all . . . when one is forced to play, he must renounce reason to preserve his life, rather than risk it for infinite gain, as likely to happen as the loss of nothingness.[25]

For Pascal, this did not constitute a good argument for the existence of God. God is 'infinitely incomprehensible' and it is impossible to prove God's existence in the way that one might try to prove the existence of a new planet. Further, it does not explain why most people have faith; it is just a possible way of convincing somebody who was struggling to take the search for faith seriously.

Pascal was not so crude as to suggest that we can force ourselves to believe, even when the reasons to do so are substantial. As Tillich observed, 'no command to believe and no will to believe can create faith'.[26] Pascal acknowledged the possibility that some people seem not to be made for faith, but suggested:

at least learn your inability to believe, since reason brings you to this, and yet you cannot believe. Endeavour then to convince yourself, not by increase of proofs of God, but by the abatement of your passions. You would like to attain faith, and do not know

---

25 http://www.gutenberg.org/files/18269/18269-h/18269-h.htm 233.
26 Tillich, *Dynamics of Faith*, London: HarperCollins, 2001. p. 44.

the way; you would like to cure yourself of unbelief, and ask the remedy for it. Learn of those who have been bound like you, and who now stake all their possessions. These are people who know the way which you would follow, and who are cured of an ill of which you would be cured. Follow the way by which they began; by acting as if they believed, taking the holy water, having masses said, etc. . . . . What have you to lose?

Modern scholars distinguish between *direct voluntarism*, the idea that the choice over what to believe is under our immediate control, and *indirect voluntarism*, the idea that the choice is not under our immediate control but that we are able to influence what we come to believe by choosing to perform intermediary actions. Pascal was an indirect voluntarist. For Pascal, faith is not just the result of an intellectual decision but must be nurtured through developing a life of faith. People need to decide to put themselves in the best position for faith to develop, by being good, worshipping and integrating into the faith community. This is not just sensible in terms of a possible afterlife, but also in terms of this life. He asked:

what harm will befall you in taking this side? You will be faithful, honest, humble, grateful, generous, a sincere friend, truthful. Certainly you will not have those poisonous pleasures, glory and luxury; but will you not have others? I will tell you that you will thereby gain in this life, and that, at each step you take on this road, you will see so great certainty of gain, so much nothingness in what you risk, that you will at last recognize that you have wagered for something certain and infinite, for which you have given nothing.

Pascal calls individuals to take the step of putting themselves in a position where they may acquire faith rather than to dismiss faith without enquiry or engagement. Pascal is really targeting indifference and seeking to persuade people to seek belief while recognizing that they may not find it.

Two main objections are often raised to Pascal's argument. First, to believe in God simply for some eventual reward is the wrong motive for belief. Such self-seeking individuals would not deserve eternal life, whatever they believed or did. Second, in order to be sure of a payoff, an individual would not know which God or gods to believe in to cover the conditions of the wager. Would the wager also hold for another God? One would have to believe in all gods in order to be sure, but if there were only one God then this strategy would defeat itself. Nevertheless, it is worth considering that these criticisms could be based on an incomplete understanding of Pascal's position.

Pascal does not suggest that anybody could simply choose to believe for personal advantage; the best they could do is to be persuaded to live a good, religious life and to put themselves in the best position for faith to develop. Faith may or may not result.

Further, the idea that religions are mutually exclusive is not conclusive. It could be that different religious stories and modes of life are simply different interpretations of a single truth. It could be that being immersed in a Sikh life would be just as likely to result in faith as being immersed in a Catholic life. The differences could just be cultural and any claims to the contrary could be reflections of human beings' natural competitiveness rather than reality. Jesus seemed to indicate something on these lines in the parable of the sheep and the goats where what seems to matter most is how one lives rather than propositional belief.

## Non-Voluntarism

A final understanding of faith is perhaps best represented by the stories of prophets in the Bible. God chose Moses as a leader for the Hebrews, Amos was 'plucked' from his work as a farmer tending sycamore trees and sent to preach to the people of Judah, and Jonah was chased across land and sea as he tried to escape God's mission for him. The prophet Mohammed could be another example of somebody chosen by God for faith. For many people of faith it seems that their relationship with God is not the result of their own ordinary will or intellect, but is the will of God.

At its most basic level, a non-voluntarist approach to faith would suggest that some people are made for faith or commanded to believe. Whether we have faith or not is, to a large extent, out of our hands.

The great Islamic philosopher Al Ghazali (1058–1111) described the process of acquiring faith in Chapter III of the *Munqidh*. Al Ghazali was a leading philosopher and teacher at the University of Baghdad. He started by looking for proof of God in normal forms of worship and through study, but realized that these would yield nothing. He wrote:

I also perceived that I could not hope for eternal happiness unless I feared God and rejected all the passions, that is to say, I should begin by breaking my heart's attachment to the world. I needed to abandon the illusions of life on earth in order to direct my attention towards my eternal home with the most intense desire for God, the Almighty. This entailed avoiding all honours and wealth, and escaping from everything that usually occupies a person and ties him down . . . Turning to look inward, I perceived that I was bound by attachments on all sides. I meditated on all that I had done, teaching and instructing being my proudest achievements, and I perceived that all my studies were futile, since they were of no value for the Way to the hereafter . . . I thought of nothing else, all the time remaining undecided. One day, I would determine to leave Baghdad and lead a new life, but the next day I would change my mind . . . This tug of war between my emotions and the summons from the Hereafter lasted nearly six months, from the month of Rajab 488 A.H. (July AD 1095), during which I lost my free will and was under compulsion . . . God tied my tongue and stopped me teaching . . . I grew weak. The physicians despaired of treating me . . . Feeling my impotence, my inability to come to a decision, I put myself in the hands of God, the ultimate refuge of all those who are in need. I was heard by the one who hears those in need when they pray to Him. He made it easy for me to renounce honours, wealth, family and friends.[27]

For Al Ghazali, faith cannot arise from a normal life, from everyday experiences or unassisted reason. It arises from the realization of the inadequacy of being human and from putting oneself in God's hands. God's grace makes it possible to know God in a new way, to have a certainty in God's existence which is otherwise impossible. For Al Ghazali real faith is total certainty, which holds the 'soul so bound that nothing could detach it'.[28]

In the Christian tradition, John Calvin (1509–64) is most associated with a non-voluntarist approach to faith. For Calvin, faith is

a firm and certain knowledge of God's benevolence towards us, founded upon the truth of the freely given promise in Christ, both revealed to our minds and sealed upon our hearts through the Holy Spirit.[29]

For Calvin and modern followers of his tradition such as Alvin Plantinga, some people have a special cognitive faculty which makes them able to sense God and truly *know* God's existence. For these people faith is not really a choice. God's reality impresses itself upon them and they cannot honestly deny it. For those without the special cognitive faculty, however, God's existence appears no more than possible.

Modern *Reformed Epistemology*, following the ideas of William Alston (1921–2009), Nicholas Woltersdorff (b. 1932) and Alvin Plantinga (b. 1932), suggests that for some people, having a 'properly ordered noetic structure', belief in God is 'properly basic', reasonable though it is not held as an inference from other truths. For those with faith, reason must then be used to 'defeat the defeaters', to demonstrate the logical possibility of a faith position, and that

27  Quoted in http://www.crvp.org/book/Series01/I-20/chapter_iii.htm.
28  Quoted by http://www.crvp.org/book/Series01/I-20/chapter_iii.htm.
29  *Institutes* III, ii, 7, 551.

challenges, such as the existence of evil and suffering, do not destroy its credibility.

In *God and Other Minds* (1967), Plantinga argued that beliefs are *warranted* without regular evidence provided they are grounded and defended against known objections. Because it is conceivably possible that God has designed some minds to know God, faith is possibly warranted apart from argument. Plantinga challenges the dominance of evidentialism, suggesting that it has a limited view of warranted belief. He argues that religious experiences, including everyday experiences such as awe and wonder, form an important part of the warrant of faith. Nevertheless it can be argued that this view applies a form of spiritual apartheid with some being chosen by God for faith and others for non-belief. Human freedom is radically compromised.

## *Summary*

Although most people see faith as being opposed to reason today, in fact the place of reason in forming or supporting faith rather depends on one's denomination and/or definition of faith.

- For Roman Catholics, many of whom have propositional faith, reason and argument will be of central importance.
- For some Protestants, many of whose faith is non-propositional, reason will not lead to faith, nor argument do much to support or erode it, though reason is the essential means of exploring and enriching faith.
- For evangelical Christians, many of whose faith is fideist, the relationship between faith and reason will be slight, though the attitude that faith and reason are naturally opposed is not held as widely as many people think.
- For voluntarists, reason and argument have an important part to play, not in terms of proving God's existence, but in demonstrating the benefits of believing in it and in seeking to persuade people away from indifference.

- For Calvinists and members of the Reformed tradition who are non-voluntarists, reason and argument are irrelevant in forming faith, but may be used to explore its nature once it exists.

Of course, the five categories overlap and fail to do justice to the complexity of people's faith, but they may still be useful in elucidating the differences which exist between what people understand by 'faith'.

# 2

# The Ethics of Belief

Exceptional claims demand exceptional evidence.
(Christopher Hitchens, *God is Not Great*)

In 1877 the mathematician and philosopher W. K. Clifford (1845–79) wrote an essay called *The Ethics of Belief*. In it, he argued that

> No real belief, however trifling and fragmentary it may seem, is ever truly insignificant; it prepares us to receive more of its like, confirms those which resembled it before, and weakens others; and so gradually it lays a stealthy train in our inmost thoughts, which may someday explode into overt action, and leave its stamp upon our character for ever.[1]

Because of the relationship between belief and action, 'no one man's belief is in any case a private matter which concerns himself alone', it is a matter for public concern if anyone chooses to believe something which is not supported by evidence, because of what they might do with that belief.

Clifford's point has resonated in the years since 9/11. The connection between belief and action has seemed to invalidate the old liberal idea that what people believe is nobody else's business. It seems obvious that 'It is wrong always, everywhere, and for anyone, to believe anything upon insufficient evidence', but this ignores an essential problem. What is *sufficient* evidence?

Take the example of a ship-owner sending out an unseaworthy vessel. The man convinces himself that there is no problem, because

---

1 http://www.infidels.org/library/historical/w_k_clifford/ethics_of_belief.
html.

if there was, it would be expensive and inconvenient. He chooses not to investigate and to dismiss nagging doubts. Clifford, who himself once survived a shipwreck, writes that

> the sincerity of his conviction can in no wise help him, because he had no right to believe on such evidence as was before him. He had acquired his belief not by honestly earning it in patient investigation, but by stifling his doubts.[2]

Clifford implies that the only way to check the facts and to base a reasonable belief is for the owner to go to the ship and examine it for himself, looking at the hull and listening to the engine.

A similar example hit the news in 2013. An eight-storey building collapsed in Dhaka, Bangladesh, killing over a thousand people. Part of the building was occupied by a manufacturer which supplied cheap clothing to the British retailer Primark and other budget fashion brands. There has been much publicity about working conditions for the four million people who work in the Bangladeshi garment industry, so it is reasonable to say that senior managers and directors of British retailers might have had doubts about the safety of suppliers' operations. Did they suppress those doubts or did they take the trouble to establish the facts for themselves? Clifford's argument on the ethical status of beliefs seems compelling.

It would be easy to interpret Clifford as a materialist, someone who valued the direct evidence of the physical senses over all other putative forms of knowledge. Of course, in the case of a ship or the factory there is no difficulty with insisting that beliefs are based on physical sense-data, with what shareholders or directors could see or touch for themselves, but if we move from that to claiming that only those beliefs which are based on what we can physically sense are valid, then there will be broader implications.

Take another example. How could I see, hear, smell, taste or touch whether 0.642 plus 0.319 really does equal 0.961? How could I *verify* this against sense-data? I can be certain that it is true, without

---

2 Ibid.

resorting to cutting cakes incredibly precisely, because of the conventions of mathematics. My belief that $0.642 + 0.319 = 0.961$ is based on a different kind of evidence, logical or *analytic* evidence.

In fact, Clifford had no difficulty with accepting logical or mathematical calculations, even those which go well beyond what can be physically tested, as sufficient evidence for beliefs. In fact, he had a world-view quite different from that of many evidentialists today.

Clifford was inspired by David Hume – but this did not make him a materialist. Hume appreciated the limitations of the senses in a way that some philosophers and scientists since have not. He used the example of seeing a red object; the redness is only a chemical property which makes the object reflect light at a particular wave-length which rods and cones in our eyes perceive as red. Redness does not belong to the object; it is a function of how we see it. We need our brains to interpret and contextualize what our senses pick up, so it would be wrong to portray Hume as relegating what is known through reason.

For Clifford,

> as the physical senses have been gradually developed out of confused and uncertain impressions, so a set of intellectual senses or insights are still in the course of development, the operation of which may ultimately be expected to be as certain and immediate as our ordinary sense-perceptions.[3]

Through our intellect, human beings have the potential to know things as they are and to grapple with ultimate reality, way beyond our limited physical existence.

Clifford dwelt on the very nature of reality. What is the universe made of? What does it mean to exist? To what extent are things such as energy, magnetism, $2 + 2 = 4$ 'real'? How is it that the human mind can engage with and begin to understand the universe? Clifford

---

3 William Kingdon Clifford, *Lectures and Essays Volume 1*, Cambridge: Cambridge University Press, 2011, p. 11. See also 'On some of the conditions of mental development' (1868).

researched into geometry, uncovering the deep regularity and inter-connectedness of things. In 1870 he wrote *On the Space-Theory of Matter*, arguing that energy and matter are simply different types of curvature of space and laying the foundations for Einstein's later work on relativity.

Inspired by Spinoza (1632–77), Leibniz (1646–1716) and Berkeley (1685–1753), Clifford understood that *mind-stuff* is primary in the universe, governing how matter and energy behave. As a mathematician, Clifford saw the power of the laws of logic and realized that the way things are can be calculated with great accuracy well before there is the facility to observe them. The mind is itself a sense (effectively a sixth sense), providing evidence about reality in itself and also by interpreting data from the five physical senses. Like the other senses, the mind can be faulty or can be used inappropriately, but when functioning well, the mind is a reliable means of engaging with reality. It made sense to Clifford that the laws of logic are real and 'exist' just as much as the existence of material reality.

As the introduction to Clifford's *Lectures and Essays* puts it,

It is an open secret to the few who know it, but a mystery and a stumbling block to many, that Science and Poetry are own sisters; insomuch that in those branches of scientific inquiry which are most abstract, most formal, and most remote from the imagination of ordinary sensible imagination, a higher power of imagination akin to the creative insight of the poet is most needed and fruitful of lasting work . . . the conception is that mind is the one ultimate reality; not mind as we know it in the complex forms of conscious feeling and thought, but the simpler elements out of which thought and feeling are built up. The hypothetical ultimate element of mind, or atom of mind-stuff, precisely corresponds to the hypothetical atom of matter, being the ultimate fact of which the material atom is the phenomenon. Matter and the sensible universe are the relations between particular organisms, that is, mind organized into consciousness, and the rest of the world. This leads to results which would in a loose and popular sense be called materialist. But the theory must, as a metaphysical theory, be

reckoned on the idealist side. To speak technically, it is an idealist monism. Indeed it is a very subtle form of idealism, and by no
means easy of apprehension at first sight . . .[4]

Clifford objected to religion in the same way as the biblical critics
of the time objected to the literalistic interpretation of texts. Clifford
wanted to open up theology and ethics to rational examination
and force accumulated dogmas and beliefs to be continually re-
evaluated in the light of the evidence. He could not accept the religious
tendency to peddle empty concepts to perpetuate political power,
to preserve traditions for their own sake or to ignore new insights,
such as Darwin's theory of evolution through natural selection. Key
to Clifford's scientific method, and his ethic, was a refusal ever to be
satisfied with an idea or theory and an insistence on reconsidering it,
and being willing to drop or modify it, as and when new evidence
came to light.

Clifford believed in evolution, not just of physical characteristics
but of the intellect. He told the following story:

Once upon a time – much longer than six thousand years ago – the
Trilobites were the only people that had eyes; and they were only
just beginning to have them, and some even of the Trilobites had
as yet no signs of coming sight. So that the utmost they could
know was that they were living in darkness, and that perhaps
there was such a thing as light. But at last one of them got so
far advanced that when he happened to come to the top of the
water in the daytime he saw the sun. So he went down and told
the others that in general the world was light, but there was one
great light which caused it all. Then they killed him for disturbing
the commonwealth; but they considered it impious to doubt that
in general the world was light, and there was one great light that
caused it all. And they had great disputes about the manner in
which they had come to know this. Afterwards another of them
got so far advanced that when he happened to come to the top of

4 Ibid., pp. 1 and 39.

the water he saw the stars. So he went down and told the others
that in general the world was dark, but that nevertheless there
were a great number of little lights in it. Then they killed him
for maintaining false doctrines: but from that time there was a
division amongst them, and all the Trilobites were split into two
parties, some maintaining one thing and some another, until such
time as so many of them had learned to see that there could be no
doubt about the matter . . .[5]

The story obviously echoed Plato's allegory of the cave, yet the new
knowledge was not the product of a chance escape from the shadows, but of the development of a whole new faculty. For Clifford,
humanity had progressed and the Church should progress with it.
Faith must be apportioned to the evidence and modulated by reason.
Maintaining the old 'tribal' beliefs made no sense and advantaged no
one except those bent on abusing the power they invested. He wrote:
'I want to take up my cross and follow the true Christ, humanity; to
accept the facts as they are, however bitter or severe, to be a student
and a lover, but never a lawgiver.'[6] For Clifford it would be morally
wrong to extend what one believes beyond the evidence – but the
range of acceptable evidence may be greater than that allowed by
later evidentialists. Yet defining what constitutes acceptable or sufficient evidence is never easy.

A man's wife says that she loves him. The man is insecure and
constantly has doubts; he asks her 'Do you love me?', and she always
says 'Yes', but this does not satisfy him. Over the years, the woman
does everything that a loving wife would do, cooking and caring
for the children, remembering his birthday and remembering not to
nag sometimes. The man still has occasional doubts. What can the
man do to establish a firm basis for his beliefs? What test can he
perform?

---

5 Quoted in http://www.lutterworth.com/pub/such%20silver%20currents
%20ch3.pdf.

6 Clifford to Lady Pollock. 1871 Quoted in http://www.lutterworth.com/
pub/such%20silver%20currents%20ch3.pdf.

Would the man be morally wrong to continue to try to believe in her love for him, suppressing the doubts which he knows probably originate in his own insecurity? Would he be right to leave his wife and children, because he is plagued by doubts which he cannot dispel through any sensory investigation or process of analysis? Does Clifford's dictum that 'It is wrong always, everywhere, and for anyone, to believe anything upon insufficient evidence' apply in this case?

An artist finds an object which she believes to be beautiful. Her friends cannot understand why she values it. They ask her 'What do you mean by "beautiful"?' They try to persuade her to justify her belief or to admit that the object does not conform to this definition of beauty or that theory of aesthetics. The artist sometimes wavers in her conviction, but when she sees the object knows in her heart that she is right, that it truly is beautiful. Is the artist *morally wrong* to persist in her belief? Must even beliefs about beauty be subject to strict standards of evidence?

Further, is it right to choose not to believe in cases where sufficient evidence cannot be obtained either one way or the other? There are cases where beliefs relate to things which can be investigated using intellectual insights and information drawn from the senses, and there are cases where beliefs relate to things which cannot so be investigated. While many people find Clifford's point about the significance of beliefs compelling, they are still willing to accept that some beliefs simply have to be maintained without what Clifford would call sufficient evidence.

In 1897 the American philosopher and psychologist William James (1842–1910) attacked Clifford's position in *The Will to Believe*. He focused on beliefs which cannot be supported on purely rational grounds, such as belief in God, pointing out the limitations of evidentialism and noting that although it fosters the attitude of continually searching for the truth, which is extremely important, it holds us back from making some *forced* choices, pushing people to make just such unreasonable decisions about belief as evidentialists claim to deplore.

In the case of God, James argued that the choice over what to believe is forced, inescapable and momentous; it involves changing one's life irreversibly. As Descartes is reputed to have said, 'to know what people really think, pay attention to what they do, rather than what they say'. Further, James argued that the choice over whether to believe in God cannot be made on purely rational grounds. Despite this, James argued, in labelling any choice wrong Clifford seeks to prevent people making the choice to believe and makes them live like unbelievers by default.

Strictly speaking, Clifford's evidentialism can only support agnosticism, not atheism. The evidence doesn't support belief in God, but it can't support belief that God does not exist either. For James, faith is not just an intellectual decision, it is a state of existence bound up with how we live our lives. It is highly unlikely that somebody who lives as an atheist will suddenly convert to real faith. Choosing not to live a religious life effectively rules most people out of developing in faith.

James suggests that Clifford forces people to choose not to believe when that choice is as indefensible as the choice to believe would be! James went on to argue that people have more to lose in being paralysed by doubt than they have to gain; that there is a pragmatic case for abandoning empiricism and choosing to believe on the basis of passion, not reason.

For James, we cannot make the decision about God and about how to live on intellectual grounds, so we have to make our best guess, putting ourselves in the best possible position as regards both living a good life now and benefiting from an afterlife, if such exists. For the heirs of Clifford such a game is not worth playing; it is stupid and wrong to encourage people to guess beyond what they can reasonably know. It would be better to refuse to choose, even if that meant potentially losing out, than to take part in such a silly show.

Nevertheless, despite the logic of James' argument, most scientists and philosophers were more persuaded by a superficial materialist reading of Clifford's position. For more than a hundred years religion has been operating in what has been described as a 'hegemony of evidentialism'. Believers either try to argue that their faith is based on sufficient evidence of one sort of another, or they try to challenge evidentialism itself, either by suggesting instances in which it is sensible or necessary to believe without evidence or, like Alvin Plantinga, by pointing out that evidentialism is self-referentially inconsistent, that there is no evidence for evidentialism.[7]

## Faith as Anti-intellectual

Richard Dawkins labelled faith anti-intellectual. In his bestselling book *The God Delusion* (2006) he wrote that '[i]t is the nature of faith that one is capable of holding a belief without adequate reason to do so'[8] and that '[r]eason is the greatest enemy of faith, it never comes to the aid of spiritual things but frequently struggles against the divine word, treating with contempt all that emanates from God'.[9] Dawkins has said that '[f]aith is the great cop-out, the great excuse to evade the need to think and evaluate evidence. Faith is the belief in spite of, even perhaps because of, the lack of evidence.'[10]

Dawkins asserts that faith is potentially dangerous, observing that

> [t]he God of the Old Testament is arguably the most unpleasant character in all fiction: jealous and proud of it; a petty, unjust, unforgiving control-freak; a vindictive, bloodthirsty ethnic cleanser; a misogynistic, homophobic, racist, infanticidal, genocidal, filicidal, pestilential, megalomaniacal, sadomasochistic, capriciously malevolent bully.[11]

For Dawkins and his fellow celebrity-atheists, as for Clifford back in the nineteenth century, the idea that tribal religion is a rational response to the human experience of the natural universe seems ludicrous.

---

7 Plantinga, 'Reason and Belief in God', p. 60.

8 Ibid., p. 51.

9 Ibid., p. 190.

10 Quoted by Alister McGrath in *Christianity: An Introduction*, 2nd edn, Oxford: Blackwell Publishing, 2006, p. 102.

11 Dawkins, *The God Delusion*, London: Bantam Press, 2006, p. 31.

Further, for Dawkins, the classical arguments for God's existence are flawed and, in any case, result in a deity so far removed from the God revealed in scripture as to make them an irrelevance as a basis for being a Christian, a Muslim or a Jew.

Dawkins dismisses all claims that religious beliefs ever could be based on sufficient evidence. Instead, in *The Selfish Gene* and subsequent works, he has developed the theory that faith and religious belief spread as a *meme*. The word *meme* is a shortening of the Greek word μίμημα which means 'something imitated'. Dawkins uses the concept to explain the spread of ideas, writing that

> examples of memes are tunes, ideas, catch-phrases, clothes fashions, ways of making pots or of building arches. Just as genes propagate themselves in the gene pool by leaping from body to body via sperms or eggs, so memes propagate themselves in the meme pool by leaping from brain to brain via a process which, in the broad sense, can be called imitation.[12]

Aaron Lynch in *Thought Contagion: How Belief Spreads through Society*[13] and Susan Blackmore in her article 'Imitation and the definition of a meme'[14] developed the meme idea and applied it to religious ideas. Dawkins adopted their argument and argued that faith is a meme which attacks the young and leaves them credulous, less able to think critically and so deprived of a full human relationship with reality.

Taking his cue from Clifford's argument in *The Ethics of Belief*, Dawkins argues that faith can be dangerous and consequently that encouraging its spread is irresponsible to the point of wickedness. Because of this he has campaigned against all forms of religion in public life and particularly against faith schools. In 2012 he founded

---

12 Dawkins, *The Selfish Gene,* 2nd edn, Oxford: Oxford University Press, 1989, p. 192.

13 New York: Basic Books, 1996.

14 *Journal of Memetics – Evolutionary Models of Information Transmission,* 2, 1998.

the Richard Dawkins Foundation for Reason and Science, to further his aims.[15] Dawkins seizes upon the special status and respect afforded to religion in most societies and on the measures taken to encourage tolerance by Western multicultural societies and seeks to show that all of this is misguided lunacy. He points to the moral character of the God of the Old Testament, the questionable readings of the Qur'an which motivate suicide bombers and the extreme literalism of Hasidic Judaism, suggesting that religion is neither quaint nor harmless, but rather insidious and corrupting.

Alister McGrath is probably the best qualified opponent of Dawkins' argument. He holds a DPhil. in biochemistry from Oxford University and is currently Professor of Theology, Ministry and Education at King's College, London and head of its Centre for Theology, Religion and Culture. Before moving to King's in 2008 he was Professor of Historical Theology at Oxford University.[16] In 2004 in *Dawkins' God: Genes, Memes, and the Meaning of Life* he attacked Dawkins' argument that religion is a *meme* specifically and in detail.

McGrath argued that there are four difficulties with the argument:

1 There is no reason to suppose that cultural evolution is Darwinian, or indeed that evolutionary biology has any particular value in accounting for the development of ideas.
2 There is no direct observational evidence for the existence of *memes* themselves.
3 The existence of the *meme* itself rests on an analogy with the gene itself, which proves incapable of bearing the weight that is placed upon it.

---

15 http://richarddawkinsfoundation.org/.

16 McGrath is the author of many widely used textbooks, including *A Fine-Tuned Universe: The Quest for God in Science and Theology*, Louisville: Westminster John Knox Press, 2009. He has been involved in public debates with leading representatives of the New Atheism, including Richard Dawkins and the late Christopher Hitchens.

4 Quite unlike the gene, there is no necessary reason to propose the existence of a *meme*. The observational data can be accounted for perfectly well by other models and mechanisms.

According to McGrath, Dawkins' own neo-Darwinian position is no more or less credible than most people's faith in God. However, while Dawkins may struggle to defend his evidentialist world-view (in the same way as Clifford's followers initially struggled to dismiss James' challenge) the faithful also struggle to explain why their religious world-view offers more than alternative world-views, that their model accounts for reality better than the alternatives, and they also struggle to provide observational evidence for God and to defend the content of claims that God is creator, designer or Father.

Dawkins utterly rejects the suggestion that his position is as much of a faith-position as the religious views he abhors. He focuses on key differences between his world-view and religious world-views.

- First, his model is *verifiable*, based on evidence which can be independently tested and observed through the five senses.
- Second, his model is *falsifiable*. He accepts that his theory could be shown to be false if particular pieces of new evidence came to light, such as fossils of a rabbit or a hippo being discovered in pre-cambrian rocks.[17]

In Dawkins' opinion, belief in anything which cannot be verified or falsified is wrong, potentially corrosive to the critical faculties, to our ability to distinguish truth from lies in the future. Like Clifford, Dawkins sees believing things without sufficient evidence as morally offensive, not just unhelpful. Dawkins, however, seems to define evidence primarily in terms of what can be known through the senses and to be more of a materialist than Clifford.

Finally, for Dawkins, a scientific world-view offers a simpler and more elegant solution to the question of origins than any

17 http://www.time.com/time/magazine/article/0,9171,1090909-6,00.html.

God-hypothesis. He asserts that seeing the universe as the product of a Big Bang caused by random quantum activity and all life as the product of four billion years of evolution, of natural environmental adaptation, is simpler than seeing it as the result of Divine creation.

The lavish use of allegory, metaphor and symbolism to explore alien concepts – and widespread tolerance of superficial thinking and talking – gives many people the impression that 'God' means an old man with a white beard sitting on a cloud, who might have said 'Let there be light' around 6,000 years ago. Dawkins dismisses belief in such a deity with scorn – and it is right to say that this explanation for the universe seems much less elegant and probable than its scientific competitor. Yet Dawkins' caricature impression of God is far from what all believers believe. It is a straw man, a false picture built up because it is easier to knock down than a more profound understanding of God.

## Summary

What we believe is not just a private matter because belief is the foundation of action. As Clifford suggested, holding beliefs that are not proportionate to the evidence may be morally wrong. Nevertheless, this begs a question over the status of beliefs concerning matters on which evidence is not forthcoming. What counts as evidence? Is empirical data the only permissible type of evidence or is it reasonable to accept beliefs founded on logical evidence or even authority?

Is it morally wrong to believe in God when there is little observable evidence for God's existence, let alone God's attributes? William James argued that the decision over whether to believe in God cannot be made on intellectual grounds, but is nonetheless *forced* and *momentous*. He made a case for choosing to put oneself in the best position for faith to develop because doing so is *pragmatic*, because doing so will yield the best results in this life and potentially in the next.

Richard Dawkins agrees with Clifford that believing beyond the evidence is morally wrong, corrosive to the intellectual faculties, both of individuals and even whole societies. He maintains that all beliefs must be based on observable evidence; they must be *verifiable* or at least *falsifiable* – in so doing he goes further than Clifford. Although the evidentialist position has been criticized by Plantinga and others for being self-referentially inconsistent, it remains highly influential, meaning that most faiths today operate within a 'hegemony of evidentialism'. Many people are closet verificationists and accept only empirical evidence, but perhaps this is far too narrow a way of understanding the nature of ultimate reality – as Clifford himself recognized.

# PART TWO

# Arguing for God

In science it often happens that scientists say, 'You know that's a really good argument; my position is mistaken,' and then they would actually change their minds and you never hear that old view from them again. They really do it. It doesn't happen as often as it should, because scientists are human and change is sometimes painful. But it happens every day. I cannot recall the last time something like that happened in politics or religion.

(Carl Sagan)

# 3

# Arguing for God

All opinions are not equal. Some are a very great deal more robust, sophisticated and well supported in logic and argument than others.

(Douglas Adams, *The Salmon of Doubt*)

Philosophers have long attempted to argue for God's existence. For Roman Catholics, many of whom have propositional faith, such arguments are part of the business of natural theology, which provides a substantial basis for *believing that* God exists. Further, even for some Protestants whose faith is non-propositional and who *believe in* God independently of arguments, they may be a useful way of defending their beliefs and of finding out more about the nature of God. Arguments for the existence of God are therefore proposed both by philosophers of religion and as part of philosophical theology. As part of the philosophy of religion the aim of such arguments will be to convince people that God exists; however, within philosophical theology the aim will be to show that belief in God is not irrational and perhaps to explain what people believe about God's nature.

Broadly speaking, there are two types of reasons or *propositions* which may be cited in an argument to support a point or conclusion.

Most commonly, propositions are based on observable *synthetic* evidence. For example, I might cite my observations of swans to support my point that all swans are white, stating 'Given my records of swans on the Thames and at Abbotsbury I conclude that swans are large white birds.' This sort of evidence appeals to people, but it is limited. Although arguments based on synthetic observations may advance human knowledge, conclusions supported by synthetic evidence are always subject to new or different evidence coming to light. This is known as the general *problem of induction*.

For example, if an Australian heard me arguing that all swans are white, they could recount their own experiences of black swans to *falsify* my argument. Scientific method requires that all conclusions are based upon observable evidence; it follows that all scientific arguments or theories are *falsifiable* or subject to revision if and when new or different evidence emerges. As another example, if the fossil of a hippo was found in pre-cambrian rocks even Richard Dawkins would be forced to admit that the current theory of evolution by natural selection was inadequate.

Synthetic arguments are normally also called *a posteriori* arguments. This is because the point is only shown to be true after (post) the observable facts are enumerated. Synthetic *a posteriori* arguments may always be criticized for offering only a probability, never a certainty, that the conclusion is true. Further, the individual observations may be irrelevant, inadequate or even misrepresented; they may not logically support the conclusion in the way that the proposer intended.

Sometimes people cite a different sort of reason to support their point. *Analytic* arguments look inside the point that is being made and suggest that the point is true by definition. For example, I might state that 'I know that Luke is a bachelor, because he is not married.' The concept of being a bachelor includes being an unmarried man. All unmarried men are bachelors. The point is necessarily true because of the meaning of the words, as philosophers would say *de dicto* (truth is based on the meaning of words). Mathematical arguments are like this: 2 + 2 = 4 is true because the concept 4 contains the concept 2 + 2. The truth of an analytic argument is certain, provided that people agree on the content of the concepts, the meaning of the words. On the other hand, analytic arguments do not advance knowledge very much. Saying 'Luke is a bachelor' and saying 'Luke is unmarried', saying '4' and saying '2 + 2' are just different ways of saying the same thing or, as philosophers would put it, they are *tautologies*.

Analytic arguments are sometimes called *a priori* arguments. This is because the definition of terms has to be agreed before (prior to) the argument working. Analytic *a priori* arguments require that people accept their definition of terms. The argument $a = 1$, $b = 2$ therefore $a + b = 3$ requires that people accept that $a$ really does equal 1 and $b$ 2, also that the numbers 1, 2 and 3 and the symbols = and + mean what they usually do, if it is to work. The first way of criticizing an analytic argument is to disagree with its definitions.

Such arguments may be valid without necessarily being sound. Take the example of a valid but unsound argument:

P1    All toasters are items made of gold.
P2    All items made of gold are time-travel devices.
C    Therefore, all toasters are time-travel devices.

It is obvious that both proposition 1 and proposition 2 are not borne out in reality and that the conclusion is pure nonsense, yet *if* P1 and P2 had been true the conclusion would indeed have followed on necessarily. The structure of the argument is *valid*, but it is not *sound* because its premises and thus its conclusion are not true.

Take another example, the argument:

P1    The Holy Qur'an is the word of God and cannot err.
P2    The Holy Qur'an teaches that Mohammed is the prophet of God.
C    Therefore, Mohammed is the prophet of God

is *valid*; if the premises are correct then the conclusion follows necessarily from them. However, many non-Muslims would not accept the first premise and, if they are right and the Qur'an is not the word of God, this would make the argument *unsound*.

In recent years some scholars have pointed to the inadequacy of the traditional synthetic/analytic categorization of arguments. Arguably, many apparently inductive arguments, which seek to infer a conclusion as being logically supported by a series of synthetic observations, are actually *abductive*. Abductive reasoning goes beyond what observations can logically support to conclude what seems to be the best explanation for the evidence.

For example, if I went out into the garden and found that my rhubarb bushes had been destroyed overnight, I might see the evidence pointing towards the guilt of a certain rabbit. Taken together, sightings of a large, fat and bold rabbit in my flower-beds (let's call him the Were-rabbit), bite-marks on stems about six inches from the ground, and the presence of a newly dug hole in the lawn make my explanation seem compelling.

However, it is possible to offer alternative explanations which would account for these observations equally well.

- Perhaps my three-year-old daughter is an insomniac trainee gardener with a passion for rhubarb. Perhaps she trotted downstairs in the dead of night, trying out her new trowel on the lawn before being overcome by temptation and stopping to gnaw on a few juicy stems?
- Perhaps my father has developed a pathological hatred of rabbits and, knowing my aversion to having them shot or poisoned, has framed the Were-rabbit for destroying my rhubarb as part of a cunning plan to get me to back down and allow him to have them exterminated.

What makes me conclude that the observations support the conclusion of the Were-rabbit's guilt? Logic doesn't make me exclude the other options; rather, it is the process of my weighing up probabilities.

Abduction is the process of moving from observations to *the best explanation* of those observations; it involves my weighing up the *probabilities* and perhaps considering a whole host of other factors to help me refine my judgement. It is probably the most common form of reasoning.

It is relatively rare to know something because it is necessarily and conceptually true or because it follows logically from personal observations. In many cases knowledge depends upon what other people have said; we weigh up their credibility, the probability that what they say is reliable, and choose to believe them and not to check the facts for ourselves. This process is generally quite reasonable, but could perpetuate beliefs which are not based on proper evidence.

Arguably, many scientific arguments are *abductive* and not truly inductive. Doctors typically use abductive reasoning when diagnosing patients. For example, in a long-running television series Hugh Laurie plays Dr Gregory House who specializes in drawing diagnoses out of assembled symptoms and other insights.[1] The philosopher of science Ernan McMullin described abduction as 'the inference that makes science',[2] explaining how important breakthroughs are made when scientists don't restrict themselves to the conclusion which is strictly supported by the observations, but use the observations to suggest the most probable hypothesis which might later be able to be tested through experiment or observation.

At the beginning of the nineteenth century it was discovered that the orbit of Uranus (one of the seven planets known at the time) departed from the orbit which had been predicted on the basis of Isaac Newton's theory of universal gravitation. One possible explanation was that Newton's theory was false, but another explanation was that there was an eighth, as yet undiscovered, planet. Adams and Leverrier both argued that the eighth planet was a better explanation than Newton's theory being false; Newton's theory had proved useful in so many other circumstances. Neptune was discovered soon afterwards.

Abduction is an important process in the philosophy of religion as well. As William James observed, strict logic cannot always help us to decide between possible explanations of the universe or allow belief in one theory to be more warranted than belief in another. Philosophers of religion, including Richard Swinburne and Alvin Plantinga, have investigated the relative probabilities of God existing and not existing and the possible warrant for believing that God does exist, but it remains difficult to defend belief when

---

1 Fox Network, 2004–2012.
2 *The Inference that Makes Science*, Milwaukee WI: Marquette University Press, 1992.

non-theistic explanations are so compelling and argument does not conclusively demonstrate God's existence, either inductively or deductively. Theists must at least make a case that God is reasonably *inferred to be a better explanation* than the alternatives. Alister McGrath is just one example of a philosopher who argues in these terms.

## Summary

Arguments for the existence of God provide reasons to believe (propositions). These propositions might consist of observations (synthetic) or an analysis of the concept of God (analytic).

Most arguments move from effect to cause, concluding that God exists by *a posteriori* argument starting from observed facts (such as motion, causation, etc.). These arguments are only ever so good as the initial observed facts as well as the logical steps that follow from the initial premises.

Ontological arguments start with a definition of God, trying to demonstrate that existence is a necessary part of the nature of God. These arguments are going to work only if people accept the initial definition of God *a priori* as well as the steps that follow from this.

There is another approach to arguing for God's existence, which would suggest that God's existence may be inferred as the best explanation for any number of other factors. This is known as *abductive* reasoning; it yields a high probability which it may be plausible to accept, but these type of arguments cannot prove God's existence conclusively. At best they may be persuasive.

# 4

# Cosmological Arguments

We know that God is everywhere; but we feel His presence most when His works are on the grandest scale spread before us; and it is in the unclouded night-sky, where His worlds wheel their silent course, that we read clearest His infinitude.

(Charlotte Brontë, *Jane Eyre*)

The cosmological argument is often presented as the simplest argument for God's existence. It infers the existence of God from the fact that anything at all exists.

The argument is certainly persuasive. Professor Richard Swinburne (b. 1934) wrote:

The human quest for explanation inevitably and rightly seeks for the ultimate explanation of everything observable – that object or objects on which everything else depends for its existence and properties . . . A may be explained by B, and B by C, but in the end there will be some one object on whom all other objects depend. We will have to acknowledge something as ultimate – the great metaphysical issue is what that is . . . Theism claims that every other object which exists is caused to exist and kept in existence by just one substance, God . . . There could in this respect be no simpler explanation than one which postulated only one cause.[1]

Today, many people even reconcile belief in the scientific theories of Big Bang and evolution through natural selection with theism by suggesting that God started the natural process.

---

1 *Is There a God?*, Oxford: Oxford University Press, 1996.

William Lane Craig (b. 1949) is an American Christian philosopher of religion. In *The Cosmological Argument from Plato to Leibniz* (1980) he argued that there are three distinct forms of cosmological argument ...

1 Arguments based on the impossibility of an actual infinity in temporal regress. E.g. Kalam arguments, based on Plato.
2 Arguments based on the impossibility of infinite contingency. E.g. Aquinas' arguments, based on Aristotle.
3 Arguments based on the Principle of Sufficient Reason. E.g. Leibniz' argument.

It is worth considering each form of cosmological argument separately here.


## Kalam Arguments

The so-called Kalam argument is a particular version of the cosmological argument which suggests that the universe must have a cause of its existence, something which is uncaused and is what everybody calls God. Kalam arguments rely on temporal causation and might be understood in terms of a line of dominoes. Each domino must be pushed by one before it, and as an infinite temporal regress of causes is impossible, there must be a first domino, which must be pushed by something which is not pushed or caused, a necessary being, God.

Kalam arguments may be understood to have their origins in the writings of Plato. Plato's cosmological argument can be found in the tenth chapter of the *Laws*, in an exchange between Clinias and an Athenian stranger. Plato began his attempt to prove the existence of the gods by arguing that, of all the different types of motion, the motion 'which can move itself' is 'necessarily the earliest and mightiest of all changes'. He wrote:

When we have one thing making a change in a second, the second, in turn, in a third, and so on – will there ever, in such a series, be a first source of change? Why, how can what is set moving by something other than itself ever be the first of the causes of alteration? The thing is an impossibility. But when something which has set itself moving alters a second thing, this second thing still a third, and the motion is thus passed on in course to thousands and tens of thousands of things, will there be any starting point for the whole movement of all, other than the change in the movements which initiated itself?

Plato's argument was founded on the belief that an infinite regress cannot occur. If an infinite regress cannot occur, then there must have been a first motion. It then follows that this first motion must have set itself into motion, for there would have been nothing else to set it into motion. Note that this sort of cause does not necessarily sustain the universe; it might no longer exist or be involved in creation. The cause of the universe in the Kalam argument could be understood as a cause *in fieri*; like a match it could 'light the blue touch paper' and start the universe, but then be taken away.

In the ninth century, Islamic *mutakallimiin*, scholars of the Kalam school, used debate and philosophical discussion to support and explore their faith in Allah and their understanding of the revealed Qur'an. They drew on the work of classical philosophers such as Plato and Aristotle as well as the neo-Platonist Plotinus and later Christian and Jewish interpreters such as John Philoponus (d. 570) and Saadia (d. 942).

One of the first great Kalam philosophers was Al-Kindi (801–73CE). He accepted the Qur'an's account of creation, which saw the universe being created at a point in time. He then argued from the existence of the universe to the existence of God, suggesting that an actual infinite regress of causes is impossible and that our present reality must have begun with an uncaused cause, Allah. For Al Kindi the world requires a creator (*mudhith*) who could generate the world out of nothing. He wrote:

We say that the true, first act is the bringing-to-be of beings from non-being. It is clear that this act is proper to God, the exalted,

49

who is the end of every cause. For the bringing-to-be of beings from non-being belongs to no other.[2]

Kalam arguments had critics from the outset. Al-Ghazali was not convinced by Al Kindi's argument. He thought that it is at least theoretically possible for there to be an infinite regress, writing that

> according to the hypothesis under consideration, it has been established that all the beings in the world have a cause. Now, let the cause itself have a cause, and the cause of the cause have yet another cause, and so on ad infinitum. It does not behove you to say that an infinite regress of causes is impossible.[3]

This criticism anticipated the conclusions of later, Western thinkers such as Bertrand Russell.

In *The Kalam Cosmological Argument*,[4] Craig developed a new version of the traditional Islamic argument, arguing that since the universe began to exist, the cause of the universe's existence must have been God. Like all versions of the cosmological argument, Craig's moves from effect to cause, relies on observation and produces an *a posteriori* argument, but also like many versions of the cosmological argument, Craig relies on some principles which cannot be conclusively proven through observation (though they may be consistent with observations). The *a priori* principle implicit in Craig's argument is that an actual infinite is impossible.

If an actual infinite is impossible, then, Craig argues, the universe must be finite in time. In other words, the universe must have begun to exist. Craig concludes that the historical Kalam arguments for the temporality of the universe 'demonstrate that the world had a

---

2 Quoted by Peter Adamson in *Al Kindi*, Great Medieval Thinkers Series, New York: Oxford University Press, 2007, p. 61.

3 Al-Ghazali, *Tahafut Al-Falasifah* (*The Incoherence of Philosophers*), trans. Sabih Ahmad Kamali, Lahore: Pakistan Philosophical Congress, 1963, pp. 90–1.

4 London: Macmillan, 1979.

beginning at a point of time. Having demonstrated the temporality of the world, the theologian may then ask why it exists'.[5]

Craig's neat argument runs as follows:

P1  Everything that begins to exist has a cause of its existence.
P2  The universe began to exist; therefore
C   the universe has a cause of its existence.

This owes a great deal to the eleventh-century statement of the argument made by Al-Ghazali (1058–1111) in the *Tahafut*, the very statement which he used as the basis for criticizing the whole Kalam approach to arguing for God.

Arguably, Craig relies upon the Islamic *principle of determination*, by which any being or effect requires a being who decides the course of an action between two likely choices. The universe may have been larger or smaller than it is, many billions of years older or younger, or it may even have failed to exist; any of these possibilities are logically possible alternatives. Ibn Rushd (1126–98) stated that 'the admissible is created and it has a creator, namely, an agent, who out of two admissibilities turns it into one rather than the other'.[6]

Only a thinking being can make the choice to create the universe at the moment that it was created; the Creator could have created the universe an hour earlier or waited several days before doing so. This principle assumes, of course, that things were in some sense bound to be this way and that the way things are cannot reasonably be seen to be by chance. It also assumes that determination must be the result of intelligence or conscious choice, rather than a blind natural force. Both assumptions would be challenged by, for instance, Richard Dawkins.

Some commentators have suggested that Craig's Kalam argument fails. In the first place he attracted criticism from scientists and their

5  Ibid., pp. 9–10.
6  Quoted by James Still in 'Eternity and Time in William Lane Craig's *Kalam Cosmological Argument*', available online at http://www.infidels.org/library/modern/james_still/ kalam.html.

interpreters, including Stephen Hawking (b. 1942) and Paul Davies (b. 1946), who suggested that Craig misinterpreted some of their findings. Craig responded to their criticisms, but Graham Oppy (b. 1960) at least found his defence unconvincing.[7]

Quentin Smith (b. 1952) argued from quantum mechanical considerations that the universe could begin to exist without an efficient cause. He also argued that the Kalam argument does not preclude the possibility of an infinite past. In 1991 Craig defended his position,[8] arguing that an actual infinite by successive addition is impossible and so the past cannot be infinite either. One can have a potentially infinite series of numbers but not an actual infinite – a library with an infinite number of books is impossible (one cannot have an actual library with an infinite number of books as one could always add another book) and so is an infinite number of past states. However, in 1995 Graham Oppy dismissed Craig's argument in favour of the impossibility of an actual infinite[9] and in 1997 and 1999 substantial critiques of Craig's argument were produced by Andrew Lias[10] and Eric Sotnak.[11]

## Arguments from Contingency

Whereas Plato's philosophy started with ideas, Aristotle's philosophy started with experience.

---

7 Graham Oppy, 'Professor William Craig's Criticisms of Critiques of Kalam Cosmological Arguments by Paul Davies, Stephen Hawking, and Adolf Grünbaum', *Faith And Philosophy* 12 (1995), pp. 237–50.

8 *The Existence of God and the Beginning of the Universe*, 'Time and Infinity', *International Philosophical Quarterly* 31, (1991), pp. 387–401.

9 'Inverse Operations with Transfinite Numbers and the Kalam Cosmological Argument', *International Philosophical Quarterly* 35:2 (1995), pp. 219–21.

10 'The Kalam Cosmological Argument: A Rebuttal', http://www.religiouseducation.co.uk/school/alevel/philosophy/cosmological/Kalam_rebuttal.htm.

11 'The Kalam Cosmological Argument and the Possibility of an Actually Infinite Future', *Philo* 2:2 (1999), pp. 41–52.

Unlike Plato, Aristotle reasoned that for all we know, the universe could be eternal; before radio telescopes, there was no observable evidence suggesting that the universe began and no observable evidence suggesting that it would end. This made Aristotle's philosophy controversial in religious circles. Both the Qur'an and the Bible teach that God created the world and that it will, one day, cease to exist in its present form. While Islamic, Jewish and Christian philosophers all found Aristotle's ideas compelling, they had difficulty in convincing authorities that they were not heretical.

One aspect of Aristotle's thought offered the possibility of reconciling his approach with belief in a creator-God. He posited the existence of a '*Prime Mover*' to account for the existence of movement, the actualizing of all forms of potential, in the universe. In Aristotle's *Physics* and in the *Metaphysics* he argued that

P1   All things that are in motion must be moved by something.[12]

P2   That mover which is ultimately responsible for moving another thing must be responsible for its own motion.

C     That which moves itself must be something unlike all other things, an unmoved *Prime Mover*.

For Aristotle, *motion* denotes *all change*, not just physical movement in space. His argument differs from that of Plato in opening up the possibility of causation leading to a sustaining cause, a cause *in esse*, rather than back in time to a cause *in fieri*, a cause which (like a spark) starts things off but may go out and have no further involvement in its effects.

For Aristotle, all change involves the actualizing of some potentiality. A human embryo has the potential to become a foetus, a crawling baby, a toddler, an adult and a geriatric. You have the potential to be here or flying over the Pacific, climbing Mount Everest or diving in the Red Sea. The nature of reality, of time and space, means that you cannot fulfil all of your potential simultaneously. Because things have potentiality, they are able to change in time and space. Potential

---

12 *Physics*, Book V.

cannot actualize itself; potential, precisely because it is potential, cannot make itself actual but must be actualized by external agent(s) within time and space. A baby, given time, will grow into an adult; if you start walking east in France, you will soon actualize your potential to be in Germany.

Nevertheless, Aristotle claimed that the first mover that is ultimately responsible for moving or changing things must be responsible for its own motion. He restated Plato's argument that, since an infinite regress cannot occur, the ultimate mover in a series must be self-moved. To make this point, he gave the example of a man who uses a stick to move a rock. It is clear that the stick, which is not ultimately responsible for moving the rock, is not self-moved; it is moved by a hand. Similarly, the hand, which also is not ultimately responsible for moving the rock, is not self-moved; it is moved by a person. Even the person is caused to move by things outside itself (including the sun, food and even gravity). All motion, Aristotle believed, must be like this, caused to move by something else that is itself moved until one reaches the ultimate cause of all motion – something that is unmoved by anything outside itself.

Aristotle reasoned that a self-moving object cannot be entirely in motion but must be fully actual and without potential to change. It must be fully what it is without any potential or capacity to change – so it must be outside both space and time (since space and time involve change). If every moving object must be moved by something else and if one is then forced to conclude that there must be a Prime Mover which is responsible for all other motion, then this, Aristotle concludes, must be what is called *theos* or God.

It is important to understand that Aristotle's God does not create the universe from nothing and really seems to have no interest in the universe or anything that happens within it. This would support *deism* at most, not *theism* or the God of Islam or Christianity. Nevertheless, Aristotle's God is perfectly fulfilled, fully actual, timeless, spaceless and unchanging. All earthly things are partial, transient, they fade and decay. Ultimately everything can be or not be. God is necessarily different and *other*. God, for Aristotle, does not do anything but God attracts or draws the universe towards God's self and thereby causes the motion in the universe. Everything in the universe is contingent, dependent, characterized by having potential and being subject to change. God is neither some-thing nor no-thing; God is pure actuality, existence itself.

Despite Aristotle's understanding leading to a rather remote 'God of the Philosophers' and not the recognizable 'God of Abraham',[13] philosophers seized upon Aristotle's argument because it offered a way of reconciling Greek philosophy with Islamic, Jewish or Christian theology – and, enticingly, of proving God's existence through a process of rational observation.

Philosophers of the Islamic *Falsafa* school such as Al-Farabi (d. 950), Ibn-Sina (d. 1037) and Ibn Rushd (d. 1198) developed cosmological arguments specifically from contingency, based on the ideas of Aristotle. Their arguments assumed that the universe is everlasting – controversially contradicting the Qur'an.

Ibn Sina interpreted the Qur'an through the lens of rational argument, rejecting the idea of bodily resurrection and arguing that the world was not created from nothing. He accepted Aristotle's view that God was timeless and spaceless, utterly unchangeable and was needed only to explain motion in the universe.

Ibn Sina's argument for God's existence runs as follows:

P1   Things cannot come into existence from nothing.
P2   There cannot be an infinite series of causes as then there would be no explanation for the whole series.
IC   Given P2, the chain of causation cannot be circular.
C    There must be a *de re necessary being* – a being having of itself its own necessity on which every other existing thing depends.

Importantly, Ibn Sina distinguishes three different kinds of existence:

1   Things that are by their natures *de re necessary*, providing the explanation for their own existence and other things' existence within themselves.

---

13  This distinction was made by Pascal.

2 Things that possibly exist that owe their existence to something else and are contingent.

3 Things that are impossible and do not exist.

God, Ibn Sina argues, is the only necessary being; there is no distinction between essence and existence in God. God IS God's existence, God is fully actual. God depends on nothing else for God's existence as otherwise God would not be God. Ibn Sina's work anticipated and directly influenced the arguments of Thomas Aquinas.

Ibn Rushd (1126–98) lived most of his life in Cordoba, Spain. He wrote a number of commentaries on the works of Aristotle and used Aristotelian ideas to argue that since God is timeless, spaceless and bodiless, *God does not act in time*. Ibn Rushd reasoned that if God is perfect and changeless, there cannot be in any meaningful sense a time when God acts to create. God cannot 'just decide' to do something. It is necessary to interpret the Qur'an through the lens of philosophy, appreciating that its account of creation, as well as the many other things it says about God's actions and will, must be understood symbolically.

Ibn Rushd agreed with Ibn Sina that heaven and hell are just allegories; they are not real in any literal sense. He also rejected the idea of a bodily resurrection and argued that only the intellectual soul which is filled with universal truths from the transcendent world survives death. Salvation, he argued, is achieved through the intellect; only those who have the knowledge of logic and philosophy can be saved.

In his famous work *The Incoherence of the Philosophers (Tahafut)*, Al Ghazali denounced such Aristotelian scholars as basically unislamic. Al Ghazali argued that faith should be independent of not just Aristotelian reason but of all reason and philosophy – God is inherently mysterious. Ibn Rushd and Ibn Sina had both argued that the Qu'ran could only be interpreted correctly by trained philosophers, and Al Ghazali's rejection of this became increasingly popular with many Muslims who held that, since God created the Qu'ran for ordinary believers, one did not have to be a philosopher to understand the text correctly. The Islamic tradition of philosophy was destroyed and the place of reason within Islam has never been restored.

Both Ibn Sina and Ibn Rushd were to have a profound effect on Western philosophy. Some of the works of Aristotle have been lost in the West for centuries; they had, however, been translated into Arabic in universities like Baghdad during the first decades of Islam and so were able to be re-imported into Europe by the twelfth century. The University of Paris became a centre for the study of Aristotle, and scholars used the work of Arabic commentators such as Ibn Sina and Ibn Rushd to help them to understand and interpret Aristotelian ideas.

The works of Aristotle, Ibn Sina (Avicenna) and Ibn Rushd (Averroes) were initially viewed with suspicion. Studying them was banned by the Bishop of Paris in 1210 (which caused the Universities of Toulouse and Oxford to gain strength in offering protection to academics who wished to continue their work) and banned again in 1270. By 1277 a group of academics called the Latin Averroists had been formally charged with heresy (if Aquinas had lived three years longer, he would almost certainly have been one of this group).

It was against this background that Thomas Aquinas (1215–74) wrote his monumental works in theology, including the *Summa Contra Gentiles* and the *Summa Theologica*. Aquinas eagerly adopted Aristotle's ideas, and was influenced in how he interpreted them by Ibn Sina and Ibn Rushd, but his towering achievement was to develop them into a philosophy which was acceptable to Christians and which eventually became the central framework of Roman Catholic Christian doctrine.

## Aquinas' Ways to God

Thomas Aquinas put forward five ways to arrive at the existence of God, summarizing them in barely two pages of his enormous *Summa Theologica*. Today these arguments are usually treated as stand-alone proofs, but this may not be how Aquinas intended them to be used. For Aquinas, the existence of God was unquestioned. The arguments demonstrated the rationality of belief, but were not intended as the primary reason for faith.

None of the Five Ways is entirely original. Anthony Kenny (b. 1931) puts them firmly in the context of Aristotelian thought, showing how they should not be understood in isolation but as part of a broader system, though this is not always considered today. All of the arguments are synthetic, *a posteriori*, they move from observations of the world to a conclusion which seeks to explain those observations. Aquinas argued from:

- Motion.
- Efficient causes.
- Contingency.
- Grades of perfection.
- Design.

Unlike Plato and Aristotle, Aquinas chose to differentiate between chains of movement, chains of efficient causation and the brute contingency of beings, developing three related but distinct cosmological arguments.

Part of the significance of this lies in the way in which Aquinas understood the universe. Aquinas accepted that the universe had a beginning in time as a matter of faith and based on revelation. As an Aristotelian he did not see that human beings are in a position to know that the universe has a beginning on the basis of logic or physical evidence. In conscience, Aquinas had to make his arguments work whether or not the universe had a beginning in time.

## The First Way

Taking the first sentence of the first argument in isolation, namely:

> The first and more manifest way is the argument from motion. It is certain, and evident to our senses, that in the world some things are in motion. Now whatever is in motion is put in motion by another . . .

you might understand that Aquinas is reiterating the old Kalam argument from temporal causation or seemingly using a crude 'domino' argument. In fact the first way is more subtle; it uses the word 'motion' in its Aristotelian sense, meaning all forms of change from potentiality to actuality.

As we have seen, for Aristotle all things have potentialities. A stick has the potential to be living on the tree, full of sap and supporting leaves, or dry on the woodpile or burning in the grate – or ash in the bucket. It cannot actualize all of its potential at the same time and place. Nothing in this world is 100 per cent actual, fully what it has the potential to be. Further, nothing changes or actualizes part of its potential without being changed by something else. The stick does not spontaneously combust – it is set alight by a lit match. Everything and every change depends on other things and other changes. Taking a step back, this does not appear to make sense. If everything must have its potential actualized by something else and nothing can be its own explanation, then nothing should exist – but it does!

Aquinas concludes that an actual infinity in movement is impossible and there must be something, unlike any other thing, that could be its own explanation, an unmoved *Prime Mover* that could go on to actualize all other potential.

It might seem that this means that God has potentiality to change since everything in the universe which moves something else changes from one state to another in the act of moving something else. However, this is not the case. Aristotle argued that God creates motion by attracting or drawing the universe towards God's self – like a magnet causing iron filings to move or a bowl of milk causing a cat to be drawn across a room. God does nothing at all and yet God is still responsible for all motion in the universe. Aquinas was to modify this idea, arguing that this was the God of Christianity.

## The Second Way

Aquinas' second argument arises from the Aristotelian theory of causation. For Aristotle all things have four causes: material causes (ingredients), efficient causes (agents which cause them to be), formal causes (a definition or essence) and a final cause (a purpose or goal). Focusing on efficient causes, nothing exists in the world which is not caused by some other thing, so Aquinas concludes that there must be a first cause, because an actual infinity of causes is impossible and things exist.

It is important to note that although the chain of efficient causes and effects is *often* a temporal one, one thing causing another thing, which in turn causes a subsequent thing and so on, this is *not necessarily* the case. Efficient causes, agents which bring another thing into being, may or may not be necessary to sustain its existence. Aquinas is not going back in time like the Kalam argument – he is seeking to show that the universe depends on God's efficient causation at every moment in time. God is the sustaining cause of the universe. Were it not for God holding the universe in being, the universe would cease to exist.

For example, some oak trees are affected by mistletoe, a parasite. The oak tree is an efficient cause of the mistletoe – it is not like the seed or spore of the plant, or like the sunlight or rain, it is not just a cause in the way that a spark is the cause of a fire. Rather it continues to sustain its being.[14]

For another example, some of the causes of a circus plate-spinning display are:

Material: Clay, glaze, gilding, bamboo etc.
Efficient: Potter, fire, sticks, circus-performer.
Formal: Design of plate and trick.
Final: Entertainment.

Some of the efficient causes might be temporal, one thing leading to another, but some are sustaining, continually needed if things are to stay as they are. The potter need not be present for the plate to spin, but the stick must – it is the sustaining cause!

None of Aquinas' ways is identical with the Kalam argument. The domino analogy is not appropriate here; the ultimate causes

---

14 William Lane Craig explains the nature of an efficient cause and how it is not necessarily a temporally prior cause at http://www.leaderu.com/offices/billcraig/docs/creation.html.

identified in all three of Aquinas' cosmological arguments are better represented by the sticks which circus performers sometimes use to support spinning plates – they are sustaining rather than originating causes. This point is important in understanding the famous radio debate between the Jesuit Frederick Copleston and Bertrand Russell.

## The Third Way

The Third Way arises from the principle of contingency, related to the Aristotelian idea of potentiality and change. Everything has the potential to be or not to be, everything is contingent. However, if time and space really existed infinitely then every possibility would have been realized and, at some time, there would once have been nothing at all. If this was once the case, then even now there would be nothing at all, since something cannot come from nothing. However, things clearly do exist – so there must be something which does not have the potential not to exist, which is not contingent but necessary. The argument can be summarized as follows:

P1 Everything can 'be' or 'not be' (so everything may or may not exist).

IC If this is so, given infinite time, at some time everything would not be (if every possibility could be realized in infinite time, there would once have been a time when there was nothing at all. This ignores, however, the Principle of Conservation of Matter which states that matter and energy may remain constant while changing their state).

P3 If there was once nothing, nothing could come from it. (Something cannot come from nothing.)

IC2 Therefore something must necessarily exist (note most carefully that this is not God).

P5 Everything necessary must be caused or uncaused (Aquinas introduces the category of caused necessary things – these are things that are caused to exist but cannot go out of existence – he is thinking of angels and human souls which, once created, cannot go out of existence).

P6  The series of necessary things cannot go on to infinity as there would then be no explanation for the series (this rules out the idea of an infinite regress of caused necessary beings, one such being causing another).

C   Therefore there must be some Being 'having of itself its own necessity' (this is the idea of something *de re necessary* – something that cannot not exist and is not dependent for its existence on anything else).

C2  This is what everyone calls God.

Aquinas' introduction of the idea of caused necessary beings is not essential for the argument. He introduces the idea of angels and human souls as caused necessary being for theological reasons and it is not a crucial step. The key idea is that it is impossible to have a universe consisting entirely of contingent things. Something must be necessary in itself for a contingent universe to exist.

Frederick Copleston simplified the argument as follows:

P1  Everything in the universe is contingent.

P2  The universe is the sum total of contingent things.

C1  The universe itself is contingent.

C2  There must be something that is not contingent and therefore necessarily exists.

C3  This is what everyone calls God.

A key feature of this argument is its first conclusion, that the universe itself is contingent. Arguably there is a leap in logic which makes the first part of the argument *invalid*.

Putting this part of the argument into other terms:

P1  All human beings have mothers.

P2  All human beings are part of the human race.

C   The human race must have a mother.

Copleston makes a jump from assuming that everything in the universe is contingent to claiming that the universe as a whole is contingent. This was one reason why Bertrand Russell rejected Copleston's argument in their famous 1947 radio debate. He argued that Copleston relied on the fallacy of composition: features of parts of the universe do not determine features of the whole universe. While things within the universe might be contingent, that does not mean that the universe is contingent. Perhaps the universe just is, perhaps it does not require an explanation and is the ultimate *brute fact*.

In a way this is the nub of the whole dependency cosmological argument. What is the ultimate brute fact? Atheists will say it is the brute fact of the universe – something that does not require an explanation. Believers will say that the ultimate brute fact is God who is necessary in and of God's self.

Any child of five is likely to ask 'Why, Mummy?' when confronted with the existence of the universe. Theists will reply that God is the answer to this question. The child may then ask 'But why God, Mummy?' (Dawkins asks the same question) and the theists' answer is that God, by being necessary in and of God's self, is the sort of explanation about which it does not make sense to ask this question. Whether this is convincing or not is, perhaps, the single most important issue in discussion of the argument.

## Arguments from Sufficient Reason

'I believe . . . that almost all the methods which have been used to prove the existence of God are sound, and could serve the purpose if rendered complete.'[15]

Gottfried Leibniz (1646–1716) was one of the first truly modern philosophers. His work laid the foundations for much of the analytic philosophy of the twentieth century. Influenced by Spinoza (1632–77) and Descartes (1596–1650), he was educated into the *scholastic*

---

15 *New Essays*, A VI.vi: RB438.

*tradition* of European philosophy. Leibniz tried to escape the human limitations of having a particular perspective on reality, bounded by time and space and dominated by physical perceptions.

Leibniz was a metaphysician, a logician and important mathematician who sought to understand the principles which govern the universe objectively. He is associated with the formalization of basic principles of logic, including *The Principle of Sufficient Reason*, which states that everything that exists, everything that happens and everything that is true has a cause, whether known or unknown. He wrote:

> There can be found no fact that is true or existent or any true proposition . . . without there being a sufficient reason for its being so and not otherwise, although we cannot know these reasons in most cases.[16]

Arguing that the Principle of Sufficient Reason points to the necessary existence of God, he wrote: 'Why is there something rather than nothing? The sufficient reason [. . .] is found in a substance which [. . .] is a necessary being bearing the reason for its existence within itself.'[17]

For Leibniz, nothing can exist without a reason or cause. That things exist presupposes the existence of something which can provide a sufficient reason for their existence. If most things exist contingently, then there really must be a necessary being which provides its own reason or explanation. Leibniz' cosmological argument is really very straightforward; he wrote:

> suppose the book of the elements of geometry to have been eternal, one copy having been written down from an earlier one. It is evident that even though a reason can be given for the present book out of a past one, we should never come to a full reason. What is true of the books is also true of the states of the world. If you suppose the

---

16 *Monadology*, Section 32.

17 Quoted in Wallace Matson, *A New History of Philosophy: From Descartes to Searle*, San Diego and London: Harcourt College Publishers, 2000, p. 386.

world eternal, you will suppose nothing but a succession of states, and will not find in any of them a sufficient reason.[18]

Geisler and Corduan summarize Leibniz' argument as follows:

1 The world we see is changing.
2 Whatever is changing lacks within itself the reason for its own existence.
3 There is a sufficient reason for everything either within itself or outside itself.
4 Therefore there must be a cause beyond itself for its existence.
5 Either this cause is itself caused or is its own sufficient reason.
6 There cannot be an infinite regress of causes.
7 Therefore there must be a first Cause of the world which has no reason beyond itself.

J. L. Mackie (1917–81) maintained that Leibniz' argument can be challenged in two ways. First, by asking 'How do we know everything must have a sufficient reason?' Leibniz asserts that this is the case but does not actually provide any compelling argument. Second, by asking 'How can there be a necessary being, one that contains its own sufficient reason?' This second criticism goes to the heart of the cosmological argument.

## Criticisms of the Cosmological Argument

### Hume's Critique

David Hume (1711–76) attacked the cosmological argument for God's existence in Part IX of *Dialogues Concerning Natural Religion*. He is generally understood to have made five separate criticisms of the argument, namely:

---

18 G VII 302–3: L486–87, quoted in Nicholas Jolley (ed.), *The Cambridge Companion to Leibniz*, Cambridge: Cambridge University Press, 1995, p. 366.

1 There is no reason to believe that everything has a cause. We have only a necessarily partial and subjective understanding of natural laws and cannot conclusively state that 'all things must have a cause'.

2 The argument commits what is called *the fallacy of composition*: it assumes that a characteristic of parts of a thing is also a characteristic of the whole thing. Consider your own body; it is alive but if I cut off an arm or a leg or poke out your eye those parts would not be alive. The whole and parts do not always share characteristics. Simply because every event in the universe may have a cause it does not mean that the universe as a whole has a cause.

3 If God is the cause of the universe, then what is the cause of God? If God is God's own cause, then why cannot the universe itself be its own cause? Perhaps the universe has itself existed for ever and needs no cause other than simply being what it is.

4 Why does the existence of anything have to have an intelligible cause? Why not accept that the sequence of causes has no particular beginning: it simply goes on endlessly, in an 'infinite regress'?

5 Even if we were to accept the argument that the universe has a cause, that would not prove that God is infinite, good, caring, etc. Since the universe is finite, it would prove only that its creator would have to be powerful and wise enough to create it, but not infinitely powerful, wise, or good. Likewise, it would prove only that God is a cause of things and might not care at all about God's creation.

Arguably, Hume's approach has been misunderstood. In 1996 Joseph Campbell of Washington State University argued that attempts to evaluate Hume's criticisms one by one are misdirected, that Hume actually intended his criticisms as parts of a single developed critique of Samuel Clarke's (1675–1729) argument in the *Demonstration of the Being and Attributes of God* (1705).

Clarke's argument represents an unusual version of the cosmological argument. The philosophy of Rene Descartes (1596–1650) dominated the scene at Cambridge University at the turn of the eighteenth century. Nevertheless, while Descartes was a Catholic, the interpretation of his philosophy had given rise to materialism and atheism. Clarke drew on the work of Isaac Newton (1642–1727) and the ideas of John Locke (1632–1704) and Baruch Spinoza (1632–77) in order to reject this interpretation of Descartes.

Clarke entered into an important philosophical correspondence with Leibniz in 1715–16. Through this, he developed an argument for the existence of God which started with observations of variety, degrees of perfection in things, order, causation and final purpose in nature, from intelligence in humans and animals and from beauty. His argument moved from these various effects to the conclusion that God must exist as the *de re necessary* cause of the universe in the usual way, but he then turned to the concept of the *de re necessary* being and began to analyse it, showing that other things could be deduced or known *a priori* from the fact of God's *necessary* existence.

Clarke argued that

1   some-thing has existed from eternity;
2   only an immutable and independent being could exist from eternity;
3   that immutable and independent being which has existed from eternity must be self-existent or *de re necessary*;
4   it is impossible for us to comprehend the substance or essence of a necessarily existing being;
5   nevertheless, the fact of its eternal existence and many of its essential attributes are demonstrable;
6   the self-existent being must of necessity be infinite and omnipresent;
7   it must be single;
8   it must be an intelligent being;
9   it must be endued with liberty and choice;
10   it must have infinite power;
11   it must be infinitely wise; and
12   it must of necessity be a being of infinite goodness, justice and truth, and all other perfections, such as to become the supreme governor and judge of the world.

For Clarke, his argument *a priori* provided a conclusive reason to believe in the God of Christian theism. Whereas other versions of the cosmological argument concluded that God must be an unmoved, uncaused, necessarily unchanging and *other* being, distant from creation and ultimately inscrutable, Clarke showed how the cosmological argument could lead directly to the God that people actually worship.

Hume's critique of the cosmological argument is couched in terms of a critique of this argument *a priori*; Hume's character Demea refers to the argument in these terms. According to Campbell, the first four of Hume's points attack the typical reasoning that Clarke employs to arrive at God's *necessary* existence and the fifth attacks the relatively unusual reasoning that he employed (above) to equate a *de re necessary* God with the God of Christian theism.

It is important to understand that Hume's objections to the argument are not in a form which *proves* that there is no God. They just show that neither Clarke's argument, nor other versions of the cosmological argument which employ some or all of the same reasoning, provides any reason to believe in God, whether as a *necessary being* or as the God of Christian theism. Hence, the result of Hume's critique is not atheism as much as agnosticism.

## Kant's Critique

Immanuel Kant (1724–1804), in his *Critique of Pure Reason* (1781), offered some of the most influential criticisms of the classical proofs of God's existence. Most distinctively, Kant believed that the cosmological argument depends on the ontological argument and, since the ontological argument can be shown to fail, the same fate must then befall the cosmological argument. The key connection between the two arguments is the idea of *necessary existence*.

Kant argues that the idea of *necessary existence* is incomprehensible. There is no way to prove that such an idea is possible, since we have no experience of necessarily existing things. Kant argues that we have no criterion of existence except existence in space and time and everything that exists in the universe might not exist. The very idea of necessary existence is meaningless.

Kant's other criticisms of the cosmological argument followed Hume, whose work influenced him in a profound way and supposedly led to his new, critical approach to philosophy – an approach that was a 'middle way' between Hume's extremely sceptical empiricism and the dominant metaphysical rationalism.

## Bertrand Russell's Critique

Like Hume and Kant, Bertrand Russell (1872–1970) argued that the idea of 'necessary existence' is basically ludicrous. If all things are moved, changed and caused, if all things are contingent, then we cannot reasonably posit the existence of something that is not in the form of God or any other thing. He wrote:

> Any particle of matter, it is said, may be conceived to be annihilated, and any form may be conceived to be altered. Such an annihilation or alteration is not therefore impossible. But it seems a great partiality not to perceive that the same argument extends equally to the Deity, so far as we have any conception of him . . .[19]

In the eleventh century Al-Ghazali (d. 1111) had also come to believe that the contingency argument was self-defeating. If the world is eternal, having no beginning or end in time, then the 'necessary being' has already been reached: it is the universe. There is no need to postulate an external cause for the universe when an assumed premise of the argument from contingency is that the universe is eternal.

Russell went on to argue that although it is natural to look for a cause for the universe, it is foolish to suppose that one will be found. For Russell, and more recently for Richard Dawkins, postulating God as the first cause of the universe is an unnecessarily complicated step. By the process of *Ockham's Razor* (the principle in logic by which the simplest solution is usually the strongest) they argue that there is no need to suppose the existence of an external body to

---

19 Hume, *Dialogues Concerning Natural Religion*, Part IX, http://www.earlymoderntexts.com/pdf/humedial.pdf, p. 39.

account for the eternal existence of the universe – the universe could just be eternal, full stop.

The reasoning employed by Russell (and, more recently, Dawkins) is not accepted by all theists. Although John Hick (1922–2012) conceded that Russell had a point in supposing the 'brute fact' explanation simpler than the God explanation, for others

> [i]t is extraordinary that there should exist anything at all. Surely the most natural state of affairs is simply nothing: no universe, no God, nothing. But there is something. And so many things. Maybe chance could have thrown up the odd electron. But so many particles! Not everything will have an explanation. But . . . the whole progress of science and all other intellectual enquiry demands that we postulate the smallest number of brute facts. If we can explain the many bits of the universe by one simple being which keeps them in existence, we should do so – even if inevitably we cannot explain the existence of that simple being.[20]

### Other Criticisms

Richard Gale has argued that, since the conclusion of all versions of the cosmological argument invokes an impossibility (a necessary existent being), then no cosmological arguments can provide examples of sound reasoning. Michael Martin, Quentin Smith and Graham Oppy have all concluded that no current version of the cosmological argument is sound. However, it is one thing to claim, as Kant does, that we can have no experience of a necessary being, but it is quite another to claim that a necessary being is impossible. There would seem to be no inherent contradiction in the idea of a necessary being, and a contradiction is needed if this idea is to be ruled as impossible.

---

20 Swinburne, *Is there a God?*, Oxford: Oxford University Press, 1996.

## Summary

Cosmological arguments are *a posteriori* inductive. They see God as the best explanation for observations of the world. If all things and all ideas are moved, caused and contingent then there must be an unmoved, uncaused, necessary being – which is what everybody calls God.

If there are unmoved, uncaused necessary things other than God, then the argument collapses. Perhaps, as Hume and Russell suggested, the universe is a brute fact and serves as its own explanation? Further, as Kant pointed out, given that our experience does not include necessary beings, it is unclear how we can postulate the existence of one as a means of explaining the apparent contingency of the universe. Finally, it may be questioned whether the unmoved mover, the uncaused cause, the *de re necessary* being is 'what everybody calls God'? Many Muslims and Christians would see God in much more personal terms.

# 5

# God and the New Physics

In the beginning there was nothing, which exploded.

(Terry Pratchett, *Lords and Ladies*)

In recent decades there has been a trend for conflating the reasoning of the cosmological argument with the basic principles of Big Bang theory, co-opting the observational data and interpretations of modern science as support for the conclusion that an uncaused creator-God brought the universe into existence *ex nihilo*.

It is not difficult to understand how the amateur scientist would be struck by similarities in language and concepts between the Big Bang theory and theology.

- In reading about Einstein's theory of relativity a theologian might recall that in the fifth century Augustine claimed that '[t]he world and time had both one beginning. The world was made, not in time, but simultaneously with time'.[1]
- Alternatively, in reading about the Singularity, a philosopher of religion might recall Aquinas' description of God as 'neither something nor nothing'.

Some highly respectable scientists have lent their support to such a drawing together of contemporary cosmology and theology – perhaps most famously John Polkinghorne – as well as some not-so-respectable ones!

---

1 Augustine, *The City of God* (trans. Marcus Dods), available online at http://newadvent.org/fathers/1201.htm. From *Nicene and Post-Nicene Fathers*, First Series, Vol. 2, edited by Philip Schalf, Buffalo, NY: Christian Literature Publishing Co., 1887; rev and edited for New Advent by Kevin Knight.

In 1978, in his book *God and the Astronomers*, astrophysicist Robert Jastrow wrote:

> For the scientist who has lived by his faith in the power of reason, the story ends like a bad dream. He has scaled the mountains of ignorance; he is about to conquer the highest peak; as he pulls himself over the final rock, he is greeted by a band of theologians who have been sitting there for centuries.[2]

As Jastrow explained later,

> [a]stronomers now find they have painted themselves into a corner because they have proven, by their own methods, that the world began abruptly in an act of creation to which you can trace the seeds of every star, every planet, every living thing in this cosmos and on the earth ... That there are what I or anyone would call supernatural forces at work is now, I think, a scientifically proven fact.[3]

Theodore Schick Jr described the growing numbers of theological interpretations for the Big Bang theory apparent during the 1990s. He wrote:

> Astronomer George Smoot suggested as much when he exclaimed at a press conference reporting the findings of the Cosmic Background Explorer (COBE) satellite, 'If you're religious, it's like looking at the face of god.' Why? Because something must have caused the big bang, and who else but god could have done such a thing? Astronomer Hugh Ross in his book *The Creator and the Cosmos* puts the argument this way: 'If the universe arose out of a big bang, it must have had a beginning. If it had a beginning, it must have a beginner.' So beguiling is this argument that astronomer Geoffrey Burbridge has

---

2 New York: W. W. Norton, 1978, p. 116.
3 'A Scientist Caught Between Two Faiths: Interview with Robert Jastrow', *Christianity Today*, 6 August 1982, pp. 15, 18.

lamented that his fellow scientists are rushing off to join the 'First Church of Christ of the Big Bang'.[4]

The philosopher of science Adolf Grünbaum (b. 1923) reacted strongly against this trend, taking on Craig and other Christian apologists in *Creation As a Pseudo-Problem in Current Physical Cosmology* (1991), *Some Comments on William Craig's 'Creation and Big Bang Cosmology'* (1994) and *Theological Misinterpretations of Current Physical Cosmology* (1998). In 1991, he concluded that 'neither the big bang cosmogony nor the steady-state cosmology validates the traditional cosmological argument for divine creation. But, as we see, that argument dies hard.'

As Craig put it,

> Grünbaum's argument is that even if we assume that $t^0$ (the moment when time and space began) is a well-defined instant at which the Big Bang singularity occurred, that 'event' cannot have a prior cause because there simply did not exist any instants before $t^0$. The Big Bang singularity 'cannot have any cause at all in the universe' (presumably because backward causation is impossible) nor can it 'be the effect of any prior cause' (because time did not exist prior to $t^0$). As Grünbaum elsewhere makes clear [(1991), p. 248], this argument does not depend essentially upon the assumption that $t^0$ was the first instant of time, rather than a singular point constituting the boundary of time, which, on the analogy of a series of fractions converging toward zero as the limit, has no first instant. In either case, the objection remains the same: since no instants of time existed prior to $t^0$, there can be no antecedent cause of the initial cosmological singularity. Therefore, that singularity must be uniquely uncaused . . .[5]

Following Grünbaum, in *Atheism, Theism, and Big Bang Cosmology* (1991) Quentin Smith argued that the Big Bang theory is incompatible with Christian theism and other theist perspectives. In *A Big*

---

4 http://www.infidels.org/library/modern/theodore_schick/bigbang.html.
5 http://www.leaderu.com/offices/billcraig/docs/creation.html.

*Bang Cosmological Argument for God's Nonexistence* (1992) he argues that it is unreasonable to believe that God created the Big Bang and in *Two Ways to Prove Atheism* (1996) he concludes that '[c]ontemporary scientific cosmology is not only not supported by any theistic theory, it is actually logically inconsistent with theism'.[6]

The development of quantum physics has added another layer of complexity to the debate. Quantum science effectively undermines previously accepted natural 'laws'. As Stephen Hawking (b. 1942) observed in *A Brief History of Time*,

> [t]here are something like ten million million million million million million million million million million million million million (1 with eighty [five] zeroes after it) particles in the region of the universe that we can observe. Where did they all come from? The answer is that, in quantum theory, particles can be created out of energy in the form of particle/antiparticle pairs. But that just raises the question of where the energy came from. The answer is that the total energy of the universe is exactly zero. The matter in the universe is made out of positive energy. However, the matter is all attracting itself by gravity. Two pieces of matter that are close to each other have less energy than the same two pieces a long way apart, because you have to expend energy to separate them against the gravitational force that is pulling them together. Thus, in a sense, the gravitational field has negative energy. In the case of a universe that is approximately uniform in space, one can show that this negative gravitational energy exactly cancels the positive energy represented by the matter. So the total energy of the universe is zero . . .[7]

In *Quantum Cosmology's Implication of Atheism* (1997) Quentin Smith (b. 1952) explores the implications of quantum science for traditional theistic arguments for God. In his article *Creation ex*

---

6 http://www.infidels.org/library/modern/quentin_smith/atheism.html.

7 Stephen Hawking, *A Brief History of Time*, Toronto: Bantam, 1988, p. 129.

*nihilo* – *without God* the atheist philosopher and blogger Mark Vuletic[8] offers a short but informed discussion of whether physical processes could have produced the universe from nothing. He quotes scientists such as Richard Morris, who wrote:

> In modern physics, there is no such thing as 'nothing.' Even in a perfect vacuum, pairs of virtual particles are constantly being created and destroyed. The existence of these particles is no mathematical fiction. Though they cannot be directly observed, the effects they create are quite real. The assumption that they exist leads to predictions that have been confirmed by experiment to a high degree of accuracy.[9]

There have also been criticisms of the easy conflation of God with the cause of the Big Bang from within theism. As Paul Davies explained in *God and the New Physics*,

> The problem about postulating a god who transcends time is that, though it may bring him into the 'here and now,' many of the qualities which most people attribute to god only make sense within the context of time. Surely god can plan, answer prayers, express pleasure or anxiety about the course of human progress, and sit in judgement afterwards? Is he not continually active in the world, doing work 'oiling the cogs of the cosmic machine' and so on? All of these activities are meaningless except in a temporal context. How can god plan and act except in time? Why, if god transcends time and so knows the future, is he concerned about human progress or the fight against evil? The outcome is already perceived by God.[10]

Despite these objections, the case for God causing the universe through the natural processes of the Big Bang continues to be

---

8 Revised edn, 2011.

9 Richard Morris, *The Edges of Science*, New York: Prentice-Hall, 1990, p. 25.

10 New York: Simon and Schuster, 1983, pp. 38–9.

made. Such cases often include the sheer improbability of the conditions necessary at the Singularity for the universe to have come into existence.

William Lane Craig is probably the best known advocate of the need to include God into Big Bang cosmology.[11] He wrote:

> We should therefore say that the cause of the origin of the universe is causally prior to the Big Bang, though not temporally prior to the Big Bang. In such a case, the cause may be said to exist spacelessly and timelessly sans the universe, but temporally subsequent to the moment of creation. But why think that such a cause exists at all? Very simply, the causal inference is based in the metaphysical intuition that something cannot come out of absolutely nothing. A pure potentiality cannot actualize itself. In the case of the universe (including any boundary points), there was not anything physically prior to the initial singularity. The potentiality for the existence of the universe could not therefore have lain in itself, since it did not exist prior to the singularity. On the theistic hypothesis, the potentiality of the universe's existence lay in the power of God to create it. On the atheistic hypothesis, there did not even exist the potentiality for the existence of the universe. But then it seems inconceivable that the universe should become actual if there did not exist any potentiality for its existence. It seems to me therefore that a little reflection leads us to the conclusion that the origin of the universe had a cause.[12]

## Summary

Cosmological arguments move from the existence of the universe, being full of *caused* or otherwise contingent things, to the existence of a *de re necessary* Prime Mover which, they claim, is 'what everybody calls God'. Unlike all other things, God is uncaused,

---

11 William Lane Craig, 'Creation and Big Bang Cosmology', *Philosophia Naturalis* 31 (1994), pp. 217–24.
12 Ibid.

unchanging and self-explaining, not contingent or dependent on any other thing. God is therefore not a 'some-thing' within the universe of space and time, but God is not no-thing either, because all things come from him and nothing comes from nothing. God is in a category of God's own – timeless, spaceless, unchanging and necessarily existent.

Cosmological arguments may be criticized for concluding that necessary beings can exist without any observable evidence to that effect, also for denying that the universe itself could be the necessary being and for too easily equating the Prime Mover with 'what everybody calls God'. However, this criticism depends on the claim that observable evidence is necessary – supporters of the cosmological argument will add that the existence of God is a necessary consequence of observing motion, causation and existence within the universe.

The Big Bang theory certainly supports the idea that the universe had a beginning, as the Kalam argument claims – although whether this beginning was uncaused or was caused by God who transcends time remains an open question.

# 6

# Teleological Arguments

> The divine power is to be found in a principle of reason that per-
> vades the whole of nature . . . When you see a sundial or a water-
> clock, you see that it tells the time by design and not by chance.
> How then can you imagine that the universe as a whole is devoid
> of purpose and intelligence, when it embraces everything, includ-
> ing these artefacts themselves and their artificers?
>
> (Cicero, *De natura deorum* ii.34)

Perhaps the most ancient of arguments for God's existence is the teleological argument, often called the *design argument*. Like all inductive arguments the teleological argument moves from observations of
the natural world to the conclusion that features of it are best caused
by 'what everybody calls God'. Also like other *a posteriori* arguments, the argument's strength lies in the accuracy and completeness
of its observations; its conclusion may always be disputed if new
evidence comes to light.

Most versions of the argument focus on the existence of complexity, order or sense of purpose in the natural world as a whole, noting
that such qualities usually signify a designer. It is then argued that
it is reasonable to expect that the universe has a designer, which
is what everybody calls God. Many philosophers proposing design
arguments look at the universe and see an ordered, predictable and
efficient machine – one with many cogs and mechanisms, yes, but a
machine none the less.

Teleological arguments have been proposed throughout human
history and by scholars from many different religious traditions.

Within the Hindu tradition several different forms of teleological
argument were proposed. Mackenzie-Brown describes how ancient

Vedas and Upanishads cast God as an architect or potter of the universe and how later writers such as Śaṅkara (c. 700–50) advanced more elaborate versions of the argument. He wrote:

Śaṅkara presents the design argument in his commentary on the Vedānta Sūtras . . . 'The creation, maintenance, and destruction of this world— differentiated by names and forms, serving as the platform for diverse agents and enjoyers to experience the fruits of action according to definite places, times, and causes, and having the nature of arrangement (racanā) that transcends comprehension – are produced from the omniscient, omnipotent Brahman as their cause.'[1]

Within the Jewish tradition Rabbeinu Bachya (c. 1000–50) of Zaragoza, Spain, asked:

Do you not realize that if ink were poured out accidentally on a blank sheet of paper, it would be impossible that proper writing should result, legible lines that are written with a pen? Imagine a person bringing a sheet of handwriting that could only have been composed with a pen. He claims that ink spilled on the paper and these written characters had accidentally emerged. We would charge him to his face with falsehood, for we could feel certain that this result could not have happened without an intelligent person's purpose. Since this seems impossible in the case of letters whose formation is conventional, how can one assert that something far subtler in its design and which manifests in its fashioning a depth and complexity infinitely beyond our comprehension could have happened without the purpose, power, and wisdom of a wise and mighty designer?[2]

---

1 See http://digitalcommons.trinity.edu/cgi/viewcontent.cgi?article=1000& context=relig_faculty.
2 'The Duties of the Heart', *The Gate of Oneness*, Chapter 6.

Within the Islamic tradition Ibn Rushd (1126–98) used his study of both Plato and Aristotle to conclude that the combination of order and continual motion in the universe cannot be accidental and requires a Prime Mover, a Supreme Principle, which is in itself pure Intelligence and can be seen to will or design the universe to be the way that it is and not any other way.

Teleological arguments and cosmological arguments are closely related; whereas cosmological arguments ask why anything at all exists, teleological arguments ask why things exist in the ordered and purposeful way that they seem to. Nevertheless, both arguments cite evidence of causation within the universe to support the conclusion that God exists.

## Aquinas' Fifth Way

Thomas Aquinas (1225–74) put forward his own design argument as the fifth of his ways to God in the *Summa Theologica*. As in his first three ways to God, Aquinas used Aristotelian arguments from causation as his starting point, in the fifth way focusing on the existence of *final causes* or *telos* in all things.

Aquinas wrote:

> The fifth way is taken from the governance of the world. We see that things which lack knowledge, such as natural bodies, act for an end, and this is evident from their acting always, or nearly always, in the same way, so as to obtain the best result. Hence it is plain that they achieve their end, not fortuitously, but designedly. Now whatever lacks knowledge cannot move towards an end, unless it be directed by some being endowed with knowledge and intelligence; as the arrow is directed by the archer. Therefore, some intelligent being exists by whom all natural things are directed to their end; and this being we call God.[3]

---

3 Aquinas, *Summa Theologica*, First part, a, Question 2, Article 3.

Aquinas' argument is an argument *qua purpose*. Aquinas focuses on the fact that all natural things appear to have a final cause, a *telos* or purpose, and moves from this to claim that the universe as a whole also seems to have a final cause, *telos* or purpose. Just as an arrow in mid-flight suggests a target and an archer, the existence of purposeful processes in nature suggests a designer God and a divinely willed end for creation.

## David Hume and the Design Argument

By the eighteenth century, the question of whether the order and complexity in the universe, revealed in ever more astonishing detail by scientists during the Enlightenment, could really be taken to imply purpose and a divine designer, was central to many philosophers' thinking. While many philosophers built on Aquinas' argument, suggesting their own teleological arguments, others saw science casting doubt on the suggestion that the universe showed signs of design.

David Hume (1711–76) was an empiricist. He rejected any attempt to use observations of the natural world to support belief in an unobservable creator or first cause; this was going beyond the limits of reason and what can ever be known. Hume criticized the Argument from Design in his *Enquiry Concerning Human Understanding* and, more fully, in *Dialogues Concerning Natural Religion*, published shortly after his death.[4] *Dialogues Concerning Natural Religion* takes the form of a conversation between three characters. Dialogues were often used by classical authors such as Plato and Cicero and, closer to Hume's time, had been used by Galileo in his *Dialogue Concerning the Two Chief World Systems*. Hume probably intended readers to recall some similarities between his work and that of Galileo.

---

4 Professing atheism, even expressing doubt about the grounds for believing in God, was not popular in the eighteenth century, and Hume kept his views on religion relatively quiet! He wrote most of *Dialogues Concerning Natural Religion* in and shortly after 1750, but they were not published until after his death.

Hume's main characters are Cleanthes, Demea and Philo, though a youth, Pamphilus, serves as the narrator and at the end loyally suggests that Cleanthes, his teacher, offered the strongest arguments.

Cleanthes bases his beliefs about God's existence and nature upon a version of the teleological argument, which uses evidence of design in the universe to argue for God's existence and resemblance to the human mind. Like Aquinas, he is an advocate of natural theology, arguing for God using observations and inductive arguments; his is a propositional faith. He explains:

Look round the world: contemplate the whole and every part of it: you will find it to be nothing but one great machine, subdivided into an infinite number of lesser machines, which again admit of subdivisions to a degree beyond what human senses and faculties can trace and explain. All these various machines, and even their most minute parts, are adjusted to each other with an accuracy which ravishes into admiration all men who have ever contemplated them. The curious adapting of means to ends, throughout all nature, resembles exactly, though it much exceeds, the productions of human contrivance; of human designs, thought, wisdom, and intelligence. Since, therefore, the effects resemble each other, we are led to infer, by all the rules of analogy, that the causes also resemble; and that the Author of Nature is somewhat similar to the mind of man, though possessed of much larger faculties, proportioned to the grandeur of the work which he has executed. By this argument *a posteriori*, and by this argument alone, do we prove at once the existence of a Deity, and his similarity to human mind and intelligence.[5]

Demea is an advocate of philosophical theology. His faith is non-propositional (pp. 11–14), so accordingly our beliefs about the nature of God should be based upon revelation and faith, though God's wholly simple existence can be demonstrated *a priori* as well.

---

5 *Dialogues Concerning Natural Religion*, Part II, 143.

Demea rejects Cleanthes' natural theology and his approach to faith for making man the measure of all things. He explains:

> I could not approve of your conclusion concerning the similarity of the Deity to men; still less can I approve of the mediums by which you endeavour to establish it. What! No demonstration of the Being of God! No abstract arguments! No proofs *a priori*! Are these, which have hitherto been so much insisted on by philosophers, all fallacy, all sophism?[6]

Later continuing,

> In reality, Cleanthes, consider what it is you assert when you represent the Deity as similar to a human mind and understanding. What is the soul of man? A composition of various faculties, passions, sentiments, ideas; united, indeed, into one self or person, but still distinct from each other . . . How is this compatible with that perfect immutability and simplicity which all true Theists ascribe to the Deity?[7]

Philo probably represents a viewpoint similar to Hume's own. He is a sceptic who attacks all attempts to prove God's existence, whether through natural theology or *a priori* reasoning.

In Part II of the *Dialogues*, he points out the inadequacy of arguments which are based on analogies for the universe:

> If we see a house, Cleanthes, we conclude, with the greatest certainty, that it had an architect or builder; because this is precisely that species of effect which we have experienced to proceed from that species of cause. But surely you will not affirm, that the universe bears such a resemblance to a house that we can with the same certainty infer a similar cause, or that the analogy is here entire and perfect. The dissimilitude is so striking, that the utmost

---

6  Ibid.
7  Part IV, 158.

you can here pretend to is a guess, a conjecture, a presumption concerning a similar cause.[8]

He continues, later, asking: 'From observing the growth of a hair, can we learn anything concerning the generation of a man?' Philo goes on to engage Cleanthes on his own terms: 'I argue with Cleanthes in his own way; and, by showing him the dangerous consequences of his tenets, hope at last to reduce him to our opinion.'[9]

He starts by making a very important point, namely that no human being can hope to judge the qualities of the universe of which they are a part. Many people look at the universe and make the assumption that things were always going to end up this way. They consider the necessary moves to get from the Big Bang to the exact situation of today and account it too improbable for words. This ignores the substantial possibility that things could just as well have ended up in a billion different ways.

The films *Sliding Doors*,[10] *Back to the Future*[11] and *Groundhog Day*[12] explore the idea that although things ending up this way appears to be by design, perhaps chance has a much greater role than is usually, or comfortably, suggested.

Through Philo, Hume then continues his attack on the teleological argument. He notes the leap in logic that occurs when Cleanthes observes that certain things are true of *parts* of the universe and then translates that into a claim about the *whole* universe. Philo suggests that Cleanthes' argument rests on a *fallacy of composition* and that he moves too quickly from the *specific to the general*. This works equally as a criticism of the cosmological argument as of the teleological argument.

Philo then points out that drawing comparison between the universe and God may be theologically problematic as well, suggesting

8 Ibid., 144.
9 Ibid., 145.
10 Peter Howitt, 1998.
11 Robert Zemeckis, 1985.
12 Harold Ramis, 1993.

that God may not be perfect. He says that 'by this method of reasoning, you renounce all claims to infinity in any of the attributes of the Deity'.[13] He continues to observe that human arguments for God's existence always put human reason in a privileged position. Writing that 'our partiality in our own favour does indeed present it on all occasions; but sound philosophy ought carefully to guard against so natural an illusion',[14] Philo concludes this part of the *Dialogues* by ridiculing Cleanthes' claim to be able to make observations concerning the pattern of whole universes, asking 'Have worlds ever been formed under your eye; and have you had leisure to observe the whole progress of the phenomenon, from the first appearance of order to its final consummation? If you have, then cite your experience, and deliver your theory.'

In Part IV of the *Dialogues*, Philo returns to his argument against natural theology, stating that 'I shall endeavour to show you, a little more distinctly, the inconveniences of that Anthropomorphism, which you have embraced . . .'[15] He goes on:

If we survey a ship, what an exalted idea must we form of the ingenuity of the carpenter who framed so complicated, useful, and beautiful a machine? And what surprize must we feel, when we find him a stupid mechanic, who imitated others . . . multiplied trials, mistakes, corrections . . . Many worlds might have been botched and bungled, throughout an eternity, ere this system was struck out . . . In such subjects, who can determine, where the truth . . .? And what shadow of an argument, continued Philo, can you produce, from your hypothesis, to prove the unity of the Deity? A great number of men join in building a house or ship, in rearing a city, in framing a commonwealth; why may not several deities combine in contriving and framing a world? . . . if such foolish, such vicious creatures as man, can yet often unite in

13 Philo, *Dialogues Concerning Natural Religion*, 166.
14 Ibid., 148.
15 Ibid., 160.

framing and executing one plan, how much more those deities or demons, whom we may suppose several degrees more perfect![16]

For Philo, if we argue from the analogy of a human designer to the existence of a designer God we are not justified in concluding that God is either perfect or single. Further, he points out that

> the two great sexes of male and female, says Milton, animate the world. Why must this circumstance, so universal, so essential, be excluded from those numerous and limited deities? . . . And why not become a perfect Anthropomorphite? Why not assert the deity or deities to be corporeal, and to have eyes, a nose, mouth, ears, etc.? Epicurus maintained, that no man had ever seen reason but in a human figure; therefore the gods must have a human figure.[17]

He concludes:

> In a word, Cleanthes, a man who follows your hypothesis is able perhaps to assert, or conjecture, that the universe, sometime, arose from something like design: but beyond that position he cannot ascertain one single circumstance; and is left afterwards to fix every point of his theology by the utmost license of fancy and hypothesis. This world, for aught he knows, is very faulty and imperfect, compared to a superior standard; and was only the first rude essay of some infant deity, who afterwards abandoned it, ashamed of his lame performance: it is the work only of some dependent, inferior deity; and is the object of derision to his superiors: it is the production of old age and dotage in some superannuated deity; and ever since his death, has run on at adventures, from the first impulse and active force which it received from him.[18]

---

16 Ibid., 167.
17 Ibid., 168.
18 Ibid., 168.

## Paley's Watchmaker Analogy

William Paley (1743–1805) was Archdeacon of Carlisle when he wrote *Natural Theology* in 1802. This work is best known today for containing the famous 'watchmaker analogy', which serves as a design argument *qua order* for the existence of God.

Textbooks rarely mention anything about Paley's background or the context in which the argument was put forward, which is a pity. Contrary to the general impression, Paley was not a naïve and bumbling clergyman. Considered a rising star at Cambridge University, Paley worked there after graduating and actually turned down the offer of senior positions at the University or in the Church of England. Paley was a radical, an early Utilitarian philosopher and political campaigner against slavery, for the rights of women and the poor and against private property – none of which views and activities would have gone unchallenged had Paley taken a higher profile establishment position. When Paley wrote *Natural Theology or, Evidences of the Existence and Attributes of the Deity*, he did so in the knowledge of the state of science at that time, and of Hume's philosophy. Charles Darwin wrote that Paley's *Natural Theology* was a standard text at Cambridge in his time – and that it contained more sense than any of the other books.

The main thrust of Paley's argument was that the general happiness or wellbeing evident in the physical and social order of things suggests a creator God. In this he was building on his argument in an earlier work, in which he had written 'God, when God created the human species, wished their happiness; and made for them the provision which God has made, with that view and for that purpose.'[19] Paley's vision of the universe as a complex, ordered and purposeful machine was shared by almost everybody at the time and, whatever Hume might have suggested through Philo, this vision of the universe naturally supported belief in a single, omnipotent and omnibenevolent creator-God.

---

19 *Principles of Moral and Political Philosophy*, 1785.

In opening *Natural Theology*, Paley wrote:

In crossing a heath, suppose I pitched my foot against a stone and were asked how the stone came to be there, I might possibly answer that for anything I knew to the contrary it had lain there forever; nor would it, perhaps, be very easy to show the absurdity of this answer. But suppose I had found a watch upon the ground, and it should be inquired how the watch happened to be in that place, I should hardly think of the answer which I had before given, that for anything I knew the watch might have always been there. Yet why should not this answer serve for the watch as well as for the stone; why is it not admissible in that second case as in the first? For this reason, and for no other, namely, that when we come to inspect the watch, we perceive what we could not discover in the stone, that its several parts are framed and put together for a purpose, e.g., that they are so formed and adjusted as to produce motion, and that motion so regulated as to point out the hour of the day; that if the different parts had been differently shaped from what they are, or placed in any other manner or in any other order than that in which they are placed, either no motion at all would have carried on in the machine, or none which would have answered the use that is now served by it. This mechanism being observed, the inference we think is inevitable, that the watch must have had a maker.[20]

Like Cleanthes' statement of the teleological argument, Paley's argument rests on an analogy. It draws a parallel between qualities in a watch and qualities in the natural world. As Philo immediately seized upon, in this type of argument the appropriateness of the analogy is always open to question. However, Paley is still relevant – he is seeking to put forward a persuasive and not a conclusive argument. Paley seeks to persuade his reader that, taking everything into account, the idea of a creator God is more plausible than any alternative and, seen in this way, his argument still has force today.

---

20 *Natural Theology*, Chapter 1.

## Paradigm Shift

Paley lived in a world that was about to undergo what Thomas Kuhn (1922–96) has called a *paradigm shift*. For millennia people had believed that God created the world a few thousand years ago and had created the plants and animals according to their kind; that God had determined the nature of things and things did not change. By the time that Paley was writing, however, scientists (many profoundly religious men and women) had begun to uncover evidence that things do change and over enormous periods of time. The earth, and in particularly geology and fossil discoveries, yielded evidence that it had been around for much longer than a few thousand years and that it was dynamic, changing, not static and determined.

The concept of evolution was not new when Paley was writing, though it was not widely accepted. Even the idea that it occurred by 'natural selection' and 'the survival of the fittest' had been proposed by Herbert Spenser (1820–1903) and others well before Charles Darwin (1809–82) set sail on *The Beagle*. Nevertheless, Darwin found and first published the evidence[21] to support the theory and so began the process by which evolution became the dominant paradigm, replacing the idea of divine creation in many parts of the world.

Western science during the Middle Ages was under the long shadow of Aristotle, many of whose works had been rediscovered by Western philosophers during the eleventh and twelfth centuries. It was not until the Renaissance period in Europe that science advanced by questioning the Aristotelian Paradigm. The work of Nicolaus Copernicus (1473–1543) started the ball rolling. He read the work of Aristotle and Euclid and that of Islamic philosophers such as Ibn Rushd, but saw contradictions in the accepted model of the universe and developed his own, heliocentric model. This model

---

21 The theory also relied on evidence collected by Alfred Russel Wallace (1823–1913), who developed his theory of evolution through natural selection independently while researching in the Malay Archipelago (modern Indonesia) and whose progress eventually prompted Darwin to publish his own earlier findings.

inspired Galileo Galilei (1564–1642) to begin a scientific revolution or, as Thomas Kuhn would later call it, a paradigm shift.

In 1632, after a bitter battle with the Inquisition, Galileo published *Dialogue Concerning the Two Chief World Systems*. According to Stephen Hawking, 'Galileo perhaps more than any other single person, was responsible for the birth of modern science.'[22] His work heightened the sense that the universe is amazingly complex and ordered. Although it undermined the revealed religious idea that the earth, and human beings, are at the centre of the universe, it did not undermine the philosophical argument that a designer is the best explanation for the complexity, order and apparent purpose that we see everywhere.

Science progressed during the seventeenth and eighteenth centuries by providing ever greater levels of detailed insight into how natural organisms operate and into the nature of the laws that govern their operation. The universe seemed mechanistic, like a complex machine. Given that machines have designers, this model of the universe naturally suggested the need for a grand designer, perhaps distant and unaware of human concerns, but recognizably a God. Enlightenment science may have erred towards deism rather than theism, but it did not necessarily lead to atheism. Science remained predicated on the belief that complete and objective knowledge is possible for human beings, even though enlightenment scientists accepted that the universe is not necessarily revolving around and leading towards human consciousness.

However, towards the end of the nineteenth century the scientific paradigm began to shift again. Darwin and then Einstein showed that the universe is not so much a steady, ordered, predictable machine as it had previously seemed. By the 1920s the universe started to seem strange to the point of being ultimately unintelligible, and not just because of the carnage on the Western Front. Quantum science identified particles that do not obey any of the standard physical laws. All

---

22 Quoted in *Time* magazine; see Manfred Weidhorn, *The Person of the Millennium: The Unique Impact of Galileo on World History*, iUniverse, 2005, p. 154.

things are made up of particles that both exist and don't exist, that can be in two places at once and which can't be observed without the act of observation having an effect. The ideas of order and purpose had little meaning when everything seemed relative, transient, subjective and perhaps chaotic. Scientists lost confidence in science as a potentially finite and objective search for knowledge; human understanding was exposed as limited and subjective. When things don't seem ordered, purposeful, predictable and logical, design arguments fall out of favour; many scientists today are atheists.

## Mill's Criticism

Like Hume's character Philo, John Stuart Mill rejected all arguments for God's existence and had a particular problem with the so-called design argument. In *On Nature* and *Three Essays on Religion* (both 1874) Mill disputes the premise of the teleological argument, that the universe is characterized by order and a sense of purposefulness. For Mill, any sign of order is outweighed by the many signs of disorder in nature, natural evil. This does not therefore allow the premises of the argument to support the conclusion, that an omnipotent and omniscient God designed the world and exists.

Mill wrote:

Nearly all the things which men are hanged or imprisoned for doing to one another are nature's everyday performances. Even the love of 'order' which is thought to be a following of the ways of nature is in fact a contradiction of them. All which people are accustomed to deprecate as 'disorder' and its consequences is precisely a counterpart of nature's ways. Anarchy and the reign of Terror are overmatched in injustice, ruin, and death by a hurricane and a pestilence . . .

He also wrote: 'If there are any marks at all of special design in creation, one of the things most evidently designed is that a large proportion of all animals should pass their existence in tormenting and devouring other animals.' This echoed Darwin's own remark, that 'I cannot persuade myself that a beneficent and omnipotent God would have designedly created the Ichneumonidae with the express intention of their feeding within the living bodies of Caterpillars, or that a cat should play with mice.'

Mill's criticisms of the teleological argument are persuasive; the existence of evil and suffering is perhaps the most significant problem that inductive arguments for the existence of God must overcome. Despite this, however, Mill's criticism did not represent the end of design arguments for God's existence.

The end of the nineteenth century led to people becoming dissatisfied with 'progress', questioning whether it really was what it purported to be. The new century brought with it conflict on a hitherto unimaginable scale. The British developed concentration camps to intern the Boers in South Africa; by the 1940s these had been used by the Nazis to exterminate millions of people in an industrial death machine.[23]

During this period teleological arguments became more focused, calling on the evidence of particular qualities in the universe rather than general evidence of order and purpose.

## F. R. Tennant

Today, none of Frederick Tennant's (1866–1957) books are available outside of specialist libraries. Yet he was one of the most original and important philosophers of religion in the early twentieth century. In particular, he originated a number of important arguments for the existence of God.

Tennant started his career as a scientist and a science teacher. He was ordained while teaching at Newcastle-under-Lyme High School (1891–94), a move which was to change his career direction radically. Nevertheless, Tennant never lost his scientific approach to the

---

23 The dubious record of being the site of the biggest ever mass murder belongs to the Polish village of Treblinka.

world – he believed that theism could and should be supported on sound evidence and argument.[24]

When he is remembered, Tennant is associated with being an early proponent of the *Anthropic Principle*. The Anthropic Principle has given rise to some confusion and controversy in recent decades, partly because the phrase has been applied to several distinct ideas. Tennant simply developed an early 'intelligent design' argument which focused on the relative improbability of chance or blind evolution leading to human consciousness. He was probably inspired by the evolutionary biologist Alfred Russel Wallace (1823–1913), who wrote:

> Such a vast and complex universe as that which we know exists around us, may have been absolutely required . . . in order to produce a world that should be precisely adapted in every detail for the orderly development of life culminating in man.[25]

In *Philosophical Theology*, Volume II, Tennant began by arguing that

> [t]he forcibleness of nature's suggestion that she is the outcome of intelligent design lies not in cases of particular adaptedness in

---

24 Tennant's study of theology led him back to Cambridge, eventually as a fellow of Trinity College during the era of Bertrand Russell and George Moore and around the time that Ludwig Wittgenstein first presented himself in Cambridge and just before the outbreak of the First World War. Perhaps it is because he was working in this context that Tennant's work has been overshadowed. During the early decades of the twentieth century the Trinity College SCR contained a 'Who's Who' of leading scientists and analytic philosophers – Tennant's work on sin and the problem of evil, though important, would not have stood out as modern and this would have been compounded by his major work *Philosophical Theology*, whose application of philosophical techniques to 'prove' Christian doctrine would not have been acceptable to many of his colleagues.

25 A. R. Wallace, *Man's Place in the Universe: A Study of the Results of Scientific Research in Relation to the Unity or Plurality of Worlds,* 4th edn, London: George Bell & Sons, 1904, pp. 256–7.

the world, nor even in the multiplicity of them, [but] . . . consists rather in the conspiration of innumerable causes to produce . . . a General Order in Nature.

before focusing on the existence of human beings as highly complex and conscious beings, suggesting that evolution through natural selection struggles to provide a complete explanation of human existence.

More recently physicists and cosmologists as well as philosophers and theologians have developed the basic idea in different directions. In particular, two variants of the Anthropic Principle, the *Strong Anthropic Principle* and the *Weak Anthropic Principle*, have emerged (though unhelpfully, these are defined differently in different books).

The physicist Roger Penrose wrote of the Weak Anthropic Principle: 'The argument can be used to explain why the conditions happen to be just right for the existence of (intelligent) life on the earth at the present time.'[26] The Strong Anthropic Principle goes beyond considering carbon-based life forms at this particular place and time and suggests that the fundamental constants of physics must have been fine-tuned to result in intelligent life.

Obviously enough, all versions of the Anthropic Principle have been accused of discouraging the search for a deeper physical understanding of the universe. For physicists these principles look at chance and probability in the wrong way. If you reflect back on all the tiny events that led to you reading this book today, it seems extraordinarily improbable. Do you conclude that you have no free will and that you are being manipulated in some grand cosmic game of SIM CITY? Alternatively, do you consider that the end point, you reading this book, is not determined; that things are genuinely open? Perhaps intelligent life such as ours is not inevitable, the fact that it has emerged just makes us think it is.

---

26 Roger Penrose, *The Emperor's New Mind: Concerning Computer, Minds and the Laws of Physics*, Oxford: Oxford University Press, 1989, Chapter 10.

## The Aesthetic Argument

> If I should ever die, God forbid, let this be my epitaph: the only proof he needed for the existence of God was music. (Kurt Vonnegut)

Tennant is also sometimes remembered for the aesthetic argument, by which he suggested that the excessive beauty in nature points to a creative mind and makes scientific explanation inadequate. As John Polkinghorne has argued, 'beauty slips through the scientist's net'. Tennant wrote:

> Whether it be subjectively constituted . . . whether beauty be wholly Objective and literally intrinsic to Nature: these controversial questions are here immaterial . . . If we minimize phenomenal Nature's gift by denying that her beauty is intrinsic . . . we must allow to Nature an intrinsic constitution such that minds can make beauty . . . out of it. And the more we magnify man's part in this making . . . the more motivation have we to believe that Nature comes to herself in man, has a significance for man that exists not for herself, and without man is a broken circle. Theologically expressed, this is the belief that Nature is meaningless and valueless without God behind it and man in front.

In the *City of God*, Augustine developed a related argument, writing:

> Beauty . . . can be appreciated only by the mind. This would be impossible, if this 'idea' of beauty were not found in the mind in a more perfect form . . . But even here, if this 'idea' of beauty were not subject to change, one person would not be a better judge of sensible beauty than another . . . nor the experienced and skilled than the novice and the untrained; and the same person could not make progress towards better judgement than

before. And it is obvious that anything which admits of increase or decrease is changeable. This consideration has readily persuaded men of ability and learning . . . that the original 'idea' is not to be found in this sphere, where it is shown to be subject to change . . . And so they saw that there must be some being in which the original form resides, unchangeable, and therefore incomparable. And they rightly believed that it is there that the origin of things is to be found, in the uncreated, which is the source of all creation.

St Bonaventure and the Franciscan tradition have taken beauty as the starting point for their theology and see it as most clearly pointing to the existence of God.

Although the horrors of the twentieth century made it more difficult to accept the objective existence of beauty, there have always been those for whom it remains the most compelling of arguments for God's existence. Nevertheless, for others the aesthetic argument makes an unjustifiable assumption about the objective nature of beauty. Hume wrote that 'beauty is no quality in things themselves: It exists merely in the mind which contemplates them; and each mind perceives a different beauty . . .'[27]

Picasso reputedly quipped that 'God is really only another artist. He invented the giraffe, the elephant and the cat. He has no real style; He just goes on trying other things.'

## C. S. Lewis

C. S. Lewis developed several arguments for the existence of God based on particular aspects of our human experience. His famous 'moral argument' was inspired by Kantian philosophy, but went

---

27 *The Philosophical Works of David Hume in Four Volumes*, Volume III, 1826, *Of The Standard of Taste* (Essay XXIII), Edinburgh: Adam Black and William Tait, p. 260.

further than Kant would allow in arguing for God's existence. The argument may be summarized as follows:

1 Everyone knows *a priori* and so believes that there are objective moral truths.
2 Objective moral laws are very peculiar in that they are quite unlike Laws of Nature and other 'natural' facts.
3 The hypothesis that there is an intelligence that implants the knowledge of right and wrong in us and serves as the foundation for the objectivity of such judgements is a good explanation of our intuitions.
4 The existence and nature of objective moral facts supports the existence of intelligence behind them serving as their basis and foundation.

While it might seem strange that Lewis argued from a universal appreciation of the moral law in the aftermath of the Shoah, perhaps it was the general human revulsion at Nazi policy and the determination on all sides never to let such a thing happen again which made the moral argument seem plausible in the 1950s and 1960s.

Lewis wrote that 'conscience reveals to us a moral law whose source cannot be found in the natural world, thus pointing to a supernatural Lawgiver'.[28] He argued that if science is accepted to provide a complete explanation for our world, human morality becomes worthless; moral statements cannot be right or wrong if we are all biologically or evolutionarily determined. Despite this, Lewis noted, those who accept evolutionary naturalism still act as if objective moral truths exist. This suggests that science cannot provide a complete explanation and theism seems the best alternative.

Lewis, like Kant, equated God with goodness and treated goodness as an essential part of reality, thus asserting God's existence.

---

28 *Mere Christianity*, London: Collins, 1955, quoted in the *Dictionary of the Philosophy of Religion* (ed. Charles Taliaferro and Elsa J. Marty), London: Continuum, 2010, p. 154.

Broadly related to the argument from morality, in that it begins with our inward experience of being human, is Lewis' *argument from desire*, which can be summarized as follows:

P1 Every natural, innate desire in us corresponds to some real object that can satisfy that desire.

P2 But there exists in us a desire which nothing in time, nothing on earth, no creature can satisfy.

IC Therefore there must exist something more than time, earth and creatures, which can satisfy this desire.

C This something is what people call 'God' and 'life with God forever'.

Drawing on a tradition that dates back to Augustine, who wrote: 'Because God has made us for Himself, our hearts are restless until they rest in Him . . .', Lewis argues that if and when we desire, we do so because what we desire exists prior to our desiring it. Religion at its basic level could be defined as a desire to please or appease a Supreme Being. Therefore this Supreme Being must exist.

He wrote:

The Christian says, 'Creatures are not born with desires unless satisfaction for those desires exists. A baby feels hunger: well, there is such a thing as food. A duckling wants to swim: well, there is such a thing as water. Men feel sexual desire: well, there is such a thing as sex. If I find in myself a desire which no experience in this world can satisfy, the most probable explanation is that I was made for another world. If none of my earthly pleasures satisfy it, that does not prove that the universe is a fraud. Probably earthly pleasures were never meant to satisfy it, but only to arouse it, to suggest the real thing. If that is so, I must take care, on the one hand, never to despise, or be unthankful for, these earthly blessings, and on the other, never to mistake them for the something else of which they are only a kind of copy, or echo, or mirage. I must keep alive in myself the desire for my true country, which I shall not find until after death; I must never let it get snowed under or turned aside; I

must make it the main object of life to press on to that other country and to help others do the same.'[29]

Nevertheless, the argument from desire is open to criticism. As Sartre
wrote, 'That God does not exist, I cannot deny. That my whole being
cries out for God, I cannot forget.' The existence of insatiate longing
in the human soul is, for some, a powerful argument against God's
goodness and consequently against the existence of the God of classical theism. As Bertrand Russell wrote,

> The centre of me is always and eternally a terrible pain – a curi-
> ous wild pain – a searching for something beyond what the world
> contains – something transfigured and infinite . . . I do not find it, I
> do not think it is to be found – but the love of it is my life.[30]

Lewis's broader argument from consciousness and reason also
deserves consideration.

P1　We experience the universe as intelligible. This intelligibility
　　means that the universe is graspable by intelligence.
P2　Either this intelligible universe and the finite minds so well
　　suited to grasp it are the products of intelligence, or both intel-
　　ligibility and intelligence are the products of blind chance.
A1　It cannot be blind chance.
C　　Therefore this intelligible universe and the finite minds so
　　well suited to grasp it are the products of intelligence.

Obviously the key assumption that Lewis makes is A1 – and this
claim atheists will simply reject, arguing that natural selection alone
can provide a complete explanation.

However, in *Miracles*, Chapter 3, Lewis argues against what
he calls naturalism, the view that everything belongs to one vast

---

29 *Mere Christianity*, pp. 136–7.

30 Bertrand Russell, 'Letter to Colette O'Neil', in *The Selected Letters of
Bertrand Russell The Public Year* 1914–1970, Taylor & Francis, 2002 p. 85.

interlocking system of physical causes and effects. He argues that if naturalism is true then it seems to leave us with no reason for believing it to be true; all judgements would equally and ultimately be the result of non-rational forces that determine how we think rather than approach what is true. If Lewis's argument is a good one then blind chance cannot be the source of our intelligence.

## Summary

Design arguments for God's existence are ancient and varied. They share the characteristic of moving from effects to cause and being *a posteriori*, but they cite different attributes of the world to support their conclusion of a designer-God. Some arguments focus on order (for example Paley's analogy) while others focus on purpose (for example Aquinas); still others focus on very particular features of the natural world such as human reason, consciousness, beauty or morality. Yet, they all struggle to account for evil and suffering and depend to a large extent on existing perspectives. All the arguments seek to persuade people that God is the best explanation. For somebody already convinced of the order, complexity and beauty of nature it is easier to accept that God exists and that evil and suffering can be explained away than for somebody who sees the world as brutish and arbitrary.

# 7

# Evolution and Fine Tuning

## Intelligent Design Arguments

Modern intelligent design arguments are usually put forward by members of the Discovery Institute, a Republican think-tank founded in Seattle in 1990, and its subsidiary The Center for Science and Culture. The Discovery Institute aimed to 'reverse the stifling materialist world view and replace it with a science consonant with Christian and theistic convictions'.[1] This is known as the Wedge Strategy, which aims to renew American culture by shaping public policy to reflect conservative Christian values.

Intelligent design arguments have also attracted some support from a vocal minority of Catholics, Jews and Muslims. The Istanbul Municipal Government hosted an international conference on intelligent design in 2007, and there is growing support for teaching of alternative perspectives on human origins in schools across Turkey, which has (perhaps surprisingly) led the anti-Darwin backlash in the Muslim world.[2]

Intelligent design arguments tend to fall into two categories, arguments from *irreducible complexity* and arguments from *specified complexity*. Both types of argument move from observations of the natural world to the conclusion that an intelligent cause is more likely than chance as an explanation of those observations. Intelligent design arguments tend to avoid all mention of the word

---

1 As explained in this policy document http://www.antievolution.org/features/wedge.pdf.

2 http://www.washingtonpost.com/wp-dyn/content/article/2009/11/07/AR2009110702233.html.

'God', both for political reasons and because saying 'and this is what everybody calls God' begs many questions about equating the God people worship with what might be suggested by the evidence.


## Irreducible Complexity

In *Darwin's Black Box* (1996) Michael Behe coined the term *irreducible complexity*. He pointed to complex systems in which each part depends on every other part; remove one part and the system ceases functioning. An example of this might be the bacterial flagellum of E. coli, the blood-clotting cascade, cilia, and the adaptive immune system. Behe argues that the necessary parts of an irreducibly complex system have always been necessary – they must have occurred together and not developed one by one. This implies a point in time when such systems were designed and created, rather than a drawn-out process of evolution. Darwin's theory of evolution by a process of natural selection is inadequate; that creation by an intelligent designer would explain the facts more completely.

One good analogy to explain the idea of irreducible complexity would be a mousetrap. No part of the mousetrap has an independent function – it only works when all the parts are present together. How could a mousetrap have evolved? Of course, it did not; it was designed and manufactured to do a job. The inference is that other irreducibly complex organisms were similarly designed and created for a purpose.

Another analogy would be the game Jenga. Blocks of wood are piled high, then blocks are removed and placed on top to try to make the tower ever taller . . . if you took a snapshot of the Jenga tower partway through the game, then it would be difficult to see how this could have evolved – each block balances on other blocks in a seemingly irreducibly complex pattern.

Arguably, this overlooks the fact that the pattern has been achieved through intermediate steps – in Jenga some blocks were previously there that are no longer there. This could be a criticism of the argument from irreducible complexity. It assumes that evolution could not have gone through intermediate steps to get to the present situation and that some once-vital elements of systems could be phased out through natural selection, just as elements which remain vital persist by the same process.

It is not uncommon for intelligent design arguments to suggest that the difficulty of explaining certain natural phenomena through evolution indicates the general inadequacy of the hypothesis. Arguably, this commits the fallacy of moving from the specific to the general. Phenomena such as love, altruism and beauty were all cited as things which evolution cannot account for in the past but today evolutionary biology and its close relative evolutionary psychology have posited explanations for almost all these things.

## Specified Complexity

William Dembski is a Christian with doctorates in both mathematics and philosophy. Sponsored by the Discovery Institute since 1996, Dembski taught at Baylor University from 1999 until 2005, and has since taught at two Baptist Theological Seminaries in the southern USA.

Dembski has written a number of popular books,[3] including *The Design Inference: Eliminating Chance through Small Probabilities*, which was a bestselling philosophical monograph for Cambridge University Press and which has been cited as good scientific evidence in support of intelligent design by the Discovery Institute.

Most closely associated with arguments for intelligent design from *specified complexity*, Dembski argues that while many highly complex things occur in nature (for example a chain of 100 protein molecules) and while highly specified things also occur (such as where a particular amino acid molecule is needed to do a particular job) *specified complex* things do not occur naturally (for example the DNA of Shakespeare).

---

3 Such as *Intelligent Design: The Bridge between Science and Theology* (with Michael Behe) IUP Academic, 2002, *The Design Revolution*, IUP Academic, 2004, *The End of Christianity*, Bate Publishing Group, 2009 and *Intelligent Design Uncensored* (with Jonathan Witt) IUP, 2010.

Dembski uses probability theory to suggest that a designer is more likely than a specified complex object arising by chance.

In his earlier papers Dembski defined specified complex information as being present in *an event whose probability did not exceed one in ten to the power of 150*, which he calls the *universal probability bound*. He asserts that specified complex information exists in numerous features of living things, such as DNA and other functional biological molecules, and argues that it cannot be generated by the only known natural mechanisms of physical law and chance, or by their combination.

## Criticisms of Intelligent Design

Most scientists have not greeted intelligent design arguments with enthusiasm. There have been many responses to Behe, Dembski and others, attacking their methodology and their calculations as well as their conclusions. There have even been criticisms from believing scientists, with writers such as John Polkinghorne and Alister McGrath remaining unconvinced that irreducible complexity or specified complexity really suggests the need for an intelligent designer.

Intelligent design arguments have been parodied. Online, people have seized on the suggestion that it is as reasonable to conclude that features of the world suggest that it has been created by a Flying Spaghetti Monster as to conclude that it has been created by a Christian God.

Richard Dawkins rejects intelligent design arguments from both irreducible complexity and from specified complexity in *The God Delusion*. He points out that any suggestion that a supernatural designer is a simpler explanation than natural processes is simply nonsensical. Suggesting that a complex system is best explained by a complex but uncaused designer is at least as incredible as suggesting that a complex universe is itself uncaused.

Further, Dawkins observes that all the probability arguments look at the end product and consider the improbability of things arising like this, as if they had to do so. For Dawkins, this misses the point.

There is nothing to suggest that things had to end up this way as opposed to a million different possible ways. The way things are is simple chance driven by random natural selection, and the improbability of this is much less astounding.

## Fine-Tuning Arguments

Dembski's argument from specified complexity recalls the famous example given by the Cambridge physicist professor Fred Hoyle (1915–2001) that the universe coming about by chance is equivalent to a tornado whipping through a scrapyard and assembling a working 747, which built on a point made previously by fellow-physicist Robert Dicke. In another example Hoyle compared 'the chance of obtaining even a single functioning protein by chance combination of amino acids to a star system full of blind men solving Rubik's Cube simultaneously'.[4]

Fine-tuning arguments focus on the sheer unlikelihood of the precise conditions necessary for things to end up as they are, such as the force needed for the Big Bang to yield our present expanding universe full of stars and planets or the many steps needed for evolution to produce Einstein from single-celled antecedents. These conclude that an intelligence shaping events is more likely than blind chance. As Stephen Hawking wrote,

> The laws of science, as we know them at present, contain many fundamental numbers, like the size of the electric charge of the electron and the ratio of the masses of the proton and the electron . . . The remarkable fact is that the values of these numbers seem to have been very finely adjusted to make possible the development of life.[5]

---

4 http://www.optcorp.com/articles/hoyle-fred, see also Hoyle, *Intelligent Universe*, Rinehart and Winston, 1983.

5 *A Brief History of Time*, New York: Bantam Books, 1988, p. 125.

Fine-tuning arguments attempt to use scientific insights into the process of the universe coming into being, such as this one from Hawking to strengthen the case for God rather than weakening it. Robin Collins put it like this:

> Suppose we went on a mission to Mars, and found a domed structure in which everything was set up just right for life to exist. The temperature, for example, was set around 70F and the humidity was at 50 per cent; moreover, there was an oxygen-recycling system, an energy gathering system, and a whole system for the production of food. Put simply, the domed structure appeared to be a fully functioning biosphere. What conclusion would we draw from finding this structure? Would we draw the conclusion that it just happened to form by chance? Certainly not! Instead, we would unanimously conclude that it was designed by some intelligent being . . . The universe is analogous to such a 'biosphere', according to recent findings in physics.[6]

Alvin Plantinga, in his article 'The Dawkins Confusion; Naturalism Ad Absurdum'[7] explained that

> [o]ne reaction to these apparent enormous coincidences is to see them as substantiating the theistic claim that the Universe has been created by a personal God and as offering the material for a properly restrained theistic argument – hence the fine-tuning argument. It's as if there are a large number of dials that have to be tuned to within extremely narrow limits for life to be possible in our Universe. It is extremely unlikely that this should happen by chance, but much more likely that this should happen if there is such a person as God.[8]

---

6 'God, Evil and Suffering', in Michael J. Murray (ed.), *Reason for the Hope Within*, Grand Rapids: Eerdmans, 1999, p. 48.

7 A 2007 review of Dawkins' *The God Delusion*, available online at http://www.booksandculture.com/articles/2007/marapr/1.21.html.

8 *Christianity Today*, March/April 2007.

Of course, from the earliest days such arguments have been criticized. As Clarence Darrow observed,

> [e]ven a human being of very limited capacity could think of countless ways in which the earth could be improved as the home of man, and from the earliest time the race has been using all sorts of efforts and resources to make it more suitable for its abode. Admitting that the earth is a fit place for life, and certainly every place in the universe where life exists is fitted for life, then what sort of life was this planet designed to support? There are some millions of different species of animals on this earth, and one-half of these are insects. In numbers, and perhaps in other ways, man is in a great minority. If the land of the earth was made for life, it seems as if it was intended for insect life, which can exist almost anywhere. If no other available place can be found they can live by the million on man, and inside of him. They generally succeed in destroying his life, and, if they have a chance, wind up by eating his body.[9]

In the decades since Martin Rees (b. 1942) explored and defended fine-tuning arguments in *Cosmic Coincidences*[10] and since Paul Davies (b. 1946) wrote that 'the impression of design is overwhelming'[11] and that 'there is now broad agreement among physicists and cosmologists that the Universe is in several respects "fine-tuned" for life',[12] many cosmologists have moved on from accepting any simple fine-tuning argument for supernatural interference in the formation of our universe.

For Sean Carroll (b. 1966) of CalTech, even sophisticated appeals to fine tuning rely on our ability to understand hypothetical alternative universes, with different conditions and laws, an ability which there is little reason to suppose that we possess. Further, he points out that the

---

9 *The Story of My Life*, New York: Charles Scribner's Sons, 1932, pp. 419–20.

10 John Gribbin and Martin Rees, *Cosmic Coincidences*, London: Black Swan, 1991.

11 *The Cosmic Blueprint: New Discoveries in Nature's Creative Ability to Order the Universe*, New York: Simon and Schuster, 1995, p. 203.

12 *International Journal of Astrobiology* 2:2 (2003), p. 115.

models used to extrapolate from early conditions to the universes they would produce are crude – and would probably predict that our own universe would be inhospitable. Carroll also observes that 'intelligent observers will only measure the values which obtain in those regions which are consistent with the existence of such observers', and that cosmology betrays unintelligent design, noting that entire classes of fundamental particles exist that would have no impact on life if they had never existed.

John Polkinghorne (b. 1930) is perhaps the best known advocate of scientific theism today. He was professor of Mathematical Physics at the University of Cambridge from 1968 to 1979, when he resigned his chair to study for the priesthood, becoming an ordained Anglican priest in 1982. He served as the president of Queens' College, Cambridge, from 1988 until 1996. The author of works such as *Quantum Physics and Theology: An Unexpected Kinship* (2005), *Exploring Reality: The Intertwining of Science and Religion* (2007) and *Questions of Truth* (2009), Polkinghorne argues that science leaves room for spirituality and for God.

Polkinghorne describes his position as one of *critical realism*. He believes that science and religion address different aspects of reality and each seeks the truth in their own ways, though these ways bear comparison. Both science and theology go through five similar stages in their searches: moments of enforced radical revision, a period of unresolved confusion, new synthesis and understanding, continued wrestling with unresolved problems, and deeper implications.

Polkinghorne has criticized scientific method, arguing that because scientific experiments try to eliminate extraneous influences, they are atypical. He suggests that the mechanistic explanations of the world should be replaced by an understanding that most of nature is cloud-like rather than clock-like. He believes that standard physical causation cannot describe the many ways in which things and people interact. He describes his philosophic position in terms of *dual aspect monism*; he writes that

> there is only one stuff in the world (not two – the material and the mental) but it can occur in two contrasting states (material and

mental phases, a physicist might say) which explain our perception of the difference between mind and matter.[13]

Polkinghorne's position does not lend itself to a simple design argument for God. His universe is stranger – more complex and less ordered and purposeful – than that of Paley. Nevertheless, God is the explanation needed to account for things as they are.

In spite of the challenges to intelligent design, there is no doubt that the conditions necessary for the singularity to give rise to a universe suitable for life are incredibly improbable. There are only three ways in which this improbability can be explained:

1 There are infinite numbers of universes and we just happen to be in the one where conditions for life are right. This is a serious scientific possibility.
2 Extraordinary things do happen and, given that we are here, then the extraordinary improbability of the universe meeting the conditions for life must have occurred and there is no need to ask for any further explanation.
3 There is an intelligence behind the universe.

It is a good scientific method to maintain that an explanation that is simpler and more plausible than its alternatives to account for the facts should be preferred, and it may be argued that the third of the above alternatives is, indeed, the simpler and more plausible explanation. This is certainly not a conclusive argument, but it may be a pointer.

## Process Theology

Process theology was a movement first associated with the ideas of Alfred North Whitehead (1861–1947) and Charles Hartshorne

---

13 *Science and Christian Belief: Theological Reflections of a Bottom-up Thinker*, London: SPCK, 1994, p. 21.

(1897–2000). It has been developed by John Cobb (b. 1925) and David Griffin (b. 1939) in more recent years.[14]

Charles Hartshorne spent time refining the classical arguments for God's existence, but his most important contribution was to our understanding of the concept of the God which those arguments point to. He saw problems in labelling God as omnipotent, in the way that Aquinas did, because it is difficult to reconcile an omnipotent God with suffering in nature, with the apparent disorder which exists alongside order, and more difficult to reconcile it with any meaningful freedom for human beings.

For Hartshorne, God's necessary existence does not necessarily lead to God's simplicity. God's existence could be unalterable but God could still act, change and be changed. For example, the existence of time within the universe is unalterable, but the rate at which it progresses varies, depending on the rate of expansion of the universe and where one is relative to large masses. This would make God capable of acting in time and responding to prayer; it would make freedom more meaningful.

For Hartshorne, God is not omnipotent, but is as powerful as it is possible to be, given the partial freedom and power of creatures. God can *persuade* human beings, but cannot coerce them or remove their freedom of choice.

Inspired by Hartshorne, modern process theologians focus on the dynamic nature of things, the fact that everything changes and is fluid, suggesting that as like effects have like causes, God must be ever-changing as well – not the static, distant wholly-simple being of Aquinas or Leibniz. God cannot be known in the way that other things are known; our understanding of God's existence and nature is glimpsed through paradox.

Whitehead's classic statement of process theology[15] takes the form of a set of antithetical statements.

---

14 Similar ideas have influenced a number of Jewish theologians, including Abraham Heschel.

15 A. N. Whitehead, *Process and Reality*, New York: The Free Press, 1978, p. 349.

- It is as true to say that God is permanent and the world fluent, as that the world is permanent and God is fluent.
- It is as true to say that God is one and the world many, as that the world is one and God many.
- It is as true to say that, in comparison with the world, God is actual eminently, as that, in comparison with God, the world is actual eminently.
- It is as true to say that the world is immanent in God, as that God is immanent in the world. It is as true to say that God transcends the world, as that the world transcends God.
- It is as true to say that God creates the world, as that the world creates God.

The problem with these statements is that they seem to be not simply in tension but to rest on what may be a contradiction. It raises the problem of how far language about God is mysterious and how far it attempts to reconcile positions that are fundamentally irreconcilable.

For process theologians then,

- God is *both* eternal *and* in time.
- God changes.
- God is not omnipotent.
- God causes things to be as they are and then tries to persuade them to fulfil God's will for them, but things are ultimately free.
- God contains the universe but is not the universe; *panentheism* not *pantheism*.

Clearly, this approach remains quite controversial and is at some distance from the mainstream of Christian, Jewish and Islamic thought.

## The Gaia Hypothesis

In the 1960s British chemist James Lovelock was working as a consultant for NASA. In his spare time he developed ideas which would be the foundation for a new way of looking at our reality, the Gaia Hypothesis. The Gaia hypothesis proposes that the earth can be thought of as a single organism 'Gaia' (named after the Greek Goddess of the earth) composed of complex, interacting and inter-dependent systems.

For Lovelock, the 'biosphere' acts to sustain life. Many processes essential for the conditions of life depend on the interaction of living forms, especially micro-organisms, with inorganic elements. These processes establish a global control system that regulates earth's surface temperature, atmosphere composition, ocean salinity etc. In *The Revenge of Gaia* he argues that the lack of respect humans have had for Gaia, through the damage done to rain forests and the reduction in biodiversity, is testing Gaia's capacity to minimize the effects of the addition of greenhouse gases in the atmosphere.[16] Similarly the warming of the oceans is preventing the rise of nutrients into the surface waters and eliminating the algal blooms on which food chains depend. According to Lovelock, most of the earth will become uninhabitable for humans and other life-forms by the middle of this century, with a massive extension of tropical deserts.

Writing in the *Independent* in January 2006, Lovelock argued that, as a result of global warming, 'billions of us will die and the few breeding pairs of people that survive will be in the Arctic where the climate remains tolerable' by the end of the twenty-first century. He has been quoted in the *Guardian* that 80 per cent of humans will perish by the year 2100, and this climate change will last 100,000 years.

The Gaia hypothesis has not been widely accepted within the scientific community. Among its more famous critics are the evolutionary biologists Richard Dawkins and Stephen Jay Gould, who have questioned how natural selection operating on individual organisms can lead to the evolution of planetary-scale homeostasis. Lovelock responded with models such as Daisyworld that illustrate how individual-level effects can translate to planetary homeostasis under the right circumstances.

---

16 New York: Basic Books, 2006.

Gaia takes the conclusions of the process theologians one step further. Process sees God and the universe as interdependent, but Gaia sees God and the universe as one – it is outright pantheism. Certainly observation of the complexity, order and purposiveness could support this conclusion but, importantly, it is not necessarily compatible with mainstream Christianity, Judaism or Islam – though some few members of each faith may be attracted by it.

Of course, pantheists must account for the existence of evil in the world and, by inference, in God. If they do so by redefining or diluting the goodness of God, then pantheism could dissolve into very impersonal religion, even deism.

## Summary

Design arguments have a particular difficulty in accounting for the apparently chaotic universe suggested by quantum science, though they remain popular today in the controversial forms of intelligent design arguments and arguments from fine tuning.

Observations of the universe in the light of modern science have led some philosophers to suggest that God might not be omnipotent, omniscient and omnibenevolent as traditionally conceived within Christianity, Judaism and Islam. For process theologians and for those inspired by Lovelock's Gaia hypothesis, creation suggests a different type of creator.

In the end, like cosmological arguments, design arguments depend on prior judgements about the world and its origins. For those already convinced of order and purpose, improbable levels of complexity and responsiveness in nature, the conclusion that God exists is acceptable. For those who see the universe in different terms, as chaotic, unpredictable, brutal, the case for a creator is never going to convince.

# 8

# Ontological Arguments

O Lord, not only are you that than which a greater cannot be thought, but you are also something greater than can be thought. For since there can be thought to exist something of this kind, if you were not this, then something greater than you could be thought – which is impossible.

(Anselm, *Proslogion* 15)

Most arguments for God's existence move from an observation of the way things are to a conclusion which seems to explain that observation; they move from synthetic, observable effect to cause and conclude *a posteriori*, after the fact, that God exists. Of course, the conclusions of such an argument will only ever be contingent; if new or additional evidence comes to light then the conclusion may be *falsified*. In this sense these arguments are always vulnerable. Inductive arguments for God's existence tend to conclude that God is *de re necessary*, that is, self-explaining and self-sustaining.

Another type of argument for God's existence is possible, however: an ontological argument. *Analytic* arguments show that there is an undeniable logical relationship between two words or concepts: 'John is a bachelor, therefore John is unmarried' or 2 + 2 = 4. Ontological arguments move from an analysis of the cause to the effects. The truth of the conclusion, existence, may be deduced from and depends only on the definition of God, which is established *a priori*, before the argument. Because of this, ontological arguments are sometimes called *strong*; the conclusions do not depend on partial observations and so are not probably true but definitely true. However, it is important to note that such an argument may be *valid* even if the premise(s) are not true, but it is only considered to be *sound* if they are, if the definitions of terms are borne out in reality.

The word 'ontological' is derived from the Greek word *ontos*, the present participle of the verb *einai*, to be. Ontology is the study of the being or nature of things and as such an ontological argument tries to demonstrate that existence is a necessary part of God's being. Although the word was first used to describe analytic arguments for the existence of God by Immanuel Kant in the *Critique of Pure Reason*,[1] the possibility of an ontological argument for the existence of God was, perhaps, first conceived of by Augustine of Hippo.

Augustine opened up three routes to proving the existence of God, though he himself explored only one. Arguments like Aristotle's that begin in the world proceed from effect to cause and have been called cosmological arguments. The second route also proceeds from effect to cause, but starts within the mind and searches out God as the ultimate cause of the mind's knowledge. This is called the illumination argument for God. Augustine also suggested a third route: the ontological argument, which saw existence as part of the essence of God.

## Anselm

Anselm (1033–1109) was a dominant figure in the medieval European church. In his late twenties Anselm joined the Abbey of Bec in Normandy, where fellow Italian Lanfranc had achieved fame as an influential philosopher and teacher. By the time that Anselm became Abbot in 1078 he was already well known as the author of *De Grammatico*, *Monologion* and *Proslogion*. In 1066 Duke William of Normandy became King of England and put Norman bishops and abbots into English ecclesiastical positions. In 1093 Anselm succeeded Lanfranc as Archbishop of Canterbury in England. Anselm's role was both spiritual and political.

Throughout his life Anselm tried to rationalize Christian belief. He wrote: 'I hold it to be a failure in duty if after we have become steadfast in our faith, we do not strive to understand what we believe.'

---

1 A591/B619

Note how faith comes first and is enriched through reason which leads to understanding. Reason is not necessarily the basis for faith, and Anselm's faith is best understood to be non-propositional.

In *De Veritate* Anselm set out the framework for his philosophical system and showed how he had been influenced by Augustine. He reasons that the existence of truth suggests that there must be a supreme principle of truth through which other things may be judged to be true. This absolute truth is God himself, who is the foundation of all things and ideas. Anselm then set out to explore God's existence through the *Monologion* and the *Proslogion*.

In the *Monologion*, Anselm wrote:

If anyone does not know, either because he has not heard or because he does not believe, that there is one nature, supreme among all existing things . . . I think he could at least convince himself of most of these things by reason alone, if he is even moderately intelligent.

In the *Monologion* Anselm argued that there must be some one thing that is supremely good, through which all good things have their goodness.

He reasoned that if I say 'That is a good table', I assume the existence of a principle of goodness through which the judgement makes sense. This principle of goodness is itself a great good – since it is the source of the goodness of all other things. Moreover, that thing is good through itself, not through some external principle of goodness. Anselm concludes: 'Now that which is supremely good is also supremely great. There is, therefore, some one thing that is supremely good and supremely great – in other words, supreme among all existing things.'

Anselm's argument might be summarized like this:

P1  Every existing thing exists either through something or through nothing.

P2  Nothing exists through nothing, so every existing thing exists through something.

P3   There must be some one thing through which all things exist.

P4   That one thing, of course, must exist through itself.

P5   That being so, it is greater than all the other things and is therefore *best and greatest and supreme among all existing things*.

C    This is what everybody calls God.

Anselm wrote that

> there is a certain nature or substance or essence who through himself is good and great and through Himself is what He is; through whom exists whatever truly is good or great or anything at all; and who is the supreme good, the supreme great thing, the supreme being or subsistent, that is, supreme among all existing things.

This supreme essence is what everybody calls God.

Anselm's argument in the *Monologion* developed the *illumination argument* found in the writings of Augustine. Like Augustine, Anselm was influenced by Neoplatonic philosophy in which ultimate 'reality' is beyond the limited, contingent physical world. What are real are ideas, principles of reason, forms – not matter which is ever changing and ever decaying. Later advocates of the ontological argument, including Descartes and Leibniz, understood 'reality' similarly. There is a sense, therefore, in which critics of the ontological argument (including Kant and Russell) fundamentally misunderstand the basis of the argument because when words such as 'real' or 'exists' appear they tend to associate them with the world of physical experience.

Anselm's argument in the *Monologion* is an *a posteriori* argument and it is not therefore, an ontological argument. The argument in the *Monologion* does not distinguish between conceptual existence and actual existence and it would be possible to conclude that God exists only in the mind at the end of the *Monologion*. Nevertheless, this argument begins to explore the concept of existence, of being, and so lays the foundations for Anselm's later attempt to demonstrate God's existence *a priori*.[2]

In the *Proslogion* Anselm began with a quotation from Psalm 14.1, 'The fool says in his heart, "There is no God"' and then reflected on its meaning.

Anselm defined God as *aliquid quo nihil maius cogitari possit*, or 'that than which no greater can be conceived'. This *a priori* being accepted, he observed that anybody who doubts God's real existence is a fool; it is always greater to exist in reality (*in re*) than just in the mind (*in intellectu*) (this claim is often discussed in terms of the relationship between formal and intentional existence).

The doubter must have a concept of God in the mind to doubt or reject. If the concept of God is that of the greatest conceivable being, it must be of a formally, really existing being. For Anselm, the doubter is essentially saying 'God, who exists, does not exist' – they are asserting a straight contradiction.

Anselm wrote:

Thus even the fool is convinced that something than which nothing greater can be conceived is in the understanding, since when he hears this, he understands it; and whatever is understood is in the understanding. And certainly that than which a greater cannot be conceived cannot be in the understanding alone. For if it is even in the understanding alone, it can be conceived to exist in reality also, which is greater. Thus if that than which a greater cannot be conceived is in the understanding alone, then that than which

---

2 Gene Fendt has argued that Anselm's proof for God should be seen as a continuous process of development through the *Monologion* to the *Proslogion*, rather than as two (or more) separate arguments as Copleston and others had previously suggested. It is fair to say that the argument in the *Proslogion* cannot be understood without first appreciating the conceptual framework established by the *Monologion*, but the arguments developed in the two works are clearly separate. Gene Fendt, 'The Relation of Monologion and Proslogion', *Heythrop Journal* 46:2 (2005), pp. 149–66. There's also a partial response – Toivo J. Holopainen, 'The Proslogion in Relation to the Monologion', *Heythrop Journal* 50:4 (2009), pp. 590–602.

a greater cannot be conceived is itself that than which a greater can be conceived. But surely this cannot be. Thus without doubt something than which a greater cannot be conceived exists, both in the understanding and in reality.

To summarize, Anselm was tackling the possibility that God may exist only as a concept in the mind, left open by his previous argument in the *Monologion*. He analysed the concept of God and what it means to be the supreme principle of greatness. He argued that actual existence must be part of the concept of God and thus that it is irrational to deny the existence of God, that those who do so are fools. Anselm argues that God's existence is known *a priori* and does not depend on observations; God *de dicto* necessarily exists. The concepts of God and existence are logically linked in the way that the concepts of bachelor and unmarried man are.

Taking it step by step . . .

- . . . even the fool is convinced that something than which nothing greater can be conceived is in the understanding . . .
- . . . that than which a greater cannot be conceived cannot be in the understanding alone. For if it is even in the understanding alone, it can be conceived to exist in reality also, which is greater . . .
- [therefore] . . . something than which a greater cannot be conceived exists, both in the understanding and in reality . . .

To put it another way, Anselm sees that God exists by definition; if God is perfect, and perfection includes real and not just imaginary existence, then God just has to exist – or not be God.


## Gaunilo

The simple argument in *Proslogion* 2 was reduced to absurdity by Anselm's fellow Benedictine monk Gaunilo in *Liber pro Insipiente* or '*On Behalf of the Fool*'. Gaunilo focused on the claim that God's nature as the greatest conceivable being must include existence, observing that

> if a man should try to prove to me by such reasoning that this [perfect] island truly exists . . . either I should believe that he was jesting, or I know not which I ought to regard as the greater fool: myself, supposing that I should allow this proof; or him, if he should suppose that he had established with any certainty the existence of this island.

Gaunilo suggested that the ontological argument, if it is to work in proving God's existence, should also prove the existence of all other perfect things – islands, unicorns, women . . . We all know that perfect unicorns do not exist in the real world; no amount of believing or arguing is going to change the fact that when you get to your paradise island there could be one more coconut on the tree or one more fish in the lagoon. The perfect island cannot be defined into existence.

This criticism cuts to the heart of the ontological argument; just because a deductive argument is valid does not make it sound. Take an unrelated example we have used before:

P1    All toasters are items made of gold.
P2    All items made of gold are time-travel devices.
C     Therefore, all toasters are time-travel devices.

If the premises support the conclusion then the argument is *valid* – but we all know that toasters are not usually made of gold and that time-travel devices do not exist, gold or not – therefore this valid argument must be rejected for being *unsound*. Gaunilo is suggesting that Anselm might have put forward *an apparently valid but unsound argument*.

To summarize Gaunilo's understanding of Anselm's argument in *Proslogion* 2:

P1    God is perfect.

IC   Perfect things must exist.
C    Therefore God must exist.

We all know that we cannot define things into existence by insert-
ing 'perfect' into their definition. How much easier it would be for
women to find the ideal man if that was the case!

Anselm wasted no time in refuting Gaunilo's criticism by saying
that only God has all perfections and the logic of his argument can,
therefore, only be applied to God. He developed the existing argument in *Proslogion* 3 into a more substantial piece of philosophy in
the *Responsio*. He wrote:

> Why then has the fool said in his heart 'There is no God', since it
> is so evident to a rational mind that Thou dost exist in the highest
> degree of all? Why, except that he is dull and a fool? . . . or it is
> possible to conceive of a being which cannot be conceived not to
> exist; and this is greater than one which can be conceived not to
> exist. Hence if that than which nothing greater can be conceived
> can be conceived not to exist, it is not that . . .[3]

In the *Responsio* Anselm stuck with his definition of God as the
greatest conceivable being and still observed that it was greater to
exist *in re* (in reality) than just *in intellectu* (in the mind) – but he
went on to ask whether it is greater for a being to have contingent
existence (i.e. existence which can be conceived not to exist) or to
have necessary existence (i.e. existence which cannot be conceived
not to exist). Naturally, necessary existence is greater and thus must
be a necessary property of the greatest conceivable being, of God.

> For it is possible to conceive of a being which cannot be conceived
> not to exist; and this is greater than one which can be conceived
> not to exist. Hence if that than which nothing greater can be con-
> ceived can be conceived not to exist, it is not that . . .

---

3  *Proslogion* 3

The property of *necessary existence* is unique – a property of the greatest conceivable being – only God *must exist*, cannot be conceived not to exist. Necessary existence is part of God's nature whereas ordinary existence is part of the natures of other things. The ontological argument cannot be applied to other things even if they seem to share in the perfection which is God's nature as well. In other words, God's greatness is not like the greatness of other things – they can be more or less great but God is greatness itself; they can contingently exist but *only God necessarily exists*.

To summarize Anselm's reasoning:

- *Definition*: God is the greatest conceivable being.
- *Analysis*: it is greater to have necessary existence (i.e. existence which cannot be conceived not to exist) than just to have contingent existence (i.e. existence which can be conceived not to exist).
- *Conclusion*: necessary existence, *in re*, must be a unique property of the greatest conceivable being, of God.

## Aquinas' Objections to the Ontological Argument

Against the whole possibility of an ontological argument for God, Thomas Aquinas argued that although God's *de re* necessity could be demonstrated through natural theology, God's *de dicto* necessity could never be known in this life. He observed that all ontological arguments depend on a definition of God which he felt to be impossible to arrive at except through reasoning from experience (arguing *a posteriori*).

For Aquinas, all claims about God are analogical – they share some meaning with similar claims made about created things but should not be understood literally, univocally. We can move from experience to the conclusion that God exists and from that conclusion to making claims about the nature of God's existence as a necessary being – but the sense of our understanding of God's nature is too limited to allow for a definition to be analysed for a *de dicto* proof of God's existence. Aquinas denied the *univocal* use of language which Anselm's proof assumed – and thus undermined the ontological approach to proving God's existence. He wrote: 'Because we do not know the essence of God, the proposition "God exists" is not self-evident to us.'[4]

Aquinas objected to the whole idea of a deductive ontological argument for God because this type of argument starts with a definition which can then be analysed – something which is not possible in the case of God.

John Duns Scotus (1265/66–1308) rejected Aquinas' scepticism about language, developing a complex defence of the possibility of speaking literally, univocally, of God as Anselm did. However, despite Scotus' argument, Aquinas' rejection of the ontological argument rendered the whole attempt to arrive at God's existence *a priori* unfashionable for several centuries.

## Descartes' Clear and Distinct Idea of God

Descartes was brought up as a devout Roman Catholic, and, although his relationship with the Church grew strained, there is no reason to believe that he ever lost his faith. Descartes used scepticism to uncover the basis for certain knowledge, on which he hoped to build a new and secure philosophical system. He was an important mathematician and his concept of truth, reality and existence was shaped by this.

In a way, Descartes' philosophical method was even more sceptical than that of Hume. While Hume argued that we can be pretty certain of what we see, hear, touch, smell and taste, for Descartes our senses deceive us regularly. For example, a stick thrust into water appears to bend – but this is an optical illusion. So, if we cannot be certain of sense-data, then what can we know? Descartes argued that the only thing that I can really know which is absolutely certain and cannot be doubted is that 'I think, therefore I am' – I exist and am

---

4 *Summa Theologica* 1.2.1

a conscious, thinking being. Yet, even this would not preclude the possibility that my thoughts are as in a dream, or matrix-world. The reason, for Descartes, that I can be certain that my thoughts relate to reality is that God exists and would not allow me to be totally deceived.

For Descartes, a mind free from philosophical prejudice (that is, not distracted and confused by sense-data) intuits the existence of God as the ground of all possibility and the basis of thought and reality. He wrote:

> as regards God, if I were not overwhelmed by philosophical preju-
> dices, and if the images of things perceived by the senses did not
> besiege my thought on every side, I would certainly acknowledge
> Him sooner and more easily than anything else. For what is more
> manifest than the fact that the supreme being exists, or that God,
> to whose essence alone existence belongs, exists?[5]

Of course, most people do not possess minds free from philosophical prejudice. They are confused by sense-data and do not intuit the existence of God. Therefore, in the *Meditations* Descartes put forward two different approaches to proving God's existence. Both arguments encourage people to reflect on the manner of their own thinking, seeing that God's existence is necessary given the nature of human consciousness.

In the Third Meditation Descartes puts forward an initial *a posteriori* argument which holds that since I have an idea of a supremely perfect being, this idea must have come from somewhere. He argues that it must have been placed in my mind and that only a supremely powerful being could place such an idea directly into the minds of human beings. Therefore, Descartes concludes, a supreme being must exist. The relationship between this argument and the more famous ontological argument in the Fifth Meditation is still a subject of debate, though it is important to note that this argument is definitely NOT an ontological argument – it is a causal argument

---

5 AT 7:68–69; CSM 2:47

starting from experience and in some ways is reminiscent of Anselm's argument in the *Monologion*.

Descartes proposed several versions of the ontological argument, the clearest of which is contained in his Fifth Meditation.[6] It is important to consider Descartes' intentions. It seems likely that he did not really intend the argument to be an axiomatic proof, in which conclusions are derived from *a priori* definitions. Although he used the analogy of a triangle and used the language of logic, it is possible to interpret the Fifth Meditation as following on from the Fourth, in which Descartes established a method of establishing truths from intuition or 'clear and distinct perception'. This approach involves unveiling the contents of our clear and distinct ideas which form the most certain form of knowledge for Descartes. Through rationally analysing our concepts we can come to understand the nature of our reality, and that God is an undeniable part of that reality.

He wrote:

> I find in myself countless ideas of things that can't be called nothing, even if they don't exist anywhere outside me. For although I am free to think of these ideas or not, as I choose, I didn't invent them . . . Even if there are not and never were any triangles outside my thought, still, when I imagine a triangle I am constrained in how I do this, because there is a determinate nature or essence or form of triangle that is eternal, unchanging, and independent of my mind . . . [I] clearly recognize these properties of the triangle, whether I want to or not, even if I didn't give them a thought when the triangle first came into my mind. So they can't have been invented by me.

Descartes denies that the idea of a triangle depends on sense-experience, on past encounters with triangular bodies. He concludes that '[t]he mere fact that I find in my thought an idea of something

---

6 He repeats it in a few other central texts including *The Principles of Philosophy* and defends it in the First, Second, and Fifth Replies against scathing objections by some of the leading intellectuals of his day.

*x*, and vividly and clearly perceive *x* to have a certain property, it follows that *x* really does have that property'.

Turning to God, Descartes asks

> Can I not turn this to account in a second argument to prove the existence of God? The idea of God (that is, of a supremely perfect being) is certainly one that I find within me, just as I find the ideas of shapes and numbers; and I understand from this idea that it belongs to God's nature that he always exists. This understanding is just as vivid and clear as what is involved in mathematical proofs of the properties of shapes and numbers. So even if I have sometimes gone wrong in my meditations in these past days, I ought still to regard the existence of God as being at least as certain as I have taken the truths of mathematics to be.

Descartes admits that '[a]t first sight, this looks like a trick . . .'. He confronts the potential problem with including existence in the essence of something, even God, writing:

> where things other than God are involved, I have been accustomed to distinguish a thing's existence from its essence. The question 'What is the essence of triangles (or flames or sparrows)?'. . . still leaves open the existence question, which asks whether there are any triangles (or flames or sparrows). I can easily believe that in the case of God, also, existence can be separated from essence . . . so that God can be thought of as not existing. But on more careful reflection it becomes quite evident that, just as having-internal-angles-equal-to-180° can't be separated from the idea or essence of a triangle, and as the idea of highlands can't be separated from the idea of lowlands, so existence can't be separated from the essence of God. Just as it is self-contradictory to think of highlands in a world where there are no lowlands, so it is self-contradictory to think of God as not existing – that is, to think of a supremely perfect being as lacking a perfection, namely the perfection of existence.

Descartes reflected on this proof. He admitted that

> [h]ow things are in reality is not settled by my thought; and just as I can imagine a winged horse even though no horse has wings, so I can attach existence to God in my thought even if no God exists.

Yet, Descartes suggests that there is a difference between the concept of a winged horse and the concept of a river with banks. The former is *an incoherent concept* and the latter *a coherent concept* so that 'river and banks – whether or not there are any in reality – are inseparable'.

Though, for Descartes

> my thought doesn't . . . create necessities really. The influence runs the opposite way: the necessity of the thing constrains how I can think, depriving me of the freedom to think of God without existence (that is, a supremely perfect being without a supreme perfection).

Descartes argues that thought is constrained by God, who determines which concepts are coherent and which are not. Because of God and the principles of thought which stem from Him, it is impossible to conceive of God as other than a supremely perfect being and possessing all perfections – whether or not I know or understand what those perfections are.

It is clear that Descartes saw existence as a perfection; he wrote:

> once I have supposed that all perfections belong to God, I must suppose that he exists, because existence is one of the perfections. This idea isn't a fiction, a creature of my thought, but rather an image of a true and unchanging nature; and I have several indications that this is so. God is the only thing I can think of whose existence necessarily belongs to its essence. I can't make sense of there being two or more Gods of this kind;

and after supposing that one God exists, I plainly see that it is necessary that he has existed from eternity and will stay in existence for eternity.

He concluded:

Whatever method of proof I use, though, I am always brought back to the fact that nothing completely convinces me except what I vividly and clearly perceive. Some things that I vividly and clearly perceive are obvious to everyone; others can be learned only through more careful investigation, but once they are discovered they are judged to be just as certain as the obvious ones. (Compare these two truths about right-angled triangles: 'The square on the hypotenuse equals the sum of the squares on the other two sides' and 'The hypotenuse is opposite the largest angle.' The former is less obvious than the latter; but once one has seen it, one believes it just as strongly.) Truths about God are not in the immediately obvious class, but they ought to be. If I were not swamped by preconceived opinions, and if my thoughts were not hemmed in and pushed around by images of things perceived by the senses, I would acknowledge God sooner and more easily than anything else. The supreme being exists; God, the only being whose essence includes existence, exists; what is more self-evident than that?

## Gottfried Leibniz (1646–1716)

Leibniz, like Descartes, was a mathematician whose philosophy began in the world of thought, logic and ideas. He thus stands, as most mathematicians do, in the tradition of Plato rather than Aristotle. For Leibniz, ultimate reality is metaphysical – physical experiences are just shadows or partial reflections of forms, substances or 'monads' which exist objectively and timelessly.

Leibniz explored the nature of possibility itself – what we can know about what is possible and what is not. Possibility is the ground of reality – for something to be possible is in some sense for it to be real.

For Leibniz, Descartes' proof for God, in beginning with the concept of God, highlighted a fascinating opportunity. If the concept of God could be shown to be non-contradictory, then Descartes' conclusion, that necessary existence was part of God's nature, might really be convincing. Leibniz focused on showing that the concept of God as the supremely perfect being is non-contradictory, filling what he saw as a shortcoming in Descartes' argument.

Leibniz made a distinction between what he took to be flawed concepts, such as the highest number and the greatest speed, and those concepts of perfection which he maintained to be possible. He argued that all possible perfections are perfect through a quality of perfection that is simple and unanalysable. All perfect things are thus ultimately compatible. They can all be drawn together within a single possible concept of supreme perfection – God. Leibniz then went on to argue that supreme perfection would entail infinite existence.

## The Concept of Existence

Anselm, Descartes and Leibniz all conclude that denying God's existence is denying an essential quality or 'predicate' of God's nature. The atheist is a fool because he/she asserts 'God, who exists, does not exist.' This is as nonsensical as talking of two-sided triangles or flat hills. This claim, that existence can be seen as an essential predicate of anything, is the focus of the criticisms of the classical argument levelled by Kant and later Russell.

One important point to note is that critics of the ontological argument tend to hold a different understanding of truth and reality. Whereas proponents of the ontological argument see ultimate reality as metaphysical and true understanding of reality as accessible through a clear conceptual understanding, critics tend to see that reality is rooted in limited human (physical) experience. To put it another way, supporters of the ontological argument tend to be mathematicians and to be influenced primarily by Plato, whereas critics tend to be influenced by the scientific and observational method of Aristotle.

## Kant v. the Ontological Argument

Kant's epistemology, his world-view, prevented him from deriving a proof of God's existence from any *a priori* definition. For Kant, knowledge is based on experience; God is beyond our experience and it would, therefore, be impossible to develop an *a priori* definition of God capable of being the subject of meaningful analysis.

Experience might well indicate regularity, order, laws etc. but it cannot extend to enable us to *know* that God exists. Although God most probably explains these features of the universe, because of the limitations of human subjective knowledge we can only *postulate* the existence of such a being.

Language is based on experience. It may be used to explore that experience – but it cannot be used to provide proof in itself of something beyond experience. Whereas Descartes argued that the conceptual relationship between perfection and existence within the idea of God rendered God's necessary existence *de dicto* necessary, Kant observed that such analytic truths are simply semantic. Certainly the relationship between 'unmarried man' and 'bachelor' is undeniable, but the sort of undeniable truth that extends only to how language should be used. Unicorns must have horns, but that does not mean that there are any unicorns. Analytic truths are, for Kant, just *tautologies* or different ways of expressing the same thing. They do not add anything to our concepts; they just clarify the relationships between concepts.

For Kant, all existential claims must be synthetic; they must refer to a state of affairs which can be experienced if they are to be meaningful. All synthetic propositions must have the possibility of being either true or false in relation to an actual state of affairs. EITHER a ball is red OR it is not; therefore the claim 'This ball is red' is meaningful (even if it may not be true), whether the ball turns out to be red or green. For Kant, there can be no analytic demonstrations concerning *the existence* of anything.

Kant noted that to argue that there is a *necessary being* is the same as to say that to deny its existence is contradictory. It is not possible, therefore, for 'God necessarily exists' to be a synthetic statement. There is no possibility of it being false and no possibility of us experiencing the state of affairs to which it might refer. 'God necessarily exists' must, therefore, be an analytic statement – but no analytic statement can also tell us anything about existence. Therefore, the concept of necessary existence is just a *'miserable tautology'*, not a proof of anything, just indicative that our concept of existence remains unclear.

Kant pointed out that Descartes and Leibniz, indeed all the proponents of the ontological argument, treat existence as if it adds something to a concept or makes a being better. Kant rejected this because he argued that existence is a necessary ground for any other perfection to be meaningful rather than just another in a list of perfections.

Imagine a job interview. The panel look through the CVs of two well-qualified candidates – but it then turns out that candidate A exists and candidate B is made up. There is no real contest between the two. Candidate B never really had any of the qualities the CV claimed and was nonsense all along. Candidate A's existence is not just another qualification which tips the balance in her favour!

Descartes and Leibniz seem to see existence as a *predicate* of God. A predicate is a word that refers to the properties of an object which adds something to our understanding of the nature of a thing. Descartes and Leibniz defined God's perfection in terms of a list of attributes. Just as a perfect flower would be colourful, scented, have petals and leaves etc., the supremely perfect being would be all-powerful, all-knowing and have necessary existence. Descartes and Leibniz add existence as just another of these describing-qualities but, Kant argued, existence adds nothing to the concept of the flower, it merely maintains that there are flowers.

What is the difference between a real hundred pounds and an imaginary hundred pounds? Kant observed that the concept in question is identical whether the notes are in my pocket or not. There is a difference between claiming something about a concept and claiming that a concept exists. He wrote:

> If I reject the predicate while retaining the subject, contradiction results; and I therefore say that the former belongs necessarily to the latter. But if we reject subject and predicate alike, there is no contradiction; for nothing is then left that can be contradicted . . . the same holds true of the concept of an absolutely necessary being. If its existence is rejected, we reject the thing itself with all its predicates; and no question of contradiction can then arise . . .

Whatever adds nothing to the concept of an essence is not part of that essence, existence adds nothing to the concept of an essence, existence is not part of the essence of a thing, it is not a perfection and

> [t]he attempt to establish the existence of a supreme being by the famous ontological argument of Descartes is therefore merely so much labour and effort lost; we can no more extend our stock of [theoretical] insight by mere ideas than a merchant can better his position by adding a few noughts to his cash account [7]

For Kant, we can have no knowledge of necessary existence – the whole category is a *cupola of judgement* (flight of fancy) and as impossible as the conclusion of any inductive argument as it is as the basis of any deductive proof.


## Bertrand Russell

The great atheist philosopher Bertrand Russell was fascinated by the ontological argument, reportedly going so far as to exclaim 'Great

---

7  Quoted by Plantinga, *The Ontological Argument from St. Anselm to Contemporary Philosophers*, New York: Macmillan, 1968, p. 64.

God in Boots! – the ontological argument is sound!'[8] at one point. Nevertheless, he ended up convinced that the argument failed, picking up and developing some of Russell's criticisms in his article *On Denoting* (1905).

Russell distinguished between two types of propositions – *predicative propositions* (those which add to the concept) and *existential propositions* (those which claim a reference between a concept and a state of affairs).

Russell argued that everyday use of language makes it possible to talk about non-existent things with apparent meaning. Russell used the example of 'The present King of France' – as soon as I start talking about this meaningless entity, even if to state that it does not exist, I imply that the concept is a valid one.

For Russell, statements can be true or false only if they refer to a meaningful concept. There is no way that I can affirm the existence of any instance of 'necessary existence' before embarking on an ontological argument which seeks to conclude that God's necessary existence is necessary – therefore the whole enterprise is meaningless.

## Summary

The central question which the ontological argument raises is, appropriately enough, that of existence. What does it mean to exist?

- For Anselm, Descartes and Leibniz, existence is metaphysical, primarily in the world of logic and ideas. They are all accepting the legacy of Plato.
- For Hume, Kant and Russell, existence is primarily in the world of sense-experience, matter and energy. They are all accepting the legacy of Aristotle.

---

8 Quoted by Melvyn Bragg at the beginning of his *In Our Time* BBC Radio 4 programme on the ontological argument.

Clearly, an argument which seeks to demonstrate that God exists is affected by the definition of existence just as much as by the definition of God.

It is worth noting that most statements of the classical ontological argument make at least one of these assumptions:

- God can be defined.
- It is better to exist formally (in reality – whatever that means) than to exist intentionally (only in the mind).
- Necessary existence is a perfection and may be used as a predicate.
- Necessary existence is not contradictory.

# 9

# Necessity or Nothing

In 1948 South African philosopher John Findlay (1903–87) published his article 'Can God's Existence Be Disproved?'[1] In it he tightened the criticisms levelled by Kant and Russell and attempted to provide an ontological proof of God's impossibility.

Findlay was a critic of Wittgenstein and argued that the meaning of words does not just lie in their common use. He stood up for there being some sort of absolute meaning in language and, unusually, his criticism of the ontological argument came from taking its approach seriously rather than from disputing the possibility of analysing words and concepts in order to arrive at truth.

Findlay began by agreeing with Anselm's point in *Proslogion* 3, that only a necessary being would really be the greatest conceivable, really be God and thus really worthy of worship. Building on Kant's dismissal of 'necessary existence' as a contradictory proposition he developed what Hartshorne later called Findlay's Paradox:

- A contingent being would not deserve worship, BUT
- a necessary being is a logical absurdity.

Findlay concluded that

it was indeed an ill day for Anselm when he hit upon his famous proof. For on that day he not only laid bare something that is of the essence of an adequate religious object, but also something that entails its necessary non-existence . . .

---

1 First published in *Mind*, April 1948.

## Charles Hartshorne

Charles Hartshorne (1897–2000) is considered by many philosophers to be one of the most important philosophers of religion of the twentieth century. The *Stanford Encyclopaedia* explains that 'throughout his career he defended the rationality of theism and for several decades was almost alone in doing so among English-language philosophers'.

Hartshorne's contribution to the attempt to argue for God's existence was considerable. Hartshorne developed versions of all of the classical arguments and was responsible for one of the first 'cumulative arguments' – that is, suggesting that although none of the arguments may stand alone as proof for God's existence, together the arguments are more than the sum of their parts.

In relation to the ontological argument, from 1941 Hartshorne argued that Hume's and Kant's criticisms of the ontological argument of Anselm are not directed at the strongest version of his argument found in the *Proslogion* 3. Hartshorne's view is that ordinary existence might not be a real predicate, but *existing necessarily* might be.

Hartshorne believed that there are necessary truths concerning existence. To say that absolute non-existence in some fashion exists is to contradict oneself; hence he thinks that absolute non-existence is unintelligible.

Hartshorne specifically criticized Findlay on two counts:

1 If it makes sense to talk about God's necessary non-existence then it makes just as much sense to talk about God's necessary existence. (Of course Russell's argument in 'On Denoting' would see both discussions as equally meaningless.)
2 Findlay, like Kant and, before him, Hume, assumes that all existential propositions are contingent. Hartshorne points out that this is not a universally accepted assumption.

For Hartshorne, it is necessarily the case that something exists, and, relying on the ontological argument, it is necessarily true that God exists. On Hartshorne's view, it is not possible to think of a pre-eminent being that only existed contingently, since if it did exist contingently rather than necessarily, it would not be pre-eminent. God's existence is either impossible or possible, and, if possible, then necessary.

He is assuming here that there are three alternatives for us to consider:

1 God is impossible.
2 God is possible, but may or may not exist.
3 God exists necessarily.

For Hartshorne, the ontological argument shows that the second alternative makes no sense since a necessary being cannot just possibly exist. Since there is nothing impossible about the idea of God necessarily existing, God must necessarily exist.

## Norman Malcolm

In 1960 Norman Malcolm (1911–90) agreed with Hartshorne on his last point.[2] A follower of Wittgenstein, Malcolm saw that meaningful propositions are not restricted to the analytic or synthetic, but that meaning is derived from the *usage* of language.

Malcolm argued that within a religious form of life, the concept of necessary existence has real meaning; its effect can be seen in the lives of believers and therefore Findlay's neat extension of Kant's critique should not be accepted. He concluded that

in those complex systems of thought, those 'language games', God has the status of a necessary being. Who can doubt that? . . . I believe we may rightly take the existence of those religious systems of thought in which God features as a necessary being as disproof of the dogma, affirmed by Hume and others, that no existential proposition may be necessary . . .[3]

---

2 *Philosophical Review* 69, 1960.
3 Anselm's Ontological Arguments.

Malcolm agreed with Hartshorne that 'God necessarily exists' is a true statement but, crucially, this statement is only true to those who participate in worship and liturgy, to those who inhabit a religious culture of 'form of life'. This tells us nothing about whether or not there is a Being who corresponds to the statement.

Malcolm's own version of the ontological argument could be expressed as follows:

1 God is, by definition, an unlimited being.
2 The existence of an unlimited being is either logically necessary or logically impossible.
3 The existence of an unlimited being is not logically impossible.
4 Therefore, the existence of God is logically necessary.[4]

On this basis, God necessarily exists to those who believe in God, who worship and pray, but that does not mean there is any independent reality to which the word 'God' refers.


## Plantinga's Modal Proof

In 1974 Plantinga dismissed Malcolm's version of the ontological argument, noting that Malcolm only showed that it is possible that a *logically necessary* being exists but not that it is necessary that God is a logically necessary being.

As a reformed epistemologist, Plantinga's complex modal version of the ontological argument is designed to evade the classic criticisms and show that belief can be defended through the argument – if not based on it. He wrote: 'What I claim for this argument therefore, is that it establishes not the TRUTH of theism, but its rational acceptability . . .'

It runs as follows:

P1 The property 'has maximal greatness' entails that the property 'has maximal excellence in every possible world'.

---

4 Adapted from http://www.iep.utm.edu/ont-arg/.

P2 Maximal excellence entails omnipotence, omniscience and omnibenevolence.

P3 Maximal greatness is possible; there is nothing contradictory in this claim and so we can claim that there is a possible world in which it exists.

P4 There is a world W and an essence E.

P5 For any object X, if X has exemplified E then X exemplifies that the property 'has maximal excellence in every possible world'.

P6 E entails that the property 'has maximal excellence in every possible world'.

IC If world W had been actual, it would be impossible that E fail to be exemplified.

C There exists a being that has maximal excellence in every possible world, so this being must exist in this world . . .

There are many technical objections that have been made to Plantinga's reasoning. At a very basic level it is worth saying that, for all his complex language, Plantinga makes the assumption, already criticized by Kant and John Hick, that whatever is non-contradictory must be possible and that whatever is logically necessary must then be factually necessary.

## Another Direction

The original title of Anselm's *Proslogion* was 'faith seeking understanding' or *fides quaerens intellectum*. When considering the success or failure of the ontological argument, it is worth remembering that there are different understandings of the relationship between faith and reason and that these will affect how the argument is conceived of and judged.

For those who understand faith to be propositional, rational argument is necessary as a basis for faith. Anselm calling his book 'faith seeking understanding' would in this case imply that the *Proslogion* provides rational reasons to believe and might constitute an argument with which to convert an unbeliever. This is the interpretation of the ontological argument held by, for example, Bertrand Russell and also Aquinas who both held that the argument fails.

For those who see faith as non-propositional, faith does not really depend on argument or evidence, but it may be defended or explored through reason. In this case, Anselm calling the *Prosologion* 'faith seeking understanding' suggests that it contains an enriching meditation on the nature of God and the nature of faith rather than something intended to convert. Karl Barth used 'faith seeking understanding' as the title of an important book about Anselm in 1960 and is associated with the re-interpretation of Anselm as somebody seeking to understand pre-existent faith rather than somebody seeking to convert.

During the twentieth century, eschewing the modal logic that came to fascinate reformed epistemologists, scholars such as Karl Barth and Iris Murdoch saw in the ontological argument a very different sort of faith-exercise, meaning that it could have value even if potentially invalid or unsound.

## Karl Barth

For Barth (1886–1968), Anselm's 'arguments' should not be seen as arguments. They begin and end with a prayer, an address to a God who is already accepted to exist. Barth sees Anselm's 'that than which nothing greater can be conceived' as a revealed 'name' of God which Anselm takes to be a norm of theological thinking, one which reinforces the limits of human understanding rather than assuming that humans can fully understand God.

Barth sees the assertion of God's necessary existence in Anselm's *Proslogion* 3 as an admission of the total dependency of contingent beings, such as ourselves, on the creator. He concluded:

The reason why there is such a thing as existence is that God exists. With his existence stands or falls the existence of all beings which are distinct from him. Thus with the prohibition against conceiving anything greater than him and with this prohibition ruling out the thought of His non-existence – thus alone does God confront man. Thus he and he alone is objective reality. . .[5]

Barth operates within a faith framework and, within this framework, God is the ultimate reality – but this does not apply if one stands outside the faith framework.

## Iris Murdoch

Iris Murdoch (1919–99) was a modern Platonist – as well as a prize-winning novelist and literary critic. She maintained that ideals such as goodness, beauty and truth have a real existence – though she stopped short of ascribing them to any definite 'world of the Forms' outside the mind.

Although no obvious theist, Murdoch was fascinated by the onto-logical argument as she saw in it a way of reaffirming the connec-tion between well-known concepts of power, knowledge, love etc. and the concept of God as supreme perfection. Like Barth, she saw the ontological argument as a faith-exercise which helps individuals to accept the reality and coherence of goodness, perfection, beauty, truth of God, within their own lives.

In *The Metaphysics of Morals* Murdoch recounted a story of believers praying to a relic that was, in fact, a dog's tooth. For the villagers, the tooth begins to 'glow' and have spiritual powers. It is the act of believing, faith, which makes the object real rather than any external factor. She wrote:

Keats says that 'what the imagination seizes as beauty must be truth, whether it existed before or not'. It must be truth. Simone

---

5 Karl Barth, *Anselm, Fides Quaerens Intellectum: Anselm's Proof of the Existence of God in the Context of His Theological Scheme*, London: SCM Press, 1960, p. 154; see also R. D. Shofner, *Anselm Revisited: A Study of the Role of the Ontological Argument in the Writings of Karl Barth and Charles Hartshorne*, Leiden: E. J. Brill, 1974.

Weil quotes Valery: 'The proper, unique, and perpetual object of thought is that which does not exist.' Here we may make sense of the idea of loving good. 'At its highest point, love is a determination to create the being which it has taken for its object.' Here indeed we come back to the Ontological Proof in its simpler version, a proof by perfection, by a certainty derived from love. The good artist, the true lover, the dedicated thinker, the unselfish moral agent solving his problem: they can create the object of love. The dog's tooth, when sincerely venerated, glows with light . . .[6]

In her essay 'On God and Good', published in the collection *Existentialists and Mystics* in 1999, Murdoch wrote:

There is no plausible 'proof' of the existence of God except some form of the ontological proof, a 'proof' incidentally which must now take on an increased importance in theology as a result of the recent 'demythologizing'. If considered carefully, however, the ontological proof is seen to be not exactly a proof but rather a clear assertion of faith (it is often admitted to be appropriate only for those already convinced), which could only be confidently made on a certain amount of experience . . .

She continued, writing:

This assertion could be put in various ways.

(1) The desire for God is certain to receive a response.
(2) My conception of God contains the certainty of its own reality.
(3) God is an object of love which uniquely excludes doubt and relativism.

---

6 *Metaphysics as Guide to Morals*, London: Vintage Classics, 2003, p. 506.

Such obscure statements would of course receive little sympathy from analytical philosophers, who would divide their content between psychological fact and metaphysical nonsense . . .[7]

## Summary

The ontological argument continues to fascinate philosophers, even if it is unlikely to convert anybody and convince them to change their life. For people who already believe, the argument is an important thought experiment, an exercise which forces them to confront the natures of existence, of reality, and of God.

The argument reminds us that reality is much bigger and stranger than we often think. What is real is not just what human beings can touch, smell, taste, hear and see. On our little planet of apes, circling a tiny star in a peripheral galaxy, we can forget that human beings may not be the measure of all things; but we can also forget to wonder at our human ability to think, reason and be conscious. Necessary existence lies beyond our experience but so do the ultimate realities of mathematics. The ontological argument lies firmly in the Platonic tradition and seeks to lead us beyond the world of experience to a different form of reality and a different mode of existence.

---

7 'On God and Good', from *Existentialists and Mystics: Writings on Philosophy and Literature*, London: Penguin, 1999.

# 10

# Probability Arguments

So far we have looked at two main types of argument for the existence of God:

1 Most forms of cosmological and teleological arguments are *a posteriori* and *inductive*. They move from synthetic observations of effects to a conclusion about the logical cause of those effects. They provide a high probability rather than a proof for God and are always subject to new or different observations being made.

2 The ontological argument is *a priori* and *deductive*; it provides a proof of God's existence by analysing the concept of God and showing that existence is a necessary part of that concept. The ontological argument depends on people accepting the *a priori* definition of God before anything can be *deduced* from that.

There is, however, a third way, another form of argument not based on induction or deduction but on *abduction*, what is more commonly called *inference to the best explanation*. It can be argued that a number of the arguments considered so far are abductive as they may be persuasive rather than being decisive.

Inference to best explanation is an idea that was developed by Gilbert Harman (b. 1938) of Princeton University. This approach might be applied to God, that God is the best *postulate* to explain the universe as it is, in the absence of other proof.

Imagine that a woman has a husband who swears he is faithful to her. Now imagine that she finds a receipt for a dinner for two for a night when he says he was working. He says that he picked it up by mistake. Then she sees on his mobile phone many calls from a number she does not recognize – he says that are wrong numbers. Then she comes to realize that he has less and less time for her; he is always working late or called away at the weekend. Finally, he starts calling her by another name when they are making love. None of these, by themselves, would prove that the husband is having an affair but, taken together with what the woman has heard about the typical symptoms of infidelity in the married man, they might make the inference that her husband is having an affair a reasonable one.

Alister McGrath suggests that given the failure of both inductive and deductive arguments to provide a conclusive reason to believe, the question of God's existence and what to believe must either be labelled unanswerable or it must be decided on other grounds. McGrath argues that abduction or inference to best explanation is used in many areas of life to decide between possible options in a sensible way, therefore it is unnecessary and unreasonable to despair of answering the question of God. God, he argues, may reasonably be inferred to be the best explanation of the universe as it is, though it is impossible to prove his existence conclusively.

## Kant's Moral Argument

A similar approach can be found in the work of Immanuel Kant (1724–1804), who demolished traditional ontological, cosmological and teleological arguments in the *Critique of Pure Reason* (1781) but who still maintained that God provides a sensible *postulate* to explain the order apparent in the universe and particularly the existence of the moral law.

Kant read Hume, whose work he claimed 'awoke me from my dogmatic slumbers'. His developed philosophy saw all certain knowledge being founded on sense-experience. Although Kant was by no means as sceptical as Hume, he dismissed metaphysics for building castles in the air. Whereas Descartes mistrusted the senses because, for example, sticks appear to bend in water, Kant saw the senses as the best possible means of experiencing reality. I can be relatively certain of something if I see, hear, taste, touch or smell it. Of course I can build on basic sense experience using reason, developing an understanding of concepts, their logical relationships and what might be expected to be the case given those relationships for examples. Nevertheless, there is a limit to what can be known through reason; beyond a certain point it becomes speculation.

For Kant, given his epistemological framework, no *inductive* argument can establish God's existence. It is unreasonable to move from the claim that all things we experience are caused to the claim that there must exist something which is uncaused. We don't experience uncaused things, and claiming to know that they exist is beyond the boundaries of possible knowledge.

Further, there can be no *deductive* proof of anything's existence. Existence is not a perfection and cannot rightly be used as a predicate; it adds nothing to any concept.

For Kant therefore, traditional cosmological and teleological arguments cannot lead to God and ontological arguments are just *miserable tautologies*. Nevertheless, Kant was no atheist and he maintained that it is reasonable to believe in God.

In his *Critique of Practical Reason* (1788) Kant developed what is sometimes referred to as his *Moral Argument* for God's existence. Through it, Kant offers a reason to believe but makes no claims that he can demonstrate or prove God's existence. His approach might be compared with that of Pascal or James (pps. 16–19, 30–31), both of whom suggested that the question of God's existence, though inescapable and momentous, cannot be decided on rational grounds and both of whom argued that the choice to believe is reasonable nonetheless.

Kant's reasoning can be summarized as follows:

P1   Reason dictates that we ought to strive to attain the perfect good (happiness arising out of complete virtue).

P2   What we ought to do, it must be possible for us to do.

P3   Attaining the perfect good is only possible if *ought implies can*, if the universe is fundamentally ordered and fair.

C  Seeing the universe as fundamentally ordered and fair is only possible if we postulate a God as the source of the universe.[1]

Professor Allen Wood of Stanford University has interpreted Kant to mean that without postulating God's existence, people would be left facing a universe that is fundamentally unfair and chaotic. If reason demands that people try to be good and they cannot be good then reason itself seems irrational and an unhelpful means of engaging with reality. God is needed if Kant's world-view is to make sense. As for Descartes, God is the guarantor that things are as they seem, that we do not inhabit a nightmare world in which we are constantly pushed to do things we just cannot do.

Kant focuses on the existence of the moral law, the *Wille* or categorical imperative which he believed appeals to all human beings directly as a *synthetic a priori* (known independently of experience but confirmed through experience). The existence of the moral law is the best evidence of order in the universe. We experience it on a very deep level, yet it cannot be reduced to any particular experiences. The world as most people find it is full of injustice; there are many examples of people acting irrationally, out of fear, habit or selfishness. Nevertheless, most people still feel the demand of reason and know what is right.

Kant's epitaph translates as 'Two things ever fill me with awe, the starry skies above me and the moral law within me' – it was order in nature and the sense of objective moral truth which led Kant to postulate the Divine. However, and to repeat, Kant did not believe that we can ever prove God or truly know that God exists, but he maintained that it makes sense to postulate or assume that God does exist, because it makes best sense of our experience. Kant's moral argument is not a formal argument for the existence of God.

---

1  Peter Byrne, 'Moral Arguments for the Existence of God', *The Stanford Encyclopedia of Philosophy* (Spring 2013 edition), Edward N. Zalta (ed.), http://plato.stanford.edu/archives/spr2013/entries/moral-arguments-god/. See also *Critique of Practical Reason*, in M. Gregor, *Practical Philosophy*, Cambridge: Cambridge University Press, 1999, Vol. 5, Gesammelte Schriften, Berlin: de Gruyter.

## Richard Swinburne's Probability Argument

Proponents of fine-tuning and intelligent design arguments often talk about God being a *more probable* explanation for order in the universe than other explanations, but they rarely unpack what they mean by this.

Richard Swinburne developed a much more complex probability argument for the existence of God in 1979.[2] Swinburne still sees *The Existence of God* as his central work in the philosophy of religion and has returned to its argument at least twice, making substantial revisions for a second edition of the book in 2004.

Swinburne began by setting out how he aims

> to reach a conclusion about whether on balance the arguments indicate that there is a God or that there is not . . . I shall, however, argue that, although reason can reach a fairly well-justified con-clusion about the existence of God, it can reach only a probable conclusion, not an indubitable one.[3]

Swinburne is only really interested in inductive arguments and does not discuss deductive approaches. He sets out the nature of induc-tive arguments for God, distinguishing between those in which the premises make the conclusion probable, but less than half (p-inductive), and those in which the premises confirm the conclusion (c-inductive).

Swinburne then developed versions of a range of inductive argu-ments for the existence of God, including cosmological and teolog-ical arguments, and explored whether these might either confirm the existence of God or render God's existence more probable. In effect, Swinburne sees each of the inductive arguments as making God more probable. He uses Bayes' theorem to calculate the overall probability of God's existence, using the individual probability scores worked

---

2 *The Existence of God*, 2nd edn, Oxford: Oxford University Press, 2004.

3 Ibid., pp. 1–2.

out from each argument. Together, Swinburne argues, they make a *cumulative case* for God which renders God's existence more than one-half probable.

It is worth noting that, as Professor Richard Gale of the University of Pittsburgh (b. 1932) observes,

> While Swinburne's overall aim is to establish that the probability that God exists is greater than one-half, he does not want the probability to be too high, for he fears that this would necessitate belief in God on the part of whoever accepts the argument, thereby negating the accepter's freedom to choose not to believe.[4]

Gale quotes Swinburne in *The Existence of God*: 'If God's existence, justice, and intentions became items of evident common knowledge, then man's freedom would in effect be vastly curtailed.'[5]

Swinburne argues that if there is a reasonable probability that God exists (and he considers that he had demonstrated that this is the case) then religious experience should be assumed to be valid and to be a key factor in pointing to the existence of God – this is dealt with in detail in Chapter 13).

Swinburne applied the same probability method to the more specific question of whether Jesus was God incarnate in *The Resurrection of God Incarnate* (2003).

The physicist Stephen D. Unwin utterly rejected the fine-tuning argument for the existence of God in *The Probability of God* (2003). He argues that if the universe were not fine-tuned we would not be here to ask why it is – and this makes the argument viciously circular. Nevertheless, like Swinburne, Unwin exploited Bayes' theorem as a means of showing that the existence of God is slightly more probable than the non-existence of God. Unwin evaluates the probability of morality existing, of miracles or religious experiences occurring

---

4 'Swinburne's Argument from Religious Experience', in Alan Padgett (ed.), *Reason and the Christian Religion*, Oxford: Oxford University Press, 1994.

5 Ibid., p. 245.

under the possibilities both that God exists and that he doesn't and overall argues that this sort of evidence is marginally more probable if God exists than if he does not.

## A Cumulative Case?

Both F. R. Tennant and Charles Hartshorne proposed a more general type of probability argument for God's existence, the cumulative case approach. Whereas

> [p]hilosophers commonly use a metaphor that suggests that the chain of an argument, say for the existence of God, is only as strong as its weakest link. Hartshorne rejects this metaphor [and] replaces it by suggesting that various arguments for the existence of God – ontological, cosmological, design, etc. – are like mutually reinforcing strands in a cable.[6]

In the words of Basil Mitchell (1917–2011), the ordinary cumulative case method does 'not conform to the ordinary pattern of deductive or inductive reasoning'. The case is more like the brief that a lawyer makes in a court of law or that a literary critic makes for a particular interpretation of a book.

Mitchell gave the example of a ship in wartime when there is radio silence (this is, of course, well before the days of satellite navigation). It is night and the ship is headed towards land. The navigator says that the ship is 200 miles off shore – but then a crew member sees seaweed in the water (seaweed is not found 200 miles from shore). The navigator dismisses it as either a mistake or due to a previous storm. Then someone else sees what looks like land on the horizon but the navigator says that this is cloud. Then someone else sees a seagull (which are not found 200 miles from shore) and the navigator says it must have been a mistake. Then someone else thinks that

---

6 Dan Dombrowski, 'Charles Hartshorne', in Edward N. Zalta (ed.), *The Stanford Encyclopedia of Philosophy* (Spring 2013 edition).

they hear the sound of waves breaking on rocks. The situation is serious. If things are left too late the ship may run aground. None of the pieces of evidence are, by themselves, conclusive, but taken together they make a cumulative case for turning the ship around before it is too late.

Paul Feinberg says that 'Christian theists are urging that [Christianity] makes better sense of all the evidence available than does any other alternative worldview, whether that alternative is some other theistic view or atheism'.

In addition to Mitchell and Feinberg, cumulative cases have been set out by C. S. Lewis and, more recently, by C. Stephen Evans.

The dominant criticism of cumulative cases for God is that they are like using 'ten leaky buckets' to hold water. Ten bad arguments are not necessarily more effective than one bad argument! This criticism is often attributed to Anthony Flew. Proponents of the cumulative case method do not accept this, pointing out that the existence of so many different arguments does itself need an adequate explanation. They see the various strands of argument like fibres in a rope; individually they hold little weight, but together they are strong. J. P. Moreland uses this analogy.

Richard Swinburne addressed the 'leaky buckets' criticism directly, writing: '[f]or clearly if you jam ten leaky buckets together in such a way as the holes in the bottom of each bucket are squashed close to the solid parts of neighbouring buckets, you will get a container that holds water.'[7] But this response may be criticized because although such a composite bucket might slow down the leaks, it is unlikely to stop them – and because the location and sizes of the holes in the arguments for God's existence do not line up so conveniently! The problems with cosmological arguments are quite similar to the problems with teleological arguments, so that one does not cancel out the problems with the other but rather accentuates them.

---

7 Quoted in Kenneth Boa and Robert M. Bowman (eds), *Faith has its Reasons: Integrative Approaches to Defending the Christian Faith*, Downers Grove, IL: InterVarsity Press, 2001, p. 212.

## Summary

In the absence of proof that God exists it might be possible to suggest that God is the most probable explanation for the way things are. Probabilistic arguments might focus on a specific feature of the universe, such as the existence of moral laws, or they might take a more general view by seeing God as the most probable explanation of the existence of so many features which require explanation.

Probability arguments are, it has to be said, unlikely to convince anybody who does not already believe. Despite the technical complexity of arguments put forward by Swinburne and Unwin, they still rely on people estimating the probabilities for themselves. Whereas believers are likely to rate the existence of God highly, atheists are not.

# PART THREE

# Encountering the God of Abraham

The God of Christians is not a God who is simply the author of mathematical truths, or of the order of the elements; that is the view of heathens and Epicureans. He is not merely a God who exercises His providence over the life and fortunes of men, to bestow on those who worship Him a long and happy life. That was the portion of the Jews. But the God of Abraham, the God of Isaac, the God of Jacob, the God of Christians, is a God of love and of comfort, a God who fills the soul and heart of those whom He possesses, a God who makes them conscious of their inward wretchedness, and His infinite mercy, who unites Himself to their inmost soul, who fills it with humility and joy, with confidence and love, who renders them incapable of any other end than Himself.

(Blaise Pascal, *Pensees*, pp. 153–4)

# 11

# Encountering the God of Abraham

At the end of each of his five arguments for God's existence, Thomas Aquinas concludes by saying 'this is what everybody calls God'.[1] Is Aquinas right? Do people really worship and *believe in* the Prime Mover, uncaused cause or necessary sustainer of the universe? Is the Divine designer really the object of prayer and devotion?

While the bringing together of philosophy and religion is understandable – it provides a basis of evidence for faith and makes belief a whole lot more justifiable – the two are not so obviously compatible.

Islamic scholars had a particular problem when they tried to use Greek philosophy to support faith in Allah. Islam demands that the Qur'an is seen as a direct revelation from God, that it is accepted as literal truth and not open to interpretation in the same way as the Bible might be within some branches of Christianity and Judaism. It is difficult to see how the Prime Mover could speak directly to the Prophet in the language of medieval Arabia. Ways around this, such as by emphasizing the role of the angel Jibriel or the Prophet himself in translating inspiration into words, have always been decried as unislamic – along with those who seemed too willing to compromise key principles of faith to make religion more rational.

The great Jewish philosopher Moses Maimonides (1135–1204) drew on the work of Islamic scholars, concluding that reason demonstrates the total inadequacy of language when it comes to describing God. God's existence is known and understood through the revelation of the Torah, prophecy and spiritual communion with the Divine. God's attributes may only be correctly expressed in negative terms (for example God is not evil, God is not limited). Using language in a positive way outside the context of revealed scripture may mislead people.

---

1 Part I, Question 2, Article 3 of Aquinas' *Summa Theologica*.

Aquinas had to engage in subtle theology to reconcile what he had sought to prove through argument with what the Church held to be true of God. Although he escaped being tried as a heretic as several fellow Aristotelian philosophers of religion were in the Paris of 1277, and though he was hailed as a Doctor of the Church after the Council of Trent, Aquinas' God seems very different from the God of the Bible. The meaning of central claims such as 'God is good' or 'God answers prayers' is far from what most Christians understand by them once they have been seen as analogies.[2]

In the seventeenth century, Blaise Pascal (1623–62) wrote 'FIRE: GOD of Abraham, GOD of Isaac, GOD of Jacob not of the philosophers and of the learned.'[3] The God we discover through scripture, religious tradition, prayer and religious experiences, the God who seizes believers mind and body, is no logical, intellectual principle. Few people *believe in* God because of arguments. They may *believe that* God exists, to use H. H. Price's distinction, but being intellectually convinced of the need for a Prime Mover rarely translates into the sort of all-consuming commitment that faith, as most people understand it, demands.

So, if arguments do not lead to faith in the God of Abraham, Isaac and Jacob, where does that compelling concept of God come from?

For many people, belief in God begins not with rational argument(s) but with an experience of God of one sort or another. Religious experiences appear to fall into several categories:

- Experiences in religious contexts (including through liturgy, individual, scriptural or organizational authority, or through beauty and wonder in nature).
- Specific religious experiences.
- Near-death experiences.
- Miracles (including answers to prayers).

Each will be discussed separately here.

---

2 See Chapter 17.

3 Pascal, *Memorial*, trans by Elizabeth T. Knuth, edited by Olivier Joseph, 1999, available online at http://www.users.csbsju.edu/~eknuth/pascal.html.

# 12

# Experiences in Religious Contexts

For most religious people this is the sort of experience which sustains their faith. A sense of awe and wonder, beauty, peace and spirituality or a sense of oneness and community with others, are all likely to feature in people's explanations of why their faith seems 'live' and worthwhile.

## Liturgy

Most commonly within Christian and Muslim denominations, experiences in religious contexts could relate to liturgy or prayer. The form of words, actions, singing, music, Bible reading, prayers and experiences which make up services in church or mosque have been developed over centuries to bring people closer to God. People who share in these experiences often feel part of something bigger than themselves. They may feel a sense of tradition which adds weight to religious teachings as well as the testimony given in the Bible and Qu'ran and elsewhere about other people's direct experience of the Divine.

Liturgy provides a framework for communal prayer and shared silence. Many people find that praying and meditating alongside others creates a special atmosphere and that the object of prayers is more readily achieved in this context.

Some psychologists seek to provide a naturalistic explanation for these experiences by suggesting that the unusual conditions engendered by taking part in extended liturgies or by long periods of prayer, whether solitary or communal, may actually cause the experiences people claim as religious. Sensory deprivation, caused by silence, long periods of sitting still, often in reduced lighting or with eyes shut, can have strange effects – whether this is within a religious context or not. For example, it is not unusual for prisoners in solitary confinement to experience delusions; psychologists would suggest that religions, whether consciously or otherwise, duplicate the conditions most likely to bring about the effects people claim as religious experiences when they occur within a religious context. However, for many the experience in liturgy and worship is so real that they are absolutely convinced of the closeness of God.

Within the Islamic tradition the *rakat*, a series of physical postures, including prostration, is an essential part of the prayers which all Muslims must take part in five times per day.[1] The physical routine of prayer is a powerful part of being Muslim, giving believers a sense of structure to their days and lives, a sense of community with other believers and a tie to a place of worship and to a religious teacher in most cases.

## Scripture

Many people's encounter with God begins with scripture, the stories of the long and turbulent relationship between human beings and God, prophecies and the Law. It is difficult to express the power that scripture has in making God real in the lives of believers or at least shaping their concept of the Divine. It provides a vocabulary with which they are able to express beliefs and human experiences, it brings individuals together into a community which transcends ordinary cultural, historical and social boundaries, and it demonstrates the longevity, prevalence and consistency of faith, thus providing a substantial reason to believe in itself.

Nevertheless, believers interpret the authority of scripture differently. Evangelical Christians, some Orthodox Jews and most Muslims insist on the literal truth of scripture, seeing it as a direct revelation from God. This causes various problems.

---

1 Part of Salah (prayer), one of the central pillars of belief in most forms of Islam.

In the first instance, scripture always has to be translated in order to be understood, whether literally from another language or just from another context – this means that there are numerous ways of reading a text, even without accepting that texts are open to interpretation. As N. T. Wright observed, 'If we are not careful, the phrase "authority of scripture" can, by such routes, come to mean simply "the authority of evangelical tradition", as opposed to Catholic or rationalist ones.'[2]

There is a great scope for religious scholars or institutions to impose their own ideas on religious communities in the guise of teaching that scripture should be taken literally. As Harper Lee wrote in *To Kill a Mockingbird*:

> Sometimes the Bible in the hand of one man is worse than a whisky bottle in the hand of (another) . . . There are just some kind of men who're so busy worrying about the next world they've never learned to live in this one, and you can look down the street and see the results.

This also applies within other religious traditions. Readings of the Torah vary between the extreme literalism of the Hasidim and the allegorical interpretations common in Liberal and Reform synagogues. Very different Jewish beliefs and behaviours may be taken from the same textual cues. There are different readings of the Qur'an and not all scholars agree on what texts mean in relation to how Muslims should live today. At the extremes there are those who see the Qur'an endorsing violence against women, the slaughter of innocent civilians and a refusal to engage with any form of modern technology – and those for whom this reading is offensive, those who read the Qur'an as a testament to peace, liberty and learning.

Secondly, scriptures tend to be composite and resist being seen as a single, linear revelation. The Judeo-Christian scriptures in particular

---

2 N. T. Wright, 'How Can the Bible Be Authoritative?', the Laing Lecture 1989 and the Griffith Thomas Lecture 1989, originally published in *Vox Evangelica* 21 (1991), pp. 7–32.

are most obviously composed of different genres of text, written by multiple authors and edited many times over more than 1,000 years. Claiming to take the Bible literally begs the question – which bits? Although reformers such as Martin Luther tried to reform the canon of texts, eliminating those he felt to be unreliable, this process is likely to be open to abuse. For example, Luther relegated the book of James from the reformed Bible, probably because it taught of the primary importance of good behaviour, something which threatened his own doctrine of justification through faith alone. Is it reasonable for a religious leader to pick and choose which bits of scripture to call authoritative? If so, is it scripture that has the authority or is it being forced to serve a higher authority?

Some people have tried to get around the issue of having to pin down which bits of scripture to take as authoritative and which not by saying that the Bible contains 'timeless truths' and essentially leaving it up to the individual to determine which insights are valuable. However, as N. T. Wright explained, in claiming that scripture contains timeless truth, 'we have thereby made the Bible into something which it basically is not'.

Nevertheless, for many God 'speaks' to them directly at times when they read the Bible or are in prayer, and these experiences are very real and powerful. For the individual who has such experiences the impact can be profound. However, the experiences are very individual and are not easily communicable to or verifiable by others.

## Authority

Prophets, saints and other influential religious leaders have always had the power to inspire faith in other people. Of course, a great deal depends on their personal charisma. It is probably fair to say that numbers of false prophets with charisma have been much more influential than more probably genuine prophets without much personal charm!

In many cases prophets and saints refer to a personal encounter with God, a specific religious experience which they have had and which has given them both the authority to persuade others and special knowledge to impart. In these cases, their credibility must be assessed in much the same way as the credibility of all other specific religious experiences, as will be discussed later in this chapter.

Belief in the possibility of individuals communicating directly with God has a long history. Within the Christian tradition, belief in the power of individuals to receive direct revelation became particularly popular in the Enlightenment and post-Enlightenment periods, perhaps as a reaction to the rise of scientific materialism.

Emanuel Swedenborg (1688–1772) was a Swedish philosopher and scientist who entered into a spiritual phase of life at the age of 53 in 1741. He had a series of dreams and visions, culminating in an 'awakening' at Easter 1744, after which Swedenborg felt that he was free to visit heaven and hell and to talk with spirits, angels and demons. Swedenborg felt that he had been called to use the insights that were revealed to him to reform Christianity. He published 18 theological works, but made no move towards founding his own church, leaving that task to followers in the years after his death, and these 'new churches' survive to this day.

Whereas the Swedish Church was Lutheran, believing that Christians would be saved by faith alone and that religious works (including charity and ethical behaviour) were of secondary importance, Swedenborg taught that both faith and works are equally important. Swedenborg and his followers were pioneers in campaigning against slavery, even taking freed slaves into their homes in the late eighteenth century.

Swedenborg's ideas, and the possibility of engaging with the spiritual realm through dreams and visions, inspired a number of leading figures during the eighteenth, nineteenth and early twentieth centuries. Immanuel Kant (1724–1804) wrote a critical essay 'Dreams of the Spirit Seer' in 1766; although he mocked Swedenborg's claims to religious experience, he was influenced by his approach to Christianity.[3] Later philosophers including Goethe, Emerson and

---

3 http://en.wikisource.org/wiki/Dreams_of_a_Spirit-Seer/Editor%27s_Preface.

Jung also found Swedenborg fascinating, if not entirely convincing. Swedenborg was even more influential within the literary community. The poets Samuel Taylor Coleridge, Walt Whitman and W. B. Yeats and the novelists Balzac, Baudelaire, Herman Melville, Henry James and even Arthur Conan Doyle were all affected by Swedenborgian ideas.

In *Divine Love and Divine Wisdom* (1788), which William Blake (1757–1827) owned and annotated, Swedenborg writes how the spiritual world is 'like a Bird of Paradise, which flieth near the Eye, and toucheth it's Pupil with it's beautiful Wings, and wisheth to be seen'. He complains how the Divine in the natural universe has been obscured by the churches, writing 'all the Things of Religion, which are called Spiritual, have been removed out of the Sight of Man', by 'Councils and certain Leaders in the Church',[4] who have used and abused religion for their own selfish and political ends. He saw his purpose as making God accessible to humanity, writing:

Linking with an invisible God is like linking the sight of the eye with the expanse of the universe, the bounds of which are not to be seen. Or it is like looking out in the middle of the ocean, when the gaze falls on the air and sea and is frustrated. But linking with a visible God is like seeing a man in the air or the sea opening His arms and inviting you to come into His embrace.[5]

In the 1820s and 1830s American religious leaders such as Joseph Smith and William Miller claimed to have received special new revelations from God. Smith's revelations are partially contained within the Book of Mormon, which members of the Church of Jesus Christ of Latter Day Saints treat as scripture alongside the Bible. Miller prophesied that the second advent of Jesus Christ would occur in or

---

4 Robert Rix, *William Blake and the Radical Swedenborgians*, available online at http://www.esoteric.msu.edu/VolumeV/Blake.htm.

5 *True Christian Religion*, p. 787.

before 1843. It did not, at least by most people's reckoning,[6] but that did not stop Miller's teaching from influencing modern churches, such as the Seventh Day Adventists.

The advent of radio, television and new media has presented more and more opportunities for individuals to gain personal influence and authority over members of religions. It becomes ever more important, though ever more difficult, for believers to uncover and evaluate the messages being given by these individuals, dispassionately and outside the frenzy which can accompany services and religious events.

It is no coincidence that fundamentalist groups often place great store by the teachings of individual leaders, and have grown since communications technology, both traditional and new, has become widely available across the globe. The authority of individual religious leaders is probably the easiest to direct and control, and can be very effective in creating a form of faith – albeit one which is most likely to deserve the label of 'anti-intellectual'.

## Aesthetic Experiences

The aesthetic experience of entering and being in places of worship also contributes to people feeling a sense of awe and wonder or of peace and spirituality.

The fabric of a church or mosque is intended to draw people into an experience which will explain as well as nourish and enrich faith. The design of the building may also create altered states of perception. The silence, echoes, the darkness and intense light, the shadows and pillars – the intense cold of shady stone and the warmth of shafts of sunlight, all of these combine to make worshipping in a church or mosque more likely to provoke an experience in a religious context.

The mosque was originally conceived as the antithesis of religious buildings which seek to depict God or the human relationship with

---

6 The Bahai think that it did, though not in the place and manner that Miller predicted.

God. As a simple, empty space, the mosque was supposed to emphasize the abstract nature of the Divine and speak against anthropomorphic tribal ideas about God's nature. Nevertheless, architecture and art were soon co-opted to teach the Islamic world-view.

The Ka'aba in Mecca, one of the first mosques, was converted from a tribal shrine. The Prophet cleared out all the statues and images, leaving just an empty space. The Ka'aba became the focus of Islam,[7] and it has long been venerated by being used to find the direction of prayer around the world, being the chief object of the Hajj pilgrimage and being draped with a rich cloth (Kiswa), which is embroidered with texts from the Qur'an. As an echo of the Jewish Temple, the Ka'aba is now in the centre of an enormous mosque, with minarets (towers, used for calling believers to prayer) around the walls. Access to this building, even to the whole city of Mecca at some times, is limited to Muslims.

In the beginning, Islamic architecture took its cue from Roman architecture in using rounded arches, columned colonnades and cloisters and domes. As in ancient churches, the dome was used as an indicator of the heavens; placing a dome over a prayer-hall suggested that prayers were being conducted in God's sight and that the mosque was an allegory for the world as a whole.

Religious buildings, then, provide a space within which individuals are encouraged to be open to the presence of the Divine. Whether they provide a channel for the Divine or themselves cause the sense of awe and wonder remains a matter for debate and will largely depend on the different initial presuppositions.

## Natural Wonder

The experience of everyday life and particularly of the natural world can become an ongoing religious experience. Of course, sometimes

---

7 Originally, Muslims had prayed towards Jerusalem, but this changed after the Prophet retook Mecca.

a particular event can trigger an appreciation of God's glory in all things, but this is not necessarily the case.

The Jesuit poet Gerard Manley Hopkins (1844–89) wrote: 'The world is charged with the grandeur of God / It will flame out, like shining from shook foil.' He was influenced by reading the work of medieval writers such as John Duns Scotus, who drew from Plato and Aristotle a belief that everything is unique but also connected through a timeless, spaceless essence or form, and interpreted this as existing within God.

Thich Nhat Hanh, the Zen Buddhist Master and author of *Peace is Every Step* (1991), teaches that everything in the world interdepends, that things we value (such as roses) and things we do not (such as rubbish) interrelate so that we can experience the Divine in mundane things just as much as in beautiful things. It is significant that string theory also points to the inter-connectedness of every aspect of reality.

The Society of Jesus is the largest Roman Catholic religious order, founded by Ignatius of Loyola in 1540. Ignatius developed spiritual exercises for training young Jesuits on retreat, modelled on the practice of the Desert Fathers in the early centuries of Christianity. Jesuits are encouraged to see God in all things, to recognize that faith is not separate from any aspect of life, from any place or person, but must be lived in every moment. The poet R. S. Thomas (1913–2000) wrote: 'There is nothing too ample for you to overflow, nothing so small that your workmanship is not revealed.'[8]

Francis of Assisi found God in the natural world, and the Bonaventurian and Franciscan approaches to theology see beauty as the means by which God reveals God's self to the world. Many people who have such experiences would prefer to see them as indications of a general spirituality rather than manifestations of any particular faith tradition. The scientist Albert Einstein wrote:

The most beautiful and profound emotion we can experience is the sensation of the mystical. It is the sower of all true art and

---

8 From *Alive*.

science. He to whom this emotion is a stranger . . . is as good as dead. To know that what is impenetrable to us really exists, manifesting itself as the highest wisdom and the most radiant beauty, which our dull faculties can comprehend only in their most primitive forms – this knowledge, this feeling, is at the center of true religiousness.[9]

The problem in terms of beauty being seen as a pointer to the existence of God is that some people will see God's presence in the night sky while others will simply see refracted light, and there seems no way to evaluate either claim.

## Summary

For most people, faith is formed by this sort of general religious experience. It can be difficult for a non-believer to understand why they make people more likely to believe in their object, but there can be little doubt that they do. People who are brought up in a religious environment are more likely to remain religious. This does not necessarily mean that their faith is not genuine; it could be that the religious life is either rewarded by revelation or makes it more possible to believe in another way, or it may mean that a religious upbringing opens people to the possibility of God in a way which a totally secular upbringing does not. Further, people often become more religious as the years pass or when they have difficult lives. This is not necessarily symptomatic of mental decay or desperation. It could be that a deeper, longer experience of being human points people towards accepting that there could be something more, that man is not the measure of all things.

---

9 Quoted in John Swanson, *God, Science and the Universe: The Integration of Religion and Science*, London: Strategic Books, 2010, pp. 225–6.

# 13

# Specific Religious Experiences

Religious experiences, experiences of some power or presence beyond oneself, may take many forms. They might involve an intensely personal one-off spiritual episode, a powerful shared experience of miraculous power or a more long-term sense of God's presence in all things. It is worth noting that the line between religious experiences and experiences in religious contexts is not a solid one, and although today most people identify religious experience as a solitary phenomenon (60 per cent of respondents in a 1987 Gallup survey agreed), in the past Emil Durkheim dismissed them as 'an effervescent group phenomenon'.

Research conducted by the Alister Hardy Religious Experience Research Centre (based in Oxford until 2000, now at the University of Wales Trinity Saint David) suggests that individual religious experiences are surprisingly common, even in our predominantly secular society. The Centre asks members of the public to tell them about any 'spiritual or religious experience', and in 2009 *The Guardian* newspaper reported that the Centre received an average of three letters each week to add to its archive of over 6,000 reports,[1] though the study had been active since the late 1960s and has not been well publicized in recent years.

The variety in these reports is substantial, but as an example, one letter said:

Vauxhall station on a murky November Saturday evening is not the setting one would choose for a revelation of God . . . The whole compartment was filled with light. I felt caught up into some tremendous sense of being within a loving, triumphant and shining purpose. All men were shining and glorious beings who in the end would enter incredible joy. In a few moments the glory had departed, all but one curious, lingering feeling. I loved everybody in that compartment. I seemed to sense the golden worth in them all.[2]

A 56-year-old British woman wrote:

On this occasion I found instead that I was overtaken by an intense feeling of affection for and unity with everyone around as they ran to catch buses, took children shopping, or joyfully met their friends. The feeling was so strong that I wanted to leave my silent vigil and join them in their urgent living. This sense of 'Oneness' is basic to what I understand of religion. Hitherto I think I had only experienced it so irresistibly towards a few individuals – sometimes toward my children or when in love. The effect of the experience has been, I think, a permanent increase in my awareness that we are 'members one of another', a consequent greater openness toward all and a widening of my concern for others.[3]

In 1977 David Hay and Ann Morisy, researchers in Oxford, used the Centre's standard question, 'Have you ever had a spiritual or religious experience or felt a presence or power, whether you call it God or not, which is different from your everyday life?', as the basis for a statistical survey, designed to provide robust data concerning the prevalence of such experiences in the population as a whole. Of a random sample of 1,865 British people, 35 per cent responded 'Yes' to the question. In Australia, a similar study the same year found 44 per cent of the population reporting 'Yes' to the same question. When Gallup repeated the exercise in the late 1980s it found that the number of British people responding 'Yes' had risen to 48 per cent.

---

2 Ibid.

3 Reported in Alister Hardy, *The Spiritual Nature of Man*, Oxford: Oxford University Press, 1979.

Andrew Greely at the National Opinion Research Center at the University of Chicago used a similar question, 'Have you ever felt as though you were very close to a powerful spiritual force that seemed to lift you out of yourself?', on a national sample of 1,467 Americans. This yielded 39 per cent responding 'Yes'.

Interestingly, Hardy and Morisy noted that people reporting mystical religious experiences tended to have greater psychological well-being than those who report no mystical religious experiences. In his survey of Americans, Andrew Greely noted the same phenomenon, that mystics are happier.

The numbers of positive responses to such surveys has typically been much higher in traditional, more religious societies such as Poland. Numbers admitting to religious experiences have been higher the younger people are (and particularly high among young children, before school age). Religious experiences tend to be more common among the middle and upper classes than among poorer people.

Most religious people feel justified in believing that many religious experiences are genuine and correctly interpreted as direct actions of God in human lives. They base belief in God's existence, God's qualities and even God's will on such experiences, which they or trusted others have had. Nevertheless, the credibility of doing this depends on the extent to which

- experiences are clearly defined and documented;
- alternative explanations are shown to be inadequate or irrelevant;
- the decision to accept the experience as the result of divine action is reasonable and not credulous.

The Alister Hardy Research Centre uses a very broad definition of religious experience. This is partly because some people do not like to admit to having a 'religious' experience but are happy to talk about events as 'spiritual' for example. The website of the Alister Hardy Society for the Study of Spiritual Experience defines religious experience as an aspect of natural human experience. It can come to us, or arise in us, suddenly, at any time, in any place, and can affect and even change our lives. It can happen to anyone, whether religiously inclined or atheist, spiritually inclined or materialist, and regardless of age, sex, nationality or culture. It is called 'spiritual' and 'religious' because it is seen as either or both. It can include mystical, transcendental, out-of-body or near-death experiences, or a deep sense of meaning in a place or event. Psychical experiences such as déjà vu, clairaudience, clairvision, telepathy and precognition can be included. It can also include such features as meaningful coincidences, or synchronicities, guidance and answers to prayer or contact with deceased loved ones. It can be triggered by music, dance, church or religious architecture, beauty in nature . . . also by pain, intense suffering and distress. It can sometimes happen through meditation, prayer, worship or other means. It can be immensely beneficial and life-enhancing though some experiences can be negative and distressing. It can raise, in itself, questions such as 'What's it about?' and 'Why me?' even, 'Am I odd, or going barmy?' These questions need answering – for the experiencer and for society – for these experiences are important and can have far-reaching consequences. Investigating these experiences is what our work is about. Evidence suggests that 'love', 'relationship', 'unity' might be, ultimately, what it is about, and these words may give clues to our understanding. 'Light', 'love', 'connecting', 'oneness', 'bliss' are key words; 'insight', 'lifting of a veil', 'altered state of consciousness', 'reality', 'the Real', 'Ultimate Reality', 'God' are other words used.[4]

This broad definition, though clearly useful for the purposes of research – meaning that reports are offered up more readily and in greater numbers – might undermine the credibility of discussions about religious experience being a pointer to the existence of God. It brackets experiences which are easily explained in cultural, physiological or

---

4  http://www.studyspiritualexperiences.org/.

psychological terms alongside those which are less easy to explain in these terms.

Throughout the twentieth century, scholars attempted to define religious experiences with varying degrees of success. Most famously, the American psychologist and philosopher William James (1842–1910) categorized religious experiences as 'the feelings, acts, and experiences of individual men in their solitude, so far as they apprehend themselves to stand in relation to whatever they may consider the divine'.[5]

In *The Varieties of Religious Experience: A Study in Human Nature* (the published text of James' 1901–2 Gifford Lectures, which were delivered at the University of Edinburgh), James argued that religious experiences, not institutions or dogmas, should be the focus of theology and the philosophy of religion. In his classic chapter on 'Mysticism' James suggests 'four marks which, when an experience has them, may justify us in calling it mystical . . .':[6]

- Ineffability: 'It defies expression . . . its quality must be directly experienced; it cannot be imparted or transferred to others.'
- Noetic Quality: Mystical states present themselves as states of knowledge.
- Transiency: The experience lasts for only a short time.
- Passivity: People are not in control of their coming and going.

James ends the chapter by asking whether these experiences are 'windows through which the mind looks out upon a more extensive and inclusive world'.[7]

It is James' definition which has given rise to the broad definitions used by, for example, the Alister Hardy Research Centre, and it is James' definition which simultaneously attracts criticism for being too woolly and inclusive and for excluding some instances of what

---

5 *The Varieties of Religious Experience*, New York: Longmans, Green, 1916, p. 31.
6 Ibid., p. 380.
7 Ibid., p. 428.

many people would accept as religious experience, such as the lifelong and active mystical state of Thomas Merton (1915–68). Naturally enough, James' definition failed to satisfy other scholars from the outset. Otto and later Stace developed narrower definitions.

Rudolf Otto (1869–1937), in his book *The Idea of the Holy*, identified the common factor in all religious experiences as 'numinous'. For Otto, 'numinal' experiences have two aspects: *mysterium tremendum*, which is the tendency to invoke fear and trembling; and *mysterium fascinans*, the tendency to attract, fascinate and compel. The numinous experience also has a personal quality to it, in that the person feels to be in communion with a holy other. Otto wrote: 'There is no religion in which it [the numinous] does not live as the real innermost core and without it no religion would be worthy of the name.'[8] Otto does not really take any other kind of religious experience seriously.

Walter Stace (1886–1967) was a civil servant for the British in India before studying philosophy and eventually becoming Professor of Philosophy at Princeton in the 1930s. Although he was an empiricist, Stace had had a conversion experience while at university in Dublin. Consequently he wrote 'either God is a mystery or He is nothing at all . . . '.[9]

For Stace, experience is central to any relationship with God. He wrote: 'To ask for a proof of the existence of God is on a par with asking for a proof of the existence of beauty. If God does not lie at the end of any telescope, neither does he lie at the end of any syllogism . . .'[10]

In *Mysticism and Philosophy* and *The Teachings of the Mystics* Stace defined mystical experience as nothing vague and sloppy, nothing to do with the mysterious, the occult, with parapsychological phenomena such as telepathy, telekinesis, clairvoyance, precognition.

---

8 See *The Idea of the Holy*, London: Oxford University Press, 1972, pp. 5–30.

9 From Alexander Leitch, *A Princeton Companion*, Princeton: Princeton University Press, 1978.

10 http://etcweb.princeton.edu/CampusWWW/Companion/stace_walter.html.

Visions and voices are not mystical experiences; for Stace, all genuine mystical experiences are *non-sensuous*. They are formless, shapeless, colourless, odourless, soundless. Stace wrote:

> The central characteristic in which all fully developed mystical experiences agree . . . is that they involve the apprehension of an ultimate nonsensuous unity in all things, a oneness or a One to which neither the senses nor the reason can penetrate. In other words, it entirely transcends our sensory-intellectual consciousness.[11]

Caroline Franks Davis, a doctoral student of Richard Swinburne, questioned the coherence of earlier definitions of religious experience, pointing out for example that James claimed that experiences were ineffable against a long tradition of mystics talking about, writing about and otherwise describing what happened. She proposed instead a broader sixfold classification:

1 Interpretive experiences – an odd experience which is interpreted to be caused by God.
2 Quasi-sensory – an experience where the primary element is a physical sensation such as hearing a voice or seeing a vision.
3 Revelatory experiences – the content of the experience provides some form of specific religious knowledge or understanding.
4 Regenerative – conversion to or renewal of faith.
5 Numinous – indescribable experience of God's holiness.
6 Mystical – a sense of apprehending ultimate reality or a oneness with God.

Richard Swinburne (b. 1934) himself drew together the tight and similar definitions proposed by Otto and Stace with the broader classification proposed by James. He acknowledged the existence of five different types of religious experience, each with a specific characteristic.

---

11 *The Teachings of the Mystics*, New York: New American Library, 1960, pp. 14–15.

# GOD MATTERS

1 An experience which can be described using everyday language (for example a dream).
2 An experience which cannot be described using everyday language (for example a mystical experience).
3 A conviction that God has been experienced in some way despite lack of material evidence.
4 Perceiving a perfectly normal phenomenon (for example a sunset).
5 Perceiving a very unusual public object (for example the resurrection).

Importantly, Swinburne's definition of religious experience would include corporate experiences, miracles and spiritual experiences as well as more conventional individual mystical and religious experiences.


## Arguments from Religious Experience

The most general sort of argument from religious experience is the suggestion that God is a good postulate to explain the prevalence of such happenings and of the faith which results from them. Believers infer that the existence of God is the best explanation for the multiplicity of religious experiences and the numbers of people who believe. Beyond that, there is an inductive argument from religious experience which moves from an observation of the world (effect) to a conclusion about its probable cause, God. Both forms of argument depend on the credibility of explaining 'religious experiences' (howsoever they are defined) as actions of God as opposed to the results of cultural, physiological or psychological phenomena.

Richard Swinburne's argument from religious experience is set out in *The Existence of God*. In the first 12 chapters of the book he explores the full range of possible inductive arguments for God's existence, in each case considering whether the argument makes God's existence more likely than not. Swinburne is attempting to develop a cumulative case for God, using the inductive arguments for God's existence as exhibits. When Swinburne turns to religious experience in Chapter 13, as Richard Gale notes,

Instead of making out the usual Bayesian case that the evidence consisting of numerous religious experiences renders *h* more probable than it would otherwise be, which would be yet another good C-inductive argument, it appeals to an *a priori* presumptive inference rule, the 'Principle of Credulity', which renders it *prima facie* probable that the apparent object of religious experience, God, exists, and which can be defeated only if our background knowledge makes it very improbable that God exists. And it is here that the foregoing highly intuitive cumulative case is appealed to for the purpose of defeating this lone possible defeater, thereby rendering it probable without qualification that God exists.

In simple terms, Swinburne's argument does not concern numbers of religious experiences as pieces of evidence in the cumulative case for God, or the credibility of individual cases. Rather, Swinburne argues that if there is a reasonable possibility or probability that God exists on the basis of other arguments, then the occurrence of religious experiences *per se* makes it reasonable to believe in God's existence. Crucially, Swinburne accepts that whether or not reports of religious experiences should be accepted depends largely on assessment of *prior probability*.

If you consider that fairies cannot possibly exist, you will not accept claims to have seen fairies even when compelling evidence is presented. If you are convinced that aliens do not exist, you will not even consider accepting claims of aliens being seen even if you are shown video footage. In the case of God, the same applies. If one is a convinced atheist, then religious experience is likely to be rejected regardless of the evidence presented. For example, Richard Dawkins wrote in *The Blind Watchmaker* that if he saw a marble statue waving at him he would be more likely to believe in the impossible scientific explanation of all the atoms moving in the same direction at the same time than that the statue was being caused to move by God.[12]

Swinburne proposed, as a basis for distinguishing between things that it is reasonable to believe and things which should be rejected,

---

12  Ibid., p. 159.

two *a priori principles* – a 'Principle of Credulity' and a 'Principle of Testimony':

- Principle of Credulity: With the absence of any reason to disbelieve it, one should accept what appears to be true (for example, if one sees someone walking on water, one should believe that it is occurring, provided that one hasn't been taking drugs etc.).
- Principle of Testimony: With the absence of any reason to disbelieve them, one should accept that eye-witnesses or believers are telling the truth when they testify about religious experiences (for example, if one hears that 5,000 people have been miraculously fed, one should believe the reports if they are from otherwise credible sources).

If Swinburne's principles are accepted, then people who accept the prior probability of God's existence may believe that religious experiences occur, and are the result of Divine action, whether the experience is either personal or reported by trusted others. The fact that God's actions are felt makes a reasonable case that God exists, which must then be shown to be flawed. Swinburne is attempting to turn the table on the sceptics by asking them to produce reasons why religious experience should not be taken seriously.

Like the cosmological argument and the design argument, Swinburne's argument from religious experience is *a posteriori*, it moves from an observation of effects to a conclusion about the cause of those effects – but also like the other arguments it depends on *a priori assumptions*. In Swinburne's case these *a priori* principles, of Credulity and Testimony, are clearly articulated, but in most versions of the cosmological and design arguments there are other assumptions – including that an actual infinite is impossible.

Critics have attacked Swinburne's argument, along with more general inductive arguments from religious experience, for assuming the veracity of religious experiences which could be explained in other ways, perhaps as cultural, physiological or psychological phenomena. The credibility of accounts of religious experiences is important to the success of any argument from religious experience to God.

In *The Evidential Force of Religious Experience* (1999) Franks Davis, after considering the nature of interpretive, quasi-sensory, revelatory, regenerative, numinous and mystical experiences and the different types of argument that can be developed from them, explains and attempts to rebut a range of criticisms. She classifies these criticisms as those relating to:

- Description: Religious experiences are too broadly and loosely defined to form a cohesive body of evidence.
- Subjects: What bearing does the type and background of the people reporting experiences have? Do we only accept the experiences of those who have been suitably trained, or is that training likely to be inducing or influencing the interpretation of experiences? What about the role of hallucinogenic drugs or periods of sensory deprivation prior to the experience? How about a record of mental illness or hormonal imbalance?
- Objects: When people have experiences of logically or otherwise impossible things, for example square circles, levitation, Martians, etc., it seems probable that the experience is not real.
- Interpretation: The interpretation of an experience as religious seems to presuppose that the person having the experience (and those accepting their interpretation) are already religious. If so, religious experiences just confirm existing opinions, beliefs etc.
- Conflicting claims: Religious experiences occur within competing and conflicting religious frameworks, seeming to confirm each, yet they can't all be true, can they?
- Reductionism: Religious experiences can be explained as merely pathological or psychological events.

Franks Davis attempts to show that these criticisms are not conclusive, that there remains the possibility of religious experiences being genuine evidence of the Divine. There may, indeed, be people who are psychologically disturbed who claim religious experiences, it may be that certain experiences occur within an existing faith framework, it may be that experiences can be induced by electrical impulses to the brain, but one cannot move from saying that some religious experiences can be explained in such ways to claiming that all religious experiences can be dismissed on these or similar grounds.

It really comes down to whether one is justified in believing what one sees, hears or otherwise senses. As William Alston (1921–2009) put it:

> Our central question is: are experiences of this sort, always or sometimes, really direct apprehensions of an objectively existing personal deity, or are they purely subjective states of feeling which have no reference to anything beyond the subject? It is clear that if I have directly experienced a personal deity (as opposed to merely having supposed that I have done so) then I have the strongest possible basis for believing that such a being exists; just as I have the strongest possible basis for believing that yaks exist if I really have seen one.[13]

There have been many attempts to explain away religious experiences in terms of epileptic episodes (St Paul), delusions triggered by hormonal imbalances or a simple need for attention (Bernadette of Lourdes) or the effects of mass hysteria (Fatima or the Toronto Blessing); however, these explanations need not necessarily invalidate the religious interpretation. As Alston wrote:

> It is noteworthy that although James suggests, and it is only a suggestion without any attempt to work out details, that mystical experiences can be explained as 'invasions from the subconscious region', he does not take this as ruling out the possibility that through his unconscious mind the individual is in contact with some supernatural reality . . . [14]

Science might provide the 'how' in terms of religious experiences, such as how an altered state of vision came about or how time

---

13  William P. Alston (ed.), *Religious Belief and Philosophical Thought: Readings in the Philosophy of Religion*, New York: Harcourt, Brace & World, 1963, p. 118.

14  Ibid., p. 120.

seemed to slow down, but God would have to work through some natural process so science cannot rule out the possibility that God caused these effects. Given the power of experiences, the dominance of a religious interpretation and the effects that they have in the lives of individuals (for example conversion, healing, inspiring missionary activity, etc.), then it is hard to gainsay them.

Alston distinguished between beliefs based on analytic knowledge (e.g. $2 + 2 = 4$ or Gerald is unmarried, therefore Gerald is a bachelor), beliefs based on synthetic knowledge (all the swans I have seen are white therefore I believe that all swans are white) and beliefs based on direct experience. Does it make sense for someone who has seen or heard God not to believe in God's existence? He wrote:

> The mystic might argue that attempts to explain the occurrence of mystical experience are quite irrelevant to the validity of his claim to have directly experienced God, on the grounds that his claim was not that one would have to postulate a supernatural personal being in order to explain his experience. On the contrary, he is not interested in explanation at all, and the fact that he has been directly aware of God obviates any need to bring God in as a term in an explanation. Clearly he has a point. When I claim to see a maple tree just outside my window, I am certainly not saying that I believe that a maple tree will have to be postulated or hypothesized in order to explain the fact that I am now having the visual experience I am having.[15]

He went on to explain:

> If, one winter morning, I discover some footprints in the snow leading up to my kitchen window, I can, by reasoning from effect to cause, come to realize that during the night someone came and peered into the house. But if during the night I had happened to look out my bedroom window at the time the intruder was approaching, I could have discovered his presence in a direct

---

15   Ibid., pp. 120–1.

fashion, without the necessity of such inferences . . . there have been many religious men who have believed that they were able to discover that God exists in a more direct fashion, by experiencing His presence in as direct a way as that in which one experiences the presence of trees, buildings, and other human beings.[16]

As Dean William Ralph Inge (1860–1954) wrote: 'Rightly or wrongly genuine mystics are convinced that they have been in contact with objective reality, with the supreme Spiritual Power beyond the world of our surface consciousness.'

Of course this does not resolve whether other people are justified in believing what mystics say, it just suggests that mystics themselves are justified in believing on the basis of their own experience. This remains a point of contention. Dean Inge continued:

The mystics are convinced that their communion with God is an authentic experience . . . If a dozen honest men tell me that they have climbed the Matterhorn, it is reasonable to believe that the summit of that mountain is accessible, although I am not likely to get there myself.

## Summary

Specific religious experiences are defined differently by different scholars. Many people have had experiences which might be accepted under at least one of these definitions. Some religious experiences are easier to explain away in physiological or psychological terms than others, though the presence of such an explanation does not, in itself, rule out a Divine cause. As Swinburne argued, as an argument for God's existence religious experiences depend, to a large extent, on one's assessment of *prior probability* and on the extent to which one is willing to believe one's own eyes (Principle of Credulity) or trust in the reports of others (Principle of Testimony). They are unlikely, therefore, to convince an unbeliever.

---

16   Ibid., p. 117.

# 14

# Near-Death Experiences

Near-death experiences have a long history, though their frequency and awareness have increased with the development of modern medical technology. Study of 'deathbed visions' really began in the 1880s with the founding of the Society for Psychical Research and later, in 1926, with the publication of Sir William Barrett's book on the subject.[1]

One of the earliest accounts is given at the end of Plato's *Republic* in the story of Er. The story begins as a man named Er (son of Armenios of Pamphylia) dies in battle. After the battle the dead bodies are collected, but ten days later Er's body remains fresh, with no signs of decomposition. He revives on his funeral pyre and then tells others of his journey to the afterlife. In particular, his story includes the idea of those who have died appearing before judges and then having to choose in which body to be reincarnated and what sort of lives they next want to live. Many choose power or wealth but it is only the philosopher who can understand that what really matters is the pursuit of justice and wisdom. This story was to have a major subsequent effect on religious beliefs, but it is also a forerunner of reports of near-death experiences.

Today, near-death experiences are quite frequent and share many features in common across all cultures and religions. More than 2,500 cases are reported to have occurred in the USA between the early 1970s and the present day. These features include the person being clear that they were dead, being able to look down on their body, being free from pain, being able to see what is happening in the area around where they had died, meeting other beings who are

---

1 Susan Blackmore, 'Near-Death Experiences: In or out of the body?', *Skeptical Inquirer* 16 (1991), pp. 34–45.

generally clothed in light and the sense of passing through a tunnel towards the light. In many cases, the person involved has no wish to return to their body, and it is a feature of those who have had near-death experiences that they lose any fear of death, but also the way they look on life is transformed, and they become far more altruistic and less concerned with money, advancement and worldly prestige.

Near-death experiences often include the experience of floating outside the body, sometimes on the ceiling. There is a sense that the essential part of the person has separated from the physical body. When Michael Sabom undertook a survey of such experiences among non-surgical cases,[2] everyone he interviewed had this sensation, but other studies indicate it is not universal. One woman recorded these feelings in the following poem:

> Hovering beneath the ceiling, I looked down
> Upon a body, untenanted – my own
> Strangely at peace, airy, weightless as light,
> I floated there freed from pain-filled days and nights
> Until a voice I heard, an urgent call,
> And again I dwelt within my body's wall.[3]

This type of out-of-body experience is typically accompanied by alertness and clarity of thought and the person who experiences it tends to be absolutely convinced that it is real – so much so that they are often reluctant to speak about it in case people try to 'explain it away'.

Personal experiences of survival of death, if credible, would be a strong challenge to the assumption that death is the end and might go some way to reinforce belief in the God of Abraham, who is often associated with raising people to eternal life in scripture.

For near-death experiences to be convincing the person in question must be clinically 'brain dead' and have had experiences which cannot simply be attributed to previous memories or, indeed, imagination.

---

2 Michael Sabom, *Recollections of Death: A Medical Investigation*, San Francisco: Harper & Row, 1982.

3 Ibid., p. 21.

By definition therefore, these experiences cannot be duplicated in the laboratory. If claims are approached with a verificationist mindset then they are almost certain to be rejected.

A. J. Ayer was one of the most prominent verificationists, but in June 1988 he choked on smoked salmon and was clinically dead for four minutes. When he came round he told Jeremy George, senior consultant in the Department of Thoracic Medicine at the Middlesex Hospital in London, that he would have to revise all his atheist ideas and that he had seen the Supreme Being.

Later Ayer wrote an article for the *Sunday Telegraph* entitled 'What I saw when I was dead'. In it he described 'a red light for governing the universe' and referred to some barrier he crossed, 'like the River Styx'. The experience, he said, 'weakened my conviction that death would be the end of me, though I continue to hope it will be'.

Despite dismissing his experience as a delusion, it is clear that Ayer's brush with death had a lasting effect on him. At the end of his life Ayer spent a great deal of time with the Jesuit priest and philosopher Professor Frederick Copleston, who attended Ayer's funeral at Golders Green crematorium. His wife Dee Wells said: 'As he got older, Freddie (Ayer) realized more and more that philosophy was just chasing its own tail.'

One of the most famous near-death experiences was reported by Pam Reynolds (1956–2010), an American singer–songwriter, who had an inexplicable experience while being operated on for a brain tumour in 1991. Reynolds' experience was unusual for occurring during a standstill operation, where cardiac arrest and all brain activity had been intentionally halted and where she was being continually monitored by an independent medical team.

Although Reynolds' case is one of the most convincing accounts of a near-death experience, not everybody is convinced that the experience was anything more than a combination of physiological and psychological events. Susan Blackmore[4] suggested that the bright light and tunnel aspect of the experience could be the result

---

4 *Dying to Live: Near-Death Experience*, Prometheus Books, reprint edn, 1983.

of a 'dying brain' with the neuro-receptors gradually being starved of oxygen.

Like Ayer and Blackmore, Michael Marsh rejects the idea that near-death experiences point to any real survival of death, transcendent realm or supreme being.[5] Instead, he accounts for these experiences in terms of the reawakening consciousness following a period of brain inactivity. Many in the medical professions explain near-death experiences away in terms of what physically happens to the brain at the time of death. Leslie Ivan (a neuro-surgeon) and Maureen Melrose (a nurse) have argued that these experiences occur as a result of chemical changes in the brain. They describe key features of the process of dying as follows:

- There is a decrease in blood oxygen levels, and this is the trigger for the other processes.
- The feeling of peace and tranquillity is due to a decrease in neural activity and originates in a similar manner to tranquillizers providing a sense of calmness.
- The feeling of euphoria and separateness from the body is due to chemical changes caused by oxygen deprivation.
- As the blood supply diminishes there is a sense of blacking out which is equivalent to entering darkness.
- There are visual hallucinations due to the stimulating of a small group of optical nerve cells.
- In the final stage, just before the part of the brain responsible for consciousness is abolished, a hallucination occurs (entering the light).[6]

Sam Parnia of Southampton University has been co-ordinating the AWARE project, a study into near-death experiences covering 25

5 *Out-of-Body and Near-Death Experiences: Brain–State Phenomena or Glimpses of Immortality?*, Oxford: Oxford University Press, 2010.

6 *The Way We Die*, Chichester: Angel, 1986.

hospitals in the USA and the UK, since 2008.[7] In basic terms, Parnia sees death as a process rather than as a point, and he sees that the evidence suggests that sight, hearing and other faculties may continue to operate until well into the process, causing so-called near-death experiences in those who are resuscitated.

Some people argue that this type of attempt to explain away the experiences, even when (as in the case of Pam Reynolds) data demonstrating brain-death prior to the experience was available, is based on a commitment to a materialist world-view and reluctance, on the part of the medical profession, to engage with the possibility that consciousness could be rather more than an illusion created by the chemical and electrical interaction of cells.

The International Association for Near-Death Studies was established in the early 1980s in the United States. It has branches in the United Kingdom, Europe, Canada and Australia. The association publishes a peer-review journal, the *Journal of Near-Death Studies*, edited from the Department of Psychiatry at the University of Virginia Medical School. Near-death experiences have become a focus of serious study; there is no doubt that such experiences occur and are surprisingly common. What is at issue is not their occurrence but their cause. Are such experiences genuine evidence for survival of death (and, possibly indirectly, for the existence of God) or are they a feature of the human psyche as it shuts down with the onset of death?

Parapsychology is the study of experiences which are held to exist outside our normal ways of understanding reality, such as telepathy, psychic visions, apparitions, messages received through spiritual mediums and past-life regression. If any one of these forms of experience could be shown to be credible, it would call into question a solely materialistic world-view.

Many people will, of course, dismiss all such reports as nonsense. Paranormal events cannot be reproduced under laboratory conditions

---

7 Sam Parnia and Josh Young, *Erasing Death: The Science that is Rewriting the Boundaries between Life and Death*, San Francisco: HarperOne, 2013.

and can often be explained in other terms, as natural if unusual events. Nevertheless, some claims are easier to dismiss than others. Good science should be willing to consider and evaluate evidence dispassionately; to reject claims *a priori* just because they seem to question a dominant world-view or paradigm would be a great mistake, one which would have been denounced by W. K. Clifford as much as any conventionally religious scientist.

Dean Radin (b. 1952) has been Chief Scientist at the Institute of Noetic Sciences and Adjunct Faculty in the Department of Psychology at Sonoma State University since 2001. Before that, he held appointments at AT&T Bell Labs, Princeton University, University of Edinburgh, and SRI International, where he worked on a classified programme investigating psychic phenomena for the US government.[8] In 1996, Radin was the subject of an article, which started:

> It was data that pushed Dean Radin to the fringe of science, and it is data that keep him there, out on the edge, in that hard country where researchers in less controversial fields will often give him the Look. The Look is delivered by other scientists and fellow rationalists and even his ophthalmologist cousin, Barry, who bug one eye and clamp the other and twist their lips around as if trying to decide, in light of his data, whether to rethink space, time and causality or to get someone from the dean's office to verify his Ph.D . . .[9]

His research has attracted scorn from other psychologists, such as Susan Blackmore (b. 1951). So much so that in 1997 Radin's book *The Conscious Universe* was vociferously attacked by the statistician I. J. Good in the journal *Nature* – and the journal initially refused

---

8 He is author or co-author of over 200 articles, a dozen book chapters and three books including the award-winning *The Conscious Universe*, San Francisco: HarperOne, 1997; *Entangled Minds*, New York: Simon & Schuster, 2006 and most recently *Supernormal*, New York: Random House, 2013.

9 Chip Brown, 'They Laughed at Galileo Too', *New York Times*, late edition, 11 August 1996, p. 41, column 2.

to publish either a rebuttal of the criticisms, letters criticizing the review (including one from Professor Brian Josephson of Cambridge University), or a correction.

For many scientists, including those who find Radin's ideas incredible, *Nature*'s actions in this case were indefensible. As Don Hewitt remarked, 'Any time a reputable news organization gives its readers or viewers details that later turn out not to be true, they are obligated to tell the truth.'[10]

The very credibility of *Nature*, one of the most respected scientific journals, was called into question when editors refused to take Radin's research seriously, simply because it fell outside the parameters of the accepted scientific paradigm. When it shielded criticisms of that research from proper scrutiny, *Nature* was finally forced to back down and to acknowledge the scientific basis for Radin's research.

As W. K. Clifford remarked, 'it is wrong . . . to believe anything without sufficient evidence'. By the standards of evidentialists, it is as wrong to believe claims about parapsychology without sufficient evidence as it is to accept criticisms of those claims without sufficient evidence. Of course, the case of parapsychology is made more difficult, because it questions the very basis of what counts as evidence, but this should not in itself be enough to rule out discussion or make using rhetorical techniques to call down ridicule on those proposing new ideas acceptable.

As in so many areas of philosophy of religion, a great deal will depend on your starting point:

Myself when young did eagerly frequent
Doctor and Saint, and heard great argument
About it and about: but evermore
Came out by the same door wherein I went.

(The Rubaiyat of Omar Khayyam, 1120)

---

10 Don Hewitt, *60 Minutes*, CBS.

# 15

# Miracles

In Christianity, there can be no greater miracle than the resurrection of Jesus from the dead. St Paul said: 'If Christ has not been raised, your faith is futile' (1 Cor. 15.7), Jesus constantly performed miracles including turning water into wine, feeding 5,000 people, healing lepers, raising Lazarus from the dead; and of course Christians hold that Jesus was born without any human agency.

In Islam, there can be no greater miracle than the dictation of the Qur'an to the Prophet Mohammed by the Archangel Gabriel. The Qur'an is held to be a work of such beauty and profundity that no human being could have written it. Mohammed was taken on a journey across the heavens mounted on a fabulous winged beast called Al-Baraq and saw the unveiled face of God. Islam also holds that Jesus was born of Mary, a virgin, with no human agency involved.

In Judaism, the miraculous deliverance of the people of Israel from slavery in Egypt and God's constant protection of his chosen people on their journey is a central miracle, as is the miracle of Abraham's wife, Sarah, giving birth to Isaac long after the menopause.

In almost every religion there are miracles that are held to be the basis for faith – arguably these are far more important reasons for religious belief than any amount of philosophical arguments.

If someone has actually experienced a miracle, then the evidence of this event may be so overwhelming that nothing could count against it. For example, a Jesuit student at Heythrop College, exceptionally intelligent and well balanced, one day said in a seminar in a matter-of-fact manner that a miracle had happened to him. He told fellow students how he had been praying the rosary while on pilgrimage and how suddenly every other one of the metal dividers had turned to gold. Everyone was incredulous – but there was no doubt at all that the Jesuit was sincere and well balanced. To this person, the reality of God's action was unquestioned. To others, the report left many questions unanswered.

The issue of miracles raises several different questions for the believer. Let us consider three of them:

- What is a miracle?
- Do miracles ever occur?
- Are miracles a basis for faith?

## What is a Miracle?

In the same way as there is disagreement over the definition of religious experience, there is some disagreement about what a miracle is. David Hume (1711–76) defined a miracle in *An Enquiry Concerning Human Understanding* (1758), Section X, as 'a transgression of a law of nature by a particular volition of the deity or by the interposition of some invisible agent'.

His definition, although generally assumed by most atheist and humanist writers, begs several questions. J. L. Mackie (1917–81) wrote: 'The laws of nature . . . describe the ways in which the world – including, of course, human beings – works when left to itself, when not interfered with. A miracle occurs when the world is not left to itself, when something distinct from the natural order as a whole intrudes into it.'[1]

Mackie uses Hume's definition and unpacks its meaning. His explanation shows how on these terms it would be impossible to claim that any event constituted a miracle. What is a 'law of nature'? Think about it! If a law really is a natural law, then the occurrence of a miracle would be impossible. We are not in a position to be able to say that a particular event breaks a law. Our understanding of nature is based on limited experience, and it would never be possible to say on that basis that a particular event breaks the laws of nature. If what we believe to be a law fails to account for a particular

---

1 *The Miracle of Theism*, Oxford: Clarendon Press, 1982, p. 20.

occurrence, then it can be argued that it is more probable that our understanding of the natural law is at fault than that a real law has been broken. A true 'law of nature' must account for all the instances of how nature works, not just most instances.

Further, science operates through a process of induction, reasoning from observation of effects to the causes of those effects. Its conclusions are only ever probabilities, never definitive 'laws'. As John Hick observed, Hume's definition, lightly assumed by Mackie and other atheist writers, seems to reflect a poor grasp of scientific method and the nature of knowledge within the verificationist framework, within which most of these writers operate.[2]

Given this, it would seem that a more plausible definition of a miracle would be useful, although Richard Swinburne has attempted to maintain Hume's definition, arguing that a miracle might be defined as 'a non-repeatable counter-instance to a law of nature'. If a law has broad scope, great explanatory power and simplicity, it may be more reasonable, Swinburne argues, to retain the law (carefully re-defined as a regularity that *virtually invariably* holds) and to accept that a claimed miracle is a non-repeatable counter-instance of the general law of nature than to throw out the law and create a vastly more complex law that accommodates the event. It is not necessary for miracles to be seen in terms of breaches in natural *laws*.

Thomas Aquinas (1215–74) states that 'those things are properly called miracles which are done by divine agency beyond the order commonly observed in nature'.[3]

Aquinas' definition is much broader than Hume's, and does not exclude the possibility of miracles by making the very concept self-contradictory. Nevertheless, arguably, Aquinas' definition could be too broad, encompassing all sorts of unusual events, conceivably ranging from the appearance of comets in the sky to eclipses to spontaneous combustion. Are all of these reasonably ascribed to divine action? Can all of these really be argued to be miraculous,

---

2 *God and the Universe of Faiths*, Oxford: Oneworld, 1973.
3 *Summa Contra Gentiles* III.

when science can account for them as rare but perfectly possible events?

Today there are many scholars who define miracles in terms of coincidences, not absolute impossibilities. R. F. Holland was one such.[4] Coincidence miracles are events which are in accordance with natural law, but which are so unlikely and so fortuitous that they are held to be brought about by God.

The following is a good example. *Life* magazine reported that all 15 members of a church choir in Beatrice, Nebraska, came at least ten minutes too late for their weekly choir practice which was supposed to start at 7.20 p.m. on 1 March 1950. They were astonishingly fortunate, because at 7.25 p.m. the building was destroyed by an explosion. The reasons for the delay of each member were fairly commonplace; none of them was marked by the slightest sign of a supernatural cause. However, nothing remotely resembling the situation that all members were prevented from being on time on the same occasion had ever happened before. Furthermore, this singular event took place precisely when it was needed, on the very night when they would otherwise have perished. Consequently, some people were inclined to see the incident as a clear case of divine intervention and a compelling manifestation of God's care and power for everyone to see. How else could one explain such a spectacular coincidence, which turned out to be the deliverance of people who were regarded as the most pious, and most intensely devoted to any church-associated work and thus the most truly worthy to be saved, in a manner which (though it did not violate any law of nature) was too startling to be mere happenstance?[5]

Any event can be interpreted in more than one way, and in relation to coincidence miracles, a great deal may turn on one's prior presuppositions. It may be fair to say that these miracles may speak to faith, but may not induce faith.

---

4 R. F. Holland, 'The Miraculous', *American Philosophical Quarterly* 2 (1965), pp. 43–51.

5 27 March 1950, p. 19.

Interestingly, however, many miracles in the New Testament could certainly be understood in this way. It was widely acknowledged that Jesus worked wonders, but this by no means meant that everyone had faith – in fact at the end of his life, he was deserted and a figure of ridicule. Most people chose to explain the events in some other way.

The fact that an extraordinary series of events occurred does not mean that these events were necessarily planned for. The odds on a lottery ticket coming up or on two people from their home town meeting in a small village on the other side of the world are incredibly small – but coincidences do happen, and this does not mean that they were brought about by God (nor, of course, does it necessarily mean that they were not).

Gareth Moore OP (d. 2002) rejected the idea of defining miracles as actions by God – instead he saw the word 'miracle' as the word that is applied by those who use religious language to describe inexplicable events. The believer is the person who uses the word 'miracle' to apply to an inexplicable event, but this does not mean, Moore considers, that an agent called God performed the event – all it means is that the event is inexplicable. Moore, however, operates with what some may regard as an anti-realist conception of God and not with the view of God as a being or spirit who can act and intervene in the world.

## Do Miracles Ever Occur?

Following on from his definition of a miracle, David Hume provided reasons why we can never be sure that miracles occur. He points out that if one balances the probability of a law of nature being breached (which he considered to be very low) against the likelihood of the testimony to miracles being false, mistaken or exaggerated (which he considered to be very high), it will always be more rational to assume that the supposed miracle has not taken place.

Take for example some of the miracles recorded in the New Testament as being performed by Jesus – water being turned into wine, Jesus walking on water, raising Lazarus from the dead and healing miracles all seem to be breaches of laws of nature (at least of our present understanding of these laws). As Hume wrote,

> [w]hen anyone tells me that he saw a dead man restored to life, I immediately consider myself whether it may be more probable that this person should either deceive or be deceived or that the fact, which he relates, should really have happened. I weigh the one miracle against the other; and according to the superiority which I discover, I pronounce my decision, and always reject the greater miracle. If the falsity of his testimony would be more miraculous, than the event he relates, then, and not till then, can he pretend to command my belief or opinion.[6]

Hume argued that people have a tendency to want to believe fantastic stories of miracles whether they have good evidence or not, that claims about miracles are often made by people who have much to gain, and accounts of miracles come disproportionately from primitive and prescientific societies. Finally, Hume argues that all the different religions – Christianity, Islam, Judaism, Buddhism, Hinduism – have miracles to support them, and that these miracles contradict each other, effectively cancelling each other out. All these points show, Hume argues, how much more likely it is that any account of a miracle is mistaken or a lie than that it is true.

Hume's argument focuses on secondhand reports of miracles rather than on personal experience of such events occurring. Nevertheless, Richard Dawkins in *The Blind Watchmaker* extended Hume's argument and applied it to personal experience, suggesting that it would always be more probable that one's perception or interpretation, even of a direct experience, was faulty than that God has acted in the world. As Anthony Flew (1923–2010) suggested, breaches of our understanding of natural laws can occur. The proper response to an inexplicable event is not to say 'God did it' but to indicate the

---

6 David Hume, *An Enquiry Concerning Human Understanding*, ed. L. A. Selby Bigge, Oxford: Clarendon Press, 1902, p. 116.

flaws in our present scientific understanding and to seek for a scientific explanation. As Immanuel Kant famously wrote: 'sanction no miracles . . . attend to the commands of reason'.[7]

It is worth noting that Hume's points concerning miracles apply quite neatly to reports of other forms of religious experiences. One could say that it is always more probable that there is a natural explanation for the experience than that it was the result of divine action, that reports may have been exaggerated or misinterpreted (perhaps because of wish-fulfilment or other forms of ignorance), that such experiences tend to involve susceptible, unreliable individuals and also occur within conflicting and competing religious paradigms.

Nevertheless, Hume's argument does not prove that miracles (or other forms of religious experience) do not happen – it just suggests that it is rarely (to the point of never) rational to accept reports of such events, let alone to use them as the basis for faith or religious observance. Hume specifically rejected miracles as a basis for faith – he did not reject the possibility of miracles if one had faith in God on other grounds.

Although not an atheist in the same sense as Hume, and although he was the very antithesis of an empiricist, Baruch Spinoza (1632–77) went one step further than Hume, arguing that 'nothing then, comes to pass in nature in contravention to [nature's] universal laws, nay, nothing does not agree with them and follow from them, for . . . she keeps a fixed and immutable order'.[8] He wrote 'a miracle, whether in contravention to, or beyond, nature, is a mere absurdity'.

Spinoza's argument can be summarized as follows:

P1    Miracles are violations of natural laws.

P2    Natural laws are immutable; it is impossible for immutable laws to be violated.

---

7 *Religion within the Limits of Reason Alone*, p. 83; Preface to the first edition available at: http//www.marxists.org/reference/subject/ethics/kant/religion/religion-within-reason.htm.

8 Benedict De Spinoza, *Tractatus Theologica-Pliticus*, in *The Chief Works of Benedict de Spinoza*, trans. R. H. M. Elwes, London: George Bell and Sons, 1883, 1:83, 87, 92.

C  Therefore, miracles are impossible – or are not violations of natural laws.

Unlike Hume, however, Spinoza did not dismiss miracles on the grounds that witnesses must have got it wrong. His attention focused on the adequacy of our understanding of natural laws. He wrote: 'We may, then, be absolutely certain that every event which is truly described in Scripture necessarily happened, like everything else, according to natural laws.'[9]

## Are Miracles a Good Basis for Faith?

Most of the world's religions are founded upon reports of miracles and other religious experiences. Moses received the Ten Commandments, the basis of the Jewish Law, directly from God on top of Mount Sinai. Even the Prophet Mohammed, though mortal, was miraculously given the gift of recitation and was transported in an amazing night journey. Nevertheless, although impossible or at least highly improbable events may seem like good evidence that an omnipotent being exists, and although such events, when they bring about positive consequences for human beings, may suggest an omnibenevolent and an omniscient being as well, miracles are arguably not a good basis for faith.

Maurice Wiles (1929–2005) was a professor at the University of Oxford, an Anglican priest and a member of the Church of England's doctrine commission. He rejected the idea of any miraculous interventions by God into the created universe. He maintained that the universe is part of a single, ongoing act of creation by God but denies God the ability to specifically intervene in the world. This is because, if God could do so, God would not be worthy of worship.[10]

If God could act to cure a child at Lourdes or to make statues weep or the blood of saints not to clot or to help some individual in

9  Ibid., p. 83.
10  See *God's Action in the World*, London: SCM Press, 1986.

relatively trivial ways, then this would mean that God would not be worthy of worship. For, if God could intervene and failed to do so in cases like Stalin's death camps, the Rwanda massacres, the Bosnian conflicts and the Kobe earthquake, God would have to be rejected, for failure to act to prevent suffering is itself a moral failure. This, therefore, relates to the problem of evil, for if God could act and does not do so when human beings suffer, this would imply a negative view of God. Wiles rejects all special interventions by God and maintains that even paradigm interventions like the incarnation or resurrection of Jesus have to be understood in alternative ways than in terms of selective divine action. It is true that Islamic theology sees all events as happening by 'the will of Allah', but this raises intractable problems with human free will, and if selective action is allowed, it is precisely the selective by God which raises the problem.

Keith Ward (b. 1938), Wiles' successor at Oxford, maintains that God is restricted in God's ability to intervene. God would only act for the best, but sometimes there is no single best possible action available. He goes on: 'If the Divine plan is to a large extent open, he may consent to realize a certain state just because it is requested', continuing: 'Our request may make it possible for (God) to help . . . in ways which would otherwise have been constrained by the structures of the natural order.'[11]

Ward claims that when Jesus says that 'if two of you on earth agree about anything you ask for, it will be done for you by my father in heaven' (Matt. 18.19), this is 'poetic hyperbole, so typical of the teaching of Jesus'.[12] Ward maintains that there are three constraints on God's ability to answer prayer:

1 *Prayer must arise in the context of worship* or a relationship of loving obedience to God. It is no use disobeying God in most things and asking for God's help when it suits us. Christians,

---

11 *Divine Action: Examining God's Role in an Open and Emergent Universe*, Oxford: Templeton, 2007, p. 159.

12 Ibid., p. 166.

Ward says, pray 'through Jesus Christ' and in so doing name their ultimate object of loyalty.

2 *Prayers must be for the good of others* and must be supported by loving action whenever possible. The believer must leave God to judge whether something that is prayed for is truly for the good of others or not.

3 *Prayers must be for what is possible.* Ward writes, 'I have suggested that what is possible for God, within the structures he has created, will depend on factors of probability, system-stability and alternative causal pathways, which cannot in principle, be known to us.'[13]

So, Ward argues, God can intervene in answer to prayers by performing miracles, but his ability to do so is much constrained.

A story from Ray Bradbury illustrates this. A package holiday company in the year 2050 sends tourists back in time to shoot dinosaurs, but they are subject to very strict rules that they may not leave laid-down paths or damage anything other than the selected target. The tour operator explains:

If you step on a mouse, you kill families of mice – a thousand, a million, a billion mice annihilated . . . For want of ten mice a fox dies, for want of ten foxes a lion starves, for want of a lion, all sorts of insects, vultures, infinite billions of life forms are thrown into chaos and destruction. Eventually, 59 million years later a caveman, one of a dozen in the entire world, goes hunting wild boar or sabre-toothed tiger for food. But you, friend, have stepped on all the tigers in that region – by stepping on a single mouse. So the caveman starves. And the caveman, note, is not just any expendable man. No! He is an entire future nation. Destroy this one man, and you destroy a race, a people, an entire history of life.[14]

13 Ibid., p. 167.

14 'A Sound of Thunder', in *R is for Rocket*, New York: Doubleday, 1952, available at: http://www.lasalle.edu/~didio/courses/hon462/hon462_assets/sound_of_thunder.htm.

Process theologians such as Alfred North Whitehead, John Cobb and David Griffin see God acting to lure the world and human beings towards God – God acts to persuade, not to control. Human freedom is strongly affirmed but this approach still has to face the challenges of David Hume and Maurice Wiles.

It is worth considering that if human beings are saved through faith, and religious experiences serve to convert or to strengthen or otherwise nourish faith, then it is difficult to understand why God would choose to act in the lives of some people and not others. Why did God not come to Hitler or Stalin, causing them to use their powers for human good rather than evil? The idea that God is so selective is difficult to reconcile with the idea of God as omnibenevolent.

## Summary

Miracles can be defined in different ways. Depending on how they are defined, miracles are either common or impossible when viewed from a materialistic perspective, so it is important to establish precisely what people understand by the term.

There is no doubt that miracles are important in creating and sustaining belief and in supporting the credibility of religious traditions. Nevertheless, miracles put strain on the relationship between faith and reason, providing material to those who suggest that believers are gullible and even undermining an otherwise defensible philosophical concept of God.

# 16

# The God of the Philosophers

Most people's faith in God is neither formed nor sustained by rational argument, though they may find rational arguments interesting and sometimes useful. Ask people why they believe in God, and, beyond the obvious answer that they have been brought up to do so, the answer is more probably going to lie in some form of religious experience than in argument. This explains why most people's concept of God is closer to the God of Abraham than the God of the philosophers.

Given the difficulties with using religious experiences, religious authority or miracles to defend belief in God, let alone beliefs about God's nature, it is not surprising that, for all its problems, the philosophy of religion has remained important in establishing what people believe and why. Nevertheless, framing God in philosophical terminology and interpreting any encounters with the God of Abraham 'through reason alone' has its own issues.

Key to the philosophical concept of God is that God is perfect, which is usually defined in terms of omnipotence and omnibenevolence. Omnipotence is usually held to entail omniscience. Yet, what can these terms really mean?

- Can an omnipotent God create a rock that is too heavy for him to lift? How about a square circle? How about an imperfect world?
- Can an omniscient God see into the future? Could God have known that human freedom would result in Auschwitz? To what extent can individuals be free, if God knows what they are going to do?
- Can an omnibenevolent God have created a world where everybody is condemned to grow old, get sick and die, where

creatures must kill each other for food and always struggle to survive and reproduce?

Describing God's attributes creates a tension between theology and philosophy. Determining philosophically satisfactory meanings is likely to create theological problems, and vice versa.

It is clear that the problem of meaning in religious language is particularly acute when one conceives of God as outside time and space, given that language tends to imply a spatio-temporal framework. Aquinas claimed that there is meaning in some descriptive terms when applied to God, but it must be severely restricted. Having sought to establish that God exists through his five *a posteriori* arguments, Aquinas switches from an *a posteriori* approach to an *a priori* one to determine the attributes which the first unmoved mover, the first efficient cause, the absolutely necessary and supremely perfect being must possess.

Aquinas argued that any description of God's qualities must be understood *analogically*, through the filter of reason. As a function of his five ways, God cannot be a material being or *thing*; every material being is capable of change and motion and is contingent. God cannot be within time or space, because that would entail God depending on this framework and changing in some sense. Being outside time and space, God must be wholly lacking in potential and be pure actuality, fully whatever it is to be God. God must be *wholly simple* and immutable, without any division between God's qualities (i.e. God's power is the same as God's goodness and it is only in our limited understanding that these seem to be separate qualities).

For Aquinas, the terms 'omnipotent' and 'omnibenevolent' have very specific analogical meaning. He wrote:

Whatever in any way whatsoever can be, comes within the range of God's power and He can make it be. In God's case, and only in His case, the possible said relatively to an active power and the possible without qualification are the same. God's power is grounded in (is identical with) His infinite being which is the sum of all perfection. Thus, what is said to be possible with respect to His power is anything whatsoever that can be.[1]

For Aquinas, God's power is limited to what is *actually possible*, that which is not internally contradictory and which does not contradict God's perfect nature. God cannot do X and not X at the same time, God cannot create a square circle, neither can God do something which contradicts God's perfect nature because both these involve contradictions. God cannot create a rock too heavy for God to lift, because creating something too heavy for God to lift contradicts God's omnipotence.

Aquinas rejects the application to God of any perfections that can only belong to finite creatures. Only 'pure perfections', which are not tied to any particular mode of being, can be applied to God. For example, for Aquinas, since God is the cause of goodness or love in creatures, it is right to call God good or loving, and yet it is still wrong to think that there is any substantial overlap between what it means to call a person good or loving and what it means to call God good or loving. Aquinas makes the lack of contact clear by saying that God's goodness resembles human goodness – but to a lesser extent than the effects of the sun, such as a tree, resembles the sun.[2]

Aquinas does not think we can know God's essence or much about God at all, but we can use words truly of God without knowing their meaning when applied to God. Aquinas maintains that we can know *that* God is but not *what* God is. God's essence is unknowable except to God (incidentally this was one reason for his rejecting the ontological argument – only God knows God's own essence and, therefore, only God could deduce God's existence from knowledge of God's essence) – which is why language applied to God has so little meaning.

It is worth considering that Aquinas' whole approach to God *might* be flawed. This is a large claim and may be wrong – certainly Gerard W.

---

1 *Summa Theologica* I, q. 25.
2 *Summa Theologica* Ia, 13, 2.

Hughes S. J. rejects it.[3] However, considering the possibility will be helpful in understanding the broader implications of Aquinas' thinking. One particular problem area has to do with Aquinas' concept of timeless choice.

Effectively, Aquinas argues:

P1    It can be established that there is an X such that this X sustains the universe.

P2    This X everyone calls God.

P3    God is wholly simple and therefore timeless, spaceless, bodiless, etc.

P4    God can be truthfully talked about even though the content of language about God is very limited indeed.

P5    God can do everything that is actually possible. What is actually possible is defined by saying that everything that does not involve a contradiction can be done by God.[4]

IC    God [can] therefore do anything provided there is no contradiction involved (the brackets round 'can' are important as, when applied to God, this cannot imply potential for God to do other than what God does),

P6    A contradiction can occur either:

     i    because the action contradicts some feature of God (for instance 'can die' would contradict God's eternal nature outside time and space);

     ii    because the action is internally contradictory (for instance acting and not acting simultaneously, doing 'p and not p at the same time').

---

3 *The Nature of God*, London: Routledge, 1995.

4 The problems start with the use of 'can'. One cannot use 'can' in this sentence, rather one should say that 'X does everything, absolutely'. Aquinas maintains that God has no potential (incidentally this is one reason why definitions of omniscience in terms of God's powers [cf Anthony Kenny] cannot be applied to the timeless and spaceless God). God is pure actuality and therefore one cannot talk of unactualized powers or abilities of God.

Because of this, an omnipotent God could not swim because swimming seems to require a body and to involve time. Nevertheless, Aquinas argues that an omnipotent God could act, despite being timeless, spaceless and bodiless, because 'God acts' should be understood as 'acts timelessly'. God cannot act other than as God does act (since this would imply potential) but God acts, in a single act, in whatever timeless manner is necessary to bring about temporal effects.

The distinction between 'timelessly swims', which Aquinas sees to involve a contradiction, and 'timelessly acts' is not clear, although because 'timelessly acts' is held not to involve time, this may be considered not to be contradictory, whereas 'timelessly swims' is contradictory since 'swims' necessarily involves time.

However, if God's timeless action is held to imply God choosing to act, then this can be argued to necessarily involve a contradiction when God is defined as wholly simple. Choice seems to involve potential just as swimming involves a physical presence in time and space.

This could be rejected by saying that 'chooses' means 'timelessly chooses' in an unknowable way which does not involve potential. This would not appear to be internally contradictory – but could one not then say that 'timelessly swims' does not involve a contradiction either? The one may be no more plausible than the other. There are limits to what words can be allowed to be true when applied to a timeless God. If 'choice' involves choosing one alternative rather than another (for instance to create or not to create), then this would mean that God would have to have potential, and this is not possible if God is timeless.

If God cannot choose in any real sense then God has to act as God acts – God is compelled to act by the very nature of God. In this case, the universe becomes necessary and not contingent and the reason for separating the universe from God and not seeing the universe itself as the necessary *brute fact*, which underpins its own existence, dissolves.

In order to maintain that God can choose in any meaningful fashion and, therefore, that God can respond to prayer (since a response involves potentiality), then God needs to be in time. If God is in time, then God can have potential – God can respond to prayer by acting after the request is made. The universe can then be created as a free choice by God and is contingent and not necessary. However, placing God in time can be held to limit the idea of God and many Christian philosophers would say that would not be religiously adequate.

## The Particular Problem of Omniscience

Traditional Christianity, Islam and Judaism hold that God is omniscient – God knows everything including the past, the present and the future. If God is wholly simple and timeless, then God sees the whole of time in one 'now'. There is no past, present and future to God. God timelessly sees the whole of time including the creation of the universe, the dinosaurs, your birth, life and death and the end of the universe. Augustine likens this to a person on a mountain looking down on the road of time below. To the person on the road some people are behind them and some are ahead of them but the person on the mountain sees them all simultaneously. Similarly your grandparents are in the past and your grandchildren are in the future but God timelessly sees the whole of time in one, eternal, 'now'. This gives God complete knowledge.

Boethius (480–525) expressed this as follows:

God sees all, seated in the skies:
Earth's bulk cannot his gaze withstand,
Nor clouds of night a hindrance be.
What is, what has been, what will be
A single glance of mind discerns,
Since He alone all things can see,
The title of 'true sun' he earns.[5]

All knowledge is timelessly present to God. Since there is no time in God, all knowledge is present at once. Boethius wrote:

---

5 Boethius, *The Consolation of Philosophy*, Book 5, trans. P. G. Walsh, Oxford: Oxford University Press, 1999, p. 103.

God ponders all things as if they were enacted in the present. Hence your judgement will be more correct should you seek to envisage the foresight by which God discerns all things not as a sort of foreknowledge of the future, but as knowledge of the unceasing present moment.[6]

It is an attractive idea but it conceals a grave problem, and this revolves around human freedom.

If God knows exactly what you will do and how the whole history of the world will unfold, how can you or other humans be free? To know means to know a true state of affairs – it is not a prediction, it is absolute knowledge. It follows that whatever God knows must necessarily happen. There are two distinct possibilities here:

1 God's knowledge can be held to cause events to happen. The causal arrow flows from God to the world. In Islam everything is said to happen by the will of Allah. This affirms God's complete knowledge but it creates a massive problem for human freedom. If God's knowledge is causal, then human freedom is an illusion. We may think we are free, but actually we are wholly determined by God.

2 The alternative is to say that it is human free decisions that cause God's knowledge. In this case, the causal arrow flows from human beings to God. But if this is the case, then God depends for God's knowledge on human free decisions, and Augustine and Aquinas and other philosophers agree that this cannot happen if God is wholly simple, timeless and spaceless. God cannot come to know things, God has no potentiality. Even if God is held to timelessly know everything, then God still depends on human beings for God's knowledge, and this cannot be for Aquinas as it would make God's knowledge depend on human actions, so all God's attributes could not be identical in God.

---

6 Ibid., p. 112.

This is a major problem. If human freedom is compromised, not only does moral praise and blame disappear, as everyone is totally determined, but any suggested solution to the problem of evil is also undermined, as human beings are no longer free – they are programmed robots. They may think they are free, but this is an illusion.

Many solutions have been attempted to this problem, including the idea put forward by Luis De Molina S. J. (1535–1600) that God has *middle knowledge* – knowledge of all possibilities. God knows every possibility, so whatever a human being chooses will be known by God. However, this does not solve the problem. I can say that I know that you will have 0, 1, 2, 3, 4, 5, 6 up to 50 children. Whichever number of children you have, I can say that I knew that. But if I do not actually know which of the number of children will be actualized, I cannot claim to know. I may claim to know the result of the FA Cup Final – either Team A or Team B will win or they will draw. However, unless I can know which of the possibilities are actualized, I cannot be held to have known the result.

Boethius addressed this problem, writing:

> There seems to be a considerable contradiction and inconsistency between God's foreknowledge of all things and the existence of any free will. If God foresees all things and cannot in any way be mistaken, then what Providence has foreseen will happen must inevitably come to pass.[7]

He wrestled with the alternatives at great length but finally is forced to effectively retreat behind mystery. He wrote: 'So the future events which God foreknows will all undoubtedly come to pass, but some of them will proceed by free choice.'[8]

There is no clear way that this position can be held – if God knows the future then freedom is eliminated and to hold that the two are incompatible requires a retreat behind mystery. This raises the

---

7  Ibid., p. 103.
8  Ibid., p. 113.

problem of when it is right to play the 'mystery card' and when there is a real contradiction that cannot be overcome.

Gerard Hughes S. J. is one of the most senior Catholic theologians, and he argues that God cannot respond to prayer since, as God is unchangeable, a response would require God to have potential and be able to change. There is a single act of God which has multitudes of effects throughout history so in God's single timeless act every effect brought about by God is included. For God to be able to respond to prayer, God would have to know what people would request in prayer logically prior to those who pray existing and even praying, and if humans are to be genuinely free (as Hughes affirms), then God could not respond to these prayers in the sole, single, creative act which the timeless God performs. This may be philosophically persuasive, but it is a very long way from the understanding of prayer held by most Christians.

The simple way of resolving the tension between omniscience and freedom is to place God in time. Some Protestant theologians take this view, and it gives rise to what has been called *Openness Theology*,[9] whereby God is held to know everything that it is logically possible to know – not including the future – and to change and develop through interaction with creation. This approach has the benefit of enabling language to be relatively literal and God to be 'personal' – which is important for those who base their faith on individuals reading the Bible. Nevertheless, 'openness theology' is absolutely rejected by Roman Catholics, who maintain that God is wholly simple, not limited and anthropomorphic, and that faith is propositional, supported by philosophic argument.[10]

9 Richard Rice, *The Openness of God: The Relationship of Divine Foreknowledge and Human Free Will*, Hagerstown, ML: Review and Herald Publishers Association, 1980.

10 It follows that discussions of this issue tend to take place within the context of philosophical theology rather than the philosophy of religion.

## Summary

How we understand God's nature will depend, to a large extent, on where our belief comes from. For Protestants, whose faith originates in the Bible, God is the 'God of Abraham' and by implication eternal-in-time, with limited power and knowledge and anthropomorphic qualities. This places strain on the relationship between faith and reason. For Catholics, whose faith is propositional, God's simplicity means God is outside time and space and truly unlimited – but this places strain on language, meaning and the point of philosophy itself.

# PART FOUR

# Challenges to Belief

It seems to us as though we had either the wrong pieces, or not enough of them, to put together our jigsaw puzzle.

(Ludwig Wittgenstein, *The Blue Book*, p. 46)

# The Limits of Language

A mind enclosed in language is in prison.

(Simone Weil)

The problem of whether God is in time or wholly simple, timeless and spaceless is one of the most important issues in the philosophy of religion and has a direct bearing on how language is used about God. There has always been a sense in which, although words have given flight to our understanding and have enabled us to master our world, they also constrain us. Language is our means, not only of describing reality, but of interpreting it. In a sense language is a prison which forces us to see reality through linguistic spectacles.

Classical thinkers such as Plato (427–347 BC) had confidence that words refer to definite concepts consistently. Plato understood that the physical world is a partial reflection of the *Forms*, ultimate metaphysical reality. Through reason, human beings are able to encounter and engage with conceptual reality. Philosophy is the business of clarifying and exploring concepts through reason and seeking the truth. Its medium is language, which is taken to represent concepts accurately and to be a window on truth.

Aristotle (384–22 BC) disagreed with his teacher Plato on many things, but retained a broadly similar view of language. For Aristotle, all things have a *formal cause*, a metaphysical definition which makes something essentially what it is and which is recognized by reason. When we look at an oak tree, we recognize it as an oak tree and are able to judge it on those terms; when we look at a good man, we can recognize him as a good man and can discuss the merits of his life on those terms. People can discuss things without confusion; there is a definite meaning to words which does not depend on the situation or the intentions of individuals. Words can be meaningful when applied to things which do not have a physical form, because the human experience of reason is shared.

Throughout history there have been philosophers who have agreed with Plato and Aristotle, being positive about the ability of language to express reality neutrally.

In the Middle Ages, thinkers such as John Duns Scotus (1266–1308) had a *univocal* approach to language, even when it was applied to God. He argued that saying 'God is good' or 'Jesus is the Word of God' can be understood unequivocally, without any confusion. Like Anselm, he held that '[t]he difference between God and creatures, at least with regard to God's possession of the pure perfections, is ultimately one of degree'.[1]

Whereas earthly things are limited by their physical existence, God is infinite and has no limitations. When we say God is good, the concept of goodness is the same as when we say 'Chris is good', but to a much greater degree. The human mind is capable of imagining 'that which is greater than anything else that can be thought of'.

For Scotus, the cause (God) and the effect (created things) share at the very least in their *being* (Latin '*ens*'); God infinitely exists and creates all existing things. Language relates to existence, and claims about God's existence and the existence of earthly things mean essentially the same. As Williams writes,

> For Scotus infinity is not only what's ontologically central about God, it's the key component of our best available concept of God and a guarantor of the success of theological language. That is, our best ontology, far from fighting with our theological semantics, both supports and is supported by our theological semantics.[2]

In other words, God's nature is to infinitely exist. Created things exist in a limited way; their existence depends on the existence of God. All

---

1 Richard Cross, *Duns Scotus*, Oxford: Oxford University Press, 1999, p. 39.
2 Thomas Williams, http://plato.stanford.edu/entriesduns-scotus/#DivInf DocUni.

human language relates to existence. Our experience of existence is through limited examples, but reason is capable of extrapolating from these and understanding something of the essence and source of existence, God.

For Scotus and fellow Franciscans as well as most Protestant theologians today, language about God can be broadly univocal – language about God has much the same sense, albeit expanded in degree, as language applied in the spatio-temporal world. This is one of the great advantages if God is in time, as language can be used about God in a relatively straightforward manner.

If, however, God is beyond time and space, wholly simple, then language about God becomes more problematic. Throughout history, there have also been philosophers who have been more sceptical about the abilities of language to convey meaning neutrally. The great Neoplatonic philosopher Plotinus (204/5–70) wrote:

> Our thought cannot grasp the One as long as any other image remains active in the soul . . . To this end, you must set free your soul from all outward things and turn wholly within yourself, with no more leaning to what lies outside, and lay your mind bare of ideal forms, as before of the objects of sense, and forget even yourself, and so come within sight of that One.[3]

The idea that human concepts become confused by physical experience, that applying concepts more usually experienced in physical terms to a metaphysical reality is likely to lead to error, was developed within the Christian tradition by scholars such as Pseudo-Dionysius (fifth to sixth centuries) and within the Jewish tradition by Maimonides (1135–1204).

Maimonides argued that since God is so radically other, nothing positive can be ascribed to God, but we can, as philosophers, use logic to say what God clearly is not. This approach is known as the *via negativa* or *apophatic way* and had been adopted for centuries

---

3 Quoted in John Gregory, *The Neoplatonists: A Reader*, 2nd edn, London: Routledge, 1991, p. 183 (from Plotinus' *Enneads*).

before Maimonides, in an attempt to avoid the anthropomorphism and over-literalism that using positive language about God can encourage. In the Christian West, a similar *via negativa* was being trodden by Gilbert of Poitiers and Alan of Lille in the twelfth century. Commenting on the writings of Augustine of Hippo (354–430) and Boethius (480–524/5) they concluded that God is wholly simple, totally *other*, and that using any positive terms to describe God's nature or attributes would be folly. It is better to remain silent before the mystery that is God.

The long tradition of the *via negativa* influenced the thinking of Ludwig Wittgenstein (1889–1951) in the twentieth century. Like Ibn Sina (980–1037, Avicenna in Europe), Wittgenstein saw that language has its origins in common, shared and mostly physical experiences. Like John Locke (1632–1704) and David Hume (1711–76), Wittgenstein took this to mean that the meaning of words is ultimately subjective rather than being potentially objective.

While serving on a battleship on the Elbe on the Eastern Front during the Second World War, Wittgenstein became fascinated by the connections between words and their meanings. He spoke the same language as his fellow soldiers, but often failed to understand them. This experience inspired Wittgenstein to develop his theory of *language games*, which sought to explain the nature and limits of language.

For Wittgenstein, words are *auditory signs* representing an agreed experience or concept. The sign does not contain meaning but points towards something beyond itself. Without agreement, signs mean nothing. A sign might mean one thing to one group of people and another to another. For example, 'thumbs up' tends to mean 'Yes' in modern Europe but during the time of the Roman Empire 'thumbs up' signified death to a gladiator. One meaning is not right and the other wrong – the meaning just depends on the context and the agreement of the people using the sign.

It follows that the meaning of words depends on what is agreed and how the words are used within a particular *form of life*. For example, the word 'gay' has been used to mean different things by different groups of people. In 1940s America and Britain it meant 'carefree and happy', in 1950s South Africa it meant 'colourful and bright', in 1990s Australia it meant 'homosexual', and in 2000s Britain, in some circles, it meant 'anything stupid or pointless'. A similar range in meanings over time, place and social strata might be said about words such as 'wicked' or 'bad'. Meaning depends on the *language game* one inhabits.[4]

As for Maimonides, for Wittgenstein silence or saying nothing may be significant. He concluded the *Tractatus*, which established the limits of language, with the claim 'whereof one cannot speak, thereof one must be silent',[5] but this did not necessarily mean that there *is* nothing beyond what one can speak of. He wrote:

> The solution of the riddle of life in space and time lies outside space and time. How the world is, is completely indifferent for what is higher. God does not reveal himself in the world. Not how the world is, is the mystical, but that it is. The contemplation of the world *sub specie aeterni* is its contemplation as a limited whole. The feeling of the world as a limited whole is the mystical feeling. For an answer which cannot be expressed, the question too cannot be expressed. The riddle does not exist. If a question can be put at all, then it can also be answered. Scepticism is not irrefutable, but palpably senseless, if it would doubt where a question cannot be asked. For doubt can only exist where there is a question; a question only where there is an answer, and this only where something can be said.[6]

Importantly, despite despairing of the ability of language to convey positive meaning about God, neither Maimonides in the Jewish tradition, nor Gilbert of Poitiers or Alan of Lille in the Christian tradition, nor indeed the *Mu'tazilah* school of Islamic theology,[7] nor even Wittgenstein took that to mean that God does not exist.

---

4 Section 4, http://www.gutenberg.org/files/5740/5740-pdf.pdf.
5 Section 7, http://www.gutenberg.org/files/5740/5740-pdf.pdf.
6 Section 6, http://www.gutenberg.org/files/5740/5740-pdf.pdf.
7 Which flourished in the cities of Basra and Baghdad during the eighth to tenth centuries.

Nevertheless, following Wittgenstein, some members of the *analytic* school of philosophy moved from claiming that it is *as if* nothing exists beyond what can be said, to claiming that nothing exists beyond what can be said.

Influenced by philosophers of the Vienna Circle such as Moritz Schlick (1882–1936),[8] in *Language, Truth and Logic,*[9] A. J. Ayer (1910–89) argued that what can be said is essentially limited to what can be experienced. Statements or *propositions* can only be meaningful if they are *verifiable*, if they refer to things which can be checked with the physical senses (sight, hearing, taste, touch and smell). *Empiricists* accept that sense experience is the best source of knowledge, and the point of reference when we try to establish meaning in language. For *logical positivists* like Schlick and Ayer, meaning can either be *analytic* (one word can be shown to mean the same as another; analytic statements are *tautologous*) or *synthetic* and refer to a sense-experience. Analytic statements do not extend the sum of human knowledge, and synthetic statements are limited as a basis for conversation, yet all other types of statement are essentially meaningless, including morality, beauty and, of course, religion.

*The falsification principle* was developed by Karl Popper (1902–94) in response to concerns about the limitations of *the verification principle* proposed by, for example, Schlick. Many scientific statements are not strictly verifiable, and yet need to be accepted as meaningful if science is to achieve anything; Popper suggested that science works by accepting as meaningful or even true those statements which have not been proved false, but which would be accepted as false should falsifying evidence be produced. This extends the range of possibly meaningful statements but still excludes religious, moral

---

8 Schlick was perhaps the most famous of the so-called 'Vienna Circle', which also included Kurt Gödel and Rudolph Carnap. Schlick was assassinated by a Nazi former student in Vienna in 1936 aged 54 for his opposition to German influence in Austria and for being part of a philosophical movement labelled 'Jewish' by the Nazis, though Schlick was not himself Jewish. Nevertheless, the assassin was given a government position after the Anschluss in 1938, rather than being punished for the murder of his teacher.

9 Harmondsworth: Penguin, 2001, p. 140.

and aesthetic statements from being meaningful unless people are prepared to accept that they would reject their beliefs if the situation changed. For example, *God is good* would be meaningful only until evidence of suffering in his creation was presented.

Anthony Flew (1923–2010) developed the *falsification principle* specifically as a challenge to religious belief. He developed a parable, originally suggested by John Wisdom (1904–93), to make his point, writing:

> Once upon a time two explorers came upon a clearing in the jungle. In the clearing were growing many flowers and many weeds. One explorer says, 'Some gardener must tend this plot.' The other disagrees, 'There is no gardener.' So they pitch their tents and set a watch. No gardener is ever seen . . . Yet still the Believer is not convinced. 'But there is a gardener, invisible, . . . a gardener who comes secretly to look after the garden which he loves.' At last the Sceptic despairs, 'But what remains of your original assertion? Just how does what you call an invisible, intangible, eternally elusive gardener differ from an imaginary gardener or even from no gardener at all?'[10]

He concluded:

> Now it often seems to people who are not religious as if there was no conceivable event or series of events the occurrence of which would be admitted by sophisticated religious people to be a sufficient reason for conceding 'there wasn't a God after all' or 'God does not really love us then.' Someone tells us that God loves us as a father loves his children. We are reassured. But then we see a child dying of inoperable cancer of the throat . . . Some qualification is made – God's love is 'not merely human love' . . . perhaps – and we realize that such suffering are quite compatible with the truth of the assertion that 'God loves us as a father . . .' We are

---

10 'Theology and Falsification', in *Reason and Responsibility* (1968), available online at http://www.stephenjaygould.org/ctrl/flew_falsification.html.

reassured again . . . I therefore put . . . the simple central questions, 'What would have to occur or to have occurred to constitute for you a disproof of the love of, or the existence of, God?

It is worth saying that Flew was criticized both by Basil Mitchell (1917–2011) and by Richard Swinburne (b. 1934). Mitchell argued that Flew ignores the concept of commitment; people promise to believe despite challenges, because that is the nature of faith. Swinburne argued that we *know* that toys don't get out of the cupboard and play when we are not looking, though we can't verify or falsify this. Nevertheless, Flew's suggestion that religious beliefs are what R. M. Hare (1919–2002) called a *blik*, an unassailable supralogical conviction, not really something which philosophers can engage with and potentially anti-intellectual, has been influential.

Some philosophers were influenced by the work of Wittgenstein, Ayer and Popper, concluding that because religious statements are couched in the terms of a particular language game and so likely to be misunderstood outside the immediate context in which they are made, because they do not refer to empirically verifiable states of affairs and because they cannot even be falsified, there is no absolute truth. What is true for one person may not be true for another; truth is just relative. This is known as *anti-realism*, and in philosophy of religion is associated with the thought of D. Z. Phillips (1934–2006).

Phillips suggested that it is perfectly proper to say that 'The Lord is my shepherd' within a religious form of life. These statements are true for religious people. It is equally true to say that 'God is dead' within an atheistic community, however; that is true for some atheists. The anti-realist approach makes much sense of much religious language. Religious writers tend to use signs, symbols and metaphors which require the reader to have an appropriate cultural background or to have learned the particular usage of terms in order for them to make any sense. Nevertheless, few religious people will accept that their claims have relevance only in terms of documenting personal or local beliefs.

One middle way between accepting that language may be used univocally and despairing of the possible meaningfulness of language when applied to God is the idea that terms may be used *analogically*.

Thomas Aquinas argued that God is wholly simple. He was aware that Maimonides had argued that, if this is the case, nothing meaningful can be said of God and we must remain silent before the Mystery that is God. However, he did not agree with Maimonides' conclusion and developed a middle way between accepting that language may be used univocally and despairing of the possible meaningfulness of language when applied to God. This is the idea that terms may be used *analogically*. This approach had its roots in Aristotle, and was discussed extensively by Islamic philosophers including Al Farabi (870–950), Ibn Sina (980–1037) and Al Ghazali (1058–1111), before their works, along with their translations of many of Aristotle's works, were reimported into Europe in the twelfth and thirteenth centuries.

Thomas Aquinas was brought up in a philosophical world that was obsessed by logic and grammar. As all aspiring academics at the University of Paris did, Aquinas commented on Aristotle's *Categories*, one of the two works available in Latin prior to the early twelfth century. In doing so, Aquinas developed the idea that terms applied to God are *analogical* (from *analogia*, the Greek for proportion), and tried to explain exactly what the proportion of shared meaning would be when a term is applied to God and to an earthly thing. Using Aristotle's distinctions, he did not believe that terms applied to God are *equivocal* (essentially meaningless), but he did not believe that they should be seen as *univocally* either. Words applied to God cannot mean exactly the same as if they were applied to things in the spatio-temporal world of experience. For Aquinas, God created the world, and therefore it must tell us something about God, but God is *other*, different from the world of time and space and potentiality that God caused to be.

For Aquinas, God is perfect and beyond time and space, so language can only be used analogically of God. He used a truly medieval example to explain what this meant.

A good bull has a sleek coat, big muscles and a strong interest in cows; it conforms to the ideal of being a bull and is as fully what a bull is supposed to be as might be possible in this world. God, being outside time and space, could hardly be said to have big muscles – but when called good, God could be understood to be fulfilling God's divine nature. God is fully what it means to be God. This is known as the *analogy of proportion*: God being good shares in what it means for earthly things to be good in that the word 'good' signifies the fulfilment of nature. Nevertheless the nature of God and of any created thing is radically different from God.

A second form of analogy is *analogy of attribution*. A good bull does good things and also produces good things. A good bull might always charge at red things, always oblige when a cow is presented, might always produce healthy urine and manure, high-quality semen and prize-winning calves. Saying that God is good might share some meaning in the sense that God also does and produces good things (the creation of the universe). Obviously God's actions and productions would have to be understood timelessly, but essentially God emanates goodness and all things which come from God themselves fulfil their natures and do whatever God intended them to do.

For Aquinas, the meaning of language is not literal but nevertheless has some content, it is proportionate to the difference between God and the spatio-temporal world. God created the world and saw that it was good; the world fulfils God's will and shares something with its creator. Nevertheless, God is timeless and spaceless, wholly simple, whereas the world is complex and constrained by time and space. Phrases such as 'God is good' must be interpreted to account for God being totally other – they must be understood analogically.

Aquinas' doctrine of analogy remains influential within the Roman Catholic tradition, within which church teaching is primary and scripture must be read through the lens of doctrine; however, other traditions struggle to accept that God is wholly simple, when the scriptures suggest a God who acts directly in the world and has potential to change. Protestant Christians, for example, struggle to reconcile the God of the Old and New Testaments with a timeless, spaceless God who by definition is unable to act in the world except timelessly in a single, simple creative act and is unable to respond to prayer (since a response requires time) (cf Chapter 16).

The question of how to interpret the meaning of religious language, therefore, remains a live one and is directly related to one's understanding of the nature of God.

Ian Ramsey argued that religious language is *symbolic*, but not any more so than language in science. According to Ramsey, in both science and religion we set up models to help us to understand. In science, we use ping-pong balls and cocktail sticks to explain how atoms combine to form molecules, talk about light and sound being 'waves' and atoms having 'hooks', when none of these models has literal truth. Ramsey claims that in religion we rarely talk in positive terms and that the main function of religious terms is to provide a model which evokes an understanding in others, rather than to set out meaning in a precise way.

Like Ramsey, Ian Crombie (1917–2010) suggested that the nature of the object of religious language meant that it could only ever be evocative, never precise in its meaning or reference, always mysterious and evocative. He explored the use of deliberate category mistakes and obviously inadequate terminology by religious writers, seeing that this could be a device to communicate about the nature of God by showing the inadequacy of language.

Paul Tillich (1886–1965) also argued that religious language is symbolic, statements are not designed to be taken literally, but through being immersed in an appropriate culture and form of religious language we come to understand the spiritual meaning towards which these symbolic words point. He wrote: 'Faith consists in being vitally concerned with that ultimate reality to which I give the symbolical name of God. Whoever reflects earnestly on the meaning of life is on the verge of an act of faith.'[11]

For Tillich, the cultural limitations of language do not suggest any limitation of God's reality. God is what is ultimately real; human beings express their encounter with the ultimate in different ways

---

11 Quoted in Jude Patterson, *Spirituality: Passages in Search of the Heart of God*, New York: Barnes and Noble Books, 2003, p. 10.

and, because that encounter is profound and different from ordinary experiences, they resort to symbolic language. Tillich wrote: 'Man's ultimate concern must be expressed symbolically, because symbolic language alone is able to express the ultimate.'[12]

Today many philosophers of religion see themselves as *critical realists*. On the one hand critical realism holds that it is possible to acquire knowledge about the external world as it really is, independently of the human mind or subjectivity. On the other hand, it rejects the naïve realist's view that the external world is simply as it is perceived. Recognizing that the mind shapes what it perceives, it holds that one can only acquire knowledge of the external world by critical reflection on the process perception and its place in the world. This means that language and knowledge, including scientific claims, are both coloured by our perspective and reflective of reality. Like Aquinas' doctrine of analogy, critical realism offers a middle way between naïve literalism and hopelessness in religious language.

Critical realism was first applied to the discourse between science and religion in the 1950s by Ian Barbour (b. 1923), and since has been adopted by Arthur Peacocke (1924–2006) and John Polkinghorne (b. 1930) and more recently by Alister McGrath (b. 1953). It has become a particularly dominant epistemology for those writing about science and religion. Quantum science suggested that traditional logic may not represent the way things really are. Quarks can be in two places at once, can exist and not exist simultaneously and are changed by being viewed. This indicates that reality is not as simple as it may once have seemed.

Bernard Lonergan (1904–84) proposed applying critical realism to theology and the philosophy of religion, and his thinking has influenced a generation of others, including N. T. Wright (b. 1948) and James Dunn (b. 1939) as biblical scholars. N. T. Wright wrote:

I propose a form of critical realism. This is a way of describing the process of 'knowing' that acknowledges the reality of the thing known, as something other than the knower (hence 'realism'), while

12 Paul Tillich, *Dynamics of Faith*, London: HarperCollins, 2011, p. 43.

fully acknowledging that the only access we have to this reality lies along the spiraling path of appropriate dialogue or conversation between the knower and the thing known (hence 'critical').[13]

In 1984, Janet Martin Soskice published a thorough study of *metaphor* in religious and scientific language, arguing that the latter can be meaningful, because the former is widespread and accepted to be meaningful in that context. Her work arose as a result of critical realist enquiries into science and religion.[14] Soskice argues that metaphor can gesture towards the reality of God without claiming to describe God. To say that God is the vine and we are the branches, that God is my shepherd or that God is a rock, are metaphors. They are not to be taken literally. Soskice drew a parallel between science and theology, arguing that both are based on realism (the claim that statements are true because they refer), but they use metaphors to express what cannot be expressed literally. She explained how even in science theoretical terms are seen as representing reality without claiming to be absolutely true.

Similarly, Soskice claims that in theology there is a distinction between referring to God and attempting to define God. In both science and theology, language is being used to represent reality in the knowledge that it may be inadequate, confusing and could be improved upon.

## Summary

The possibility of the philosophy of religion depends on the meaningfulness of language when applied to God.

Maintaining the *univocity* of language requires holding that God is in time and space. The future is future to God. Although this approach means that language about God can be relatively literal, it does hold

---

13 *Christian Origins and the Question of God: Vol. 1: The New Testament and the People of God*, London: SPCK, 1996, p. 35.

14 *Metaphor and Religious Language*, Oxford: Oxford University Press, 1984, p. 78.

the danger of making God perhaps too anthropomorphic. This might encourage naïve literalism, which can lead to problems in the interpretation of texts. It might also suggest a God whose existence and attributes cannot be uncovered through rational argument alone, so making faith dependent more on revelation than on reason.

Seeing God as wholly simple, outside of time and space, as most of the arguments for God's existence suggest, leads some philosophers to see that language is *equivocal*, that it can convey no positive meaning about God. Nevertheless, the consequences of such an approach can be devastating for religion – or at least for the relationship between faith and reason. The *via negativa* has attractions for those whose faith is solitary and nourished by personal religious experiences, but it makes communal worship, organized religion, very difficult indeed.

A middle way is to hold that language about God conveys restricted meaning through analogy and metaphor. This is the Catholic position and is the aim of philosophers from Aquinas to Soskice. The difficulty with this is to define exactly how much meaning can be drawn from terms applied to God, retaining both philosophical coherence and the sense of what believers want to say. It is probably fair to say that no middle way has yet achieved a perfect balance. For example, Aquinas' doctrine of *analogy* restricts meaning very severely, so that there is almost no overlap between what might be meant by saying that God acts and saying that Peter acts.

# 18

# The Problem of Evil

As a challenge to theism, the problem of evil has traditionally been posed in the form of a dilemma; if God is perfectly loving, He must wish to abolish evil; and if He is all-powerful, He must be able to abolish evil. But evil exists; therefore God cannot be both omnipotent and perfectly loving.

(John Hick, *Philosophy of Religion*[1])

In his famous essay 'Evil and Omnipotence', J. L. Mackie tried to develop a clear argument against God's existence based on the apparent conflict between evil and a world created by an omnipotent God.[2]

Mackie began by observing that traditional arguments for the existence of God have been criticized to the extent that 'no rational proof of God's existence is possible'[3] and that believers must at least hold that God's existence is 'known in some other, non-rational way'. He then suggested that 'here it can be shown, not that religious beliefs lack rational support, but that they are positively irrational, that the several parts of the theological doctrine are inconsistent with one another'.

This would push faith far from being possibly propositional, even non-propositional, into the realm of being fideist in the most *anti-intellectual* sense. Not only would it be irrational to believe that God exists, but the believer 'can only maintain his position as a whole by a much more extreme rejection of reason'.[4]

---

1 John Hick, *Philosophy of Religion*, Chapter 4, currently out of print but can be found online at http://kslinker.com/Hick-God%20Can%20Allow%20Evil.pdf [check reference, link doesn't work].

2 First published in *Mind* 64 (1955), pp. 200–12.

3 Marilyn McCord Adams and Robert Merrihew Adams (eds), *The Problem of Evil*, Oxford: Oxford University Press, 1990, p. 25.

4 Ibid.

Mackie listed the beliefs which most Christians, and indeed members of other faiths, have:

P1 God exists and is omnipotent.
P2 God exists and is omnibenevolent.
P3 Evil exists.

This forms what David Hume called an 'inconsistent triad'[5] of beliefs.

Mackie noted that 'there seems to be some contradiction between these three propositions, so that if any two of them were true, the third would be false. But at the same time all three are essential parts of most theological positions'.[6]

He admitted that the contradiction is not necessary unless additional premises or assumptions are added – such as that a good thing always eliminates evil so far as it can – but Mackie contends that it is still a big enough problem for believers to make it difficult for them to *consistently* uphold P1 + P2 + P3, though doing so is essential.

Mackie reviewed possible solutions to the problem of evil, but found them all lacking, concluding that 'of the proposed solutions of the problem of evil . . . none has stood up to criticism'.[7] While either dropping one of the propositions by denying the existence of evil, denying God's omnipotence or omnibenevolence, or reducing the content of those concepts by means of a redefinition of terms would provide an adequate solution to the problem, it would also have major consequences for other aspects of belief.

For example, if a believer is willing to say that God's power is limited in respect of addressing evil, how could he or she still use the teleological argument for God's existence, which supposes the need for an all-powerful designer?

Mackie is particularly scathing about the tendency for believers to be inconsistent, saying 'often enough these adequate solutions are

---

5 *Dialogues Concerning Natural Religion*, ed. by H. D. Aiken, New York: Oxford University Press, 1955, p. 66.
6 Ibid.
7 Ibid., p. 36.

only *almost* adopted . . .'.[8] He notes how believers may accept God's limitation or the non-existence of evil only when confronted with the problem of evil, only to revert to a more traditional position in other matters. Also how believers can redefine their terms to such an extent that although they *appear* to have an acceptable theological position and be holding P1 + P2 + P3, in fact their position is far from clear and probably unacceptable to fellow believers, were it widely realized. For these reasons, he labels many attempts at resolving the problem of evil *almost adequate* or *fallacious*.

For Mackie, the problem of evil also serves to highlight the limitation of religious language as well as inconsistency and confusion surrounding believers' concept of God. If people believe that God is omnipotent, what can they possibly mean by that?

- If God is eternal but in time, watching events as they unfold, then there must be a question over whether God could act to change past events or whether God could know what happens in the future.
- On the other hand, if God is outside time and space and creation exists wholly and simply from God's perspective, then to what extent could God act directly in time or know how things seem from the perspective of beings within time and space?

Mackie wrote:

> God's omnipotence must in any case be restricted in one way or another, that unqualified omnipotence cannot be ascribed to any being that continues through time. And if God and his actions are not in time, can omnipotence, or power of any sort, be meaningfully ascribed to him?[9]

If God's omnipotence cannot mean that God could act to prevent what seems to be evil, then the 'inconsistent triad' becomes stable,

---

8  Ibid., p. 26.
9  Ibid., p. 37.

but at the price of removing a large part of what makes God worthy of worship and the basis of saying 'and this is what everybody means by God' at the end of classical arguments for God's existence.

- Is it worth praying to a God who could not hear you and could not do anything to help if God could?
- Can miracles be ascribed to a being who cannot act directly in time? If miracles are pre-programmed into creation from the beginning, or brought about by angelic beings, is that really the same as the position most believers wish to maintain?
- What can heaven or life after death really mean if God is wholly simple, outside time and space? If human beings become time-less to be with God, then no sense of personal identity could remain.
- Is the *de re* necessary Prime Mover of the universe limited? If God is no more than a quantum blip, that can both exist and not exist simultaneously and act without cause, then can this be the same as the God of Abraham?
- Can the divine designer be constrained by the time and space that God himself created?

Mackie's criticism of traditional theodicies, attempts to defend God against charges of creating or allowing evil, is worth serious consideration.

To summarize Mackie's analysis, there are four possible approaches to theodicy:

1 Deny P1 or P2 – or redefine the attributes of God.
2 Deny or redefine P3, evil.
3 Provide a P4, a 'morally sufficient reason' for a perfect God to have created and/or allowed evil.
4 Demonstrate that P1 + P2 + P3 is not actually irrational!

Serious thinkers attempt all possible strategies, though most efforts focus on 3, providing a morally sufficient reason for a perfect God to have allowed evil.

## Augustine

Augustine (354–430) argued that evil has no positive existence – it is *privatio boni*, a lack of good which causes suffering just as a lack of health causes illness and a lack of wealth causes poverty. God cannot be accused of creating evil if it does not actually exist. God merely allows evil – and because a world containing it is better than one without.[10]

For Augustine, evil is necessary for free will. If God forced everything to operate according to God's will and to be good, there would be no evil – but then there would also be no possibility of freedom or moral good. Moral goodness, the goodness which is freely chosen, is much better than automatic goodness. Companies reward the conscientious waiter and not the electronic ordering system with an 'employee of the month' award, precisely because the waiter is free to act in other ways. In order to make moral goodness possible, God allows the possibility of things falling short of God's plan.

That people choose to misuse their free will is their fault and not God's. Nothing forces people to go against the natural order and cause innocent suffering in the process – yet this misuse happened corporately at the beginning of time, at the fall from grace in the Garden of Eden, and happens again and again, hour by hour throughout the lives of almost every individual.

For Augustine, God's goodness has to include justice. A good God cannot allow sin, the misuse of freewill to fall short of what we are capable, to go unpunished. Without punishment for sin, there would be no incentive to do good and indeed no real way to know what is good. What sort of God would allow freedom for the sake of moral goodness and not teach us how we should use it to achieve that end?

God's justice requires God to punish human beings for falling short. According to Augustine, as a race we fell short at the fall; we were all 'seminally present' in Adam and participated in his betrayal. Consequently all humans are punished through inherited

---

*original sin* – through mortality, hard work, fear, responsibility and pain in childbirth (Genesis 2–3), but most through distance from God. Nevertheless, Christian baptism provides us with a way back, redeeming us from original sin and making it possible to enter into God's kingdom through a life of faith and good works. Humans are individually punished for sin as well, either in this life or the next.

Augustine considered whether a perfect God might have been better not to create anything if the best possible creation must contain evil and suffering. Drawing on Plato's *Timaeus*, Augustine argued that the world is perfect because it contains diversity and that without infinite variety God's infinite creativity could not be expressed. This is known as Augustine's Principle of Plenitude.

Why God would allow the suffering of animals was difficult for Augustine to explain. He held that neither have the freedom that would allow sin and make their punishment just. Augustine argues that the suffering of plants and animals is *illusory*, it occurs to teach humans by the mercy of God.

- It is better that one should learn not to be violent from the yelping of a puppy than from the screams of another person.
- It is better that one should learn the value of dignity and fortitude in dying from autumn leaves than from repeated familial exposure to terminal illness.

All real natural evil, Augustine maintains, results from the world falling short of its original perfect state due to the disobedience of Adam and Eve.

One of the difficulties that arose from Augustine's theodicy caused him to argue with Pelagius (354–440), a British monk. According to Augustine, doing good works was never going to be enough to achieve salvation; without baptism, without God's grace enabling us to be released from original sin, we would all be justly damned. Pelagius argued that this encouraged people to think that taking part in religious rituals would take away any need for them to consider their behaviour and was contrary to the gospel message of Jesus. Nevertheless, like so many reformers who tried to return Christianity to the gospel message, Pelagius was declared a heretic at the Council of Carthage in 418. Strangely, institutional churches tend to not like the idea that people could earn salvation simply by doing what is right!

## Thomas Aquinas

Thomas Aquinas built on the work of Augustine, but his theodicy emerges from his wider system.[11] As we have previously seen, his arguments for the existence of God established that the Thomist God is a *de-re necessary* being, who is 'neither something nor nothing'. As such, God is placed at a distance from the universe that God created and is seen as intrinsically *other* – while God is necessary, creation is contingent, while God is perfectly unlimited, creation is limited.

Like Augustine, Aquinas started by arguing that evil has no positive existence and cannot be caused directly by God. For Aquinas, as for Aristotle, goodness is determined in relation to an object fulfilling its nature. It follows that evil is only possible for things which exist in time and space, things which have contingent existence rather than necessary existence. To fall short of one's nature implies time and space in which to do so; a wholly simple, unchanging God cannot fall short of what it is to be God. Necessary existence precludes change and therefore precludes evil. God cannot, therefore, as a matter of logic ever be described as evil, since God cannot fall short of what it is to be God.

Nevertheless, there is no doubt that evil causes horrendous suffering. Aquinas seeks to provide a 'morally sufficient reason' for God to allow evil and its consequences in creation. Like Augustine, Aquinas starts by arguing that a world containing evil is better than one without. Aquinas wrote:

The good of the whole is of more account than the good of the part. Therefore it belongs to the prudent governor to overlook the lack of goodness in a part that there may be an increase of goodness

---

11 Recommended reading: Brian Davies, *Aquinas*, London: Continuum, 2002.

in the whole. Thus the builder hides the foundation of the house underground, that the house may stand firm. Now if evil was taken away from certain parts of the universe, the perfection of the whole universe would be much diminished, since its beauty results from the ordered unity of good and evil things. Seeing that evil arises from a failure of good, and yet certain goods are occasioned from those very evils through the providence of the governor, even as the silent pause gives sweetness to the chant. Therefore evil should not be excluded from things by the divine providence.[12]

Like Augustine, Aquinas argued that variety in creation is necessary as it reflects God's infinite majesty. Though the material of contingent creation is necessarily limited, through God's genius the limitations of individual forms is overcome. He wrote:

The distinctiveness and plurality of things is because the first agent, who is God, intended them. For he brought things into existence so that his goodness might be communicated to creatures and re-enacted through them. And because one single creature was not enough, he produced many and diverse, so that what was wanting in one expression of the divine goodness might be supplied by another, for goodness, which in God is single and all together, is in creatures multiple and scattered.[13]

Aquinas differed from Augustine, who argued that all genuine natural evils are just punishments for general or specific misuse of free will. For Aquinas, earthquakes are part of God's design and are good because they do what they are meant to do (releasing tectonic pressure) and enable the world to do what it is supposed to do (to sustain life).

Aquinas had the option of defining evil as a necessary part of creation. It is not possible for God to do the actually impossible, such as by creating a universe that is not contingent. God would

---

12  *Summa Contra Gentiles* LXXI.
13  *Summa Theologica* 1a, 47, 1 (8/95).

have a perfect excuse for allowing evil, provided that creation with all its flaws is better than no creation at all, but Aquinas worried that we are not in a position to *know* whether this is the best possible world, whether a world without evil would have been better or worse. Swinburne agrees, arguing that it does not make sense to argue that there are greater goods that justify the presence of evil in the world, unless we have experience of them, which is impossible.[14] Aquinas concluded that '[t]his world could not be better arranged, but there could be a better world, different from this one'.[15]

For Aquinas, as Brian Davies O. P. explains, 'God makes the best possible this-world, but not the best possible world'.[16] Remember, God is under no moral obligation as God is not a moral agent – this universe perfectly fulfils its nature and is rightly therefore called perfectly good. Aquinas seriously considered the question of whether God would have been better to create no world than this world. Gerard Hughes S. J. wrote:

Plainly all evils could have been avoided had God decided to create nothing at all. And all the evils of this world could have been avoided had God created a quite different world . . . But whether such a state of affairs, in which God alone existed, or in which no moral beings other than God existed, would be overall better than the present state of affairs is just the question I think cannot confidently be answered.[17]

Certainly this world contains evil; whether a better world could have been created without these evils we simply cannot know. Hughes concludes his discussions of the problem of whether this is the best possible world with a dilemma:

---

14 'Evil, the problem of', in Ted Honderich (ed.), *The Oxford Companion to Philosophy*, Oxford: Oxford University Press, 2005.

15 *Summa Theologica* 1a, 25, 6 rep.3.

16 Brian Davies, *The Thought of Thomas Aquinas*, Oxford: Oxford University Press, 1992, p. 148.

17 *The Nature of God*, London: Routledge, 1995, p. 176.

1  Either we can imagine a better version of this world, but without much confidence that what we imagine would be causally possible;

2  or we can suppose that a radically different creation might be causally possible, but we would then have no way of knowing whether it would be better or worse than the present one, since it would be beyond our power to describe it.[18]

Hughes concludes that we lack any perspective from which we are able to judge whether this is, on the whole, a good universe – still less can we judge whether this is the best possible universe. Too often human beings look at the world from their own narrow perspective.

- The rabbit who narrowly escapes being eaten might well see the fox as evil – but, if it was a philosophic rabbit, it could appreciate that the fox was just trying to fulfil its nature, providing food for itself and its cubs, and that in doing so the fox was actually good.
- The man dying of AIDS could bemoan the evil of the world and question the existence of a God who could allow such suffering – or he could marvel at the efficiency of the HIV virus and appreciate that all forms of life are necessarily finite, varied and revelatory of the majesty of God.

However philosophical we try to be, we cannot see the world from a God's-eye view or understand the mind of God. We cannot realistically analyse or weigh up the qualities of possible-worlds. While this might seem like 'playing the mystery card' and fail to satisfy critics, it stems from the reality of the human condition and is probably more rational than supposing that man can be the measure of all things.

In the end, the limits of our contingent existence place such a strain on language and conceptualization, that what it might mean for a wholly simple, timeless God to create anything is baffling. Aquinas' theodicy ends up relying on his doctrine of analogy – and analogy

---

18  Ibid., pp. 173 and 176–83.

places a necessary distance between human beings and God, invalidating any literal reading of scripture or tradition and emphasizing God's otherness and inscrutability.

Aquinas can truthfully say that God is omnipotent, omniscient and omnibenevolent – but only if the *meaning* of each term is carefully delineated. God's power and knowledge are limited to the actually possible and his goodness simply lies in being God. God cannot create anything but the best possible world containing evil.

## Interim Summary

Both the Augustinian and the Thomist theodicies are sophisticated and multi-layered. They both approach the problem of evil by:

- denying P1 or P2, redefining God's attributes;
- denying P3, the positive existence of evil;
- providing a P4, a 'morally sufficient reason' for a perfect God to have allowed evil;
- ultimately, demonstrating that P1 + P2 + P3 is not irrational.

Yet, in the end, neither approach is very pastorally satisfying.

- Can one respond to the victims of the Japanese tsunami by saying that it was a just punishment from God?
- Can one comfort the parents of a still-born baby by saying that God, in his justice, will punish their infant for the sins of Adam by keeping it out of heaven?
- Can an omniscient God who creates freedom really not be responsible for its inevitable consequences?
- Is the evil which inspired the Final Solution really analogous to the pauses in Gregorian plainchant as Aquinas indicated?
- Is a God whose nature prevents God from creating a better world, and from understanding or caring about people who experience the worst of this one, really worthy of worship?

Despite what may be seen as the pastoral shortcomings of the traditional best-possible-worlds theodicies of Augustine and Aquinas, Leibniz (1646–1716) saw this approach as the most philosophically sound, writing:

> Now as there is an infinite number of possible universes in the ideas of God, and as only one can exist, there must be a sufficient reason for God's choice . . . And this reason can only be found in the fitness, or in the degrees of perfection, which those worlds contain, each world having the right to claim existence in proportion to the perfection which it involves. And it is this which causes the existence of the best, which God knows through his wisdom, chooses through his goodness, and produces through his power . . .[19]

He was roundly mocked for asserting the goodness of creation in the face of overwhelming evidence.[20] In 1755, an enormous earthquake struck Lisbon and underlined the dangers of this sort of argument for philosophers' reputations. Saying that this is the best possible world, as bodies were being recovered from wrecked homes, seemed in poor taste!

Despite the dangers, the puzzle of reconciling God's perfection with the apparent limitations of God's creation retains its fascination today, though scholars tend to reserve such discussions to academic papers rather than explaining the issues in sermons.

## Is this REALLY the Best Possible World?

Robert Adams, Alvin Plantinga and Richard Swinburne all reject the idea that there is such a thing as a 'best of all possible worlds'. Swinburne claims that if there is going to be a world, there is no reason to suppose that a world with one more or less individuals would be less good. Like Aquinas, Swinburne tries to see the world from

---

19  Leibniz, *Monadology* (1714), 53, 54, 55.

20  In 1759 Voltaire caricatured Leibniz as the character Dr Pangloss in his hit play *Candide*.

God's perspective and broadly considers a good world as one which fulfils God's intentions.

Swinburne warns against drawing either of two false conclusions. First, it would be wrong to say that God would not create any world, even a less good one. Aquinas suggested that God's goodness effectively forced him to create worlds which fulfil God's purpose, although he acknowledged that God could have created a variety of worlds with different purposes. Leibniz went further, arguing that if there were not a best-possible-world God would not create any world, that God is constrained to create only the best. Whereas, for Swinburne, God would have reason to create a world but no overriding reason to create this world. Chris and Mary have a reason to buy a house within commuting distance of Cambridge, that is close to where Mary works in London – and which does not cost too much. This does not mean that there is *one* such house that they must buy – there may be many alternatives which fit these descriptions.

Second, for Swinburne, it is false to say that God *might create any world*. God might have reason not to create worlds in which there is excessive innocent suffering. There might not be any house at all which fits Chris and Mary's requirements and, after years of searching, they might decide not to buy at all rather than compromise.

It follows that God has reason to create a world or worlds of a broad type or group that fulfils God's intentions – and might have reason not to create a world or worlds of a type or group that would not fulfil God's intentions, such as a world which contains excessive innocent suffering. Swinburne considered that there are four possible-world groups:

1 Group 1 contains a limited number of immortal free beings who can improve the world to a limited extent before it is perfect.
2 Group 2 contains a limited number of immortal free beings who can improve the world to an unlimited extent.
3 Group 3 contains an unlimited number of immortal free beings who can reproduce and improve the world to an unlimited extent.
4 Group 4 contains an unlimited number of mortal free beings who can reproduce and improve the world to an unlimited extent.

First, Swinburne argued that human freedom is an obvious condition of the best-possible-world and that part of this is the ability to make unlimited improvements to our world. Further, Swinburne claims that reproduction adds to people's ability to enjoy and perfect the world – without having children, we would be constrained in expressing our creativity, love and joy in humanity just as God might be constrained, if he had never created a world. It follows that God has reason to create a world of Groups 3 or 4, not Groups 1 or 2.

Swinburne went on to argue that God would have reason to create a world falling into Group 4, but *not* a world in Group 3. A world with death in it is better than one without, because death has advantages, beyond the obvious lack of space if the human population eternally expanded. For examples:

- The old will die; young people need a chance, otherwise the old will dominate.
- It limits the amount of suffering humans have to undergo.
- It allows for the possibility of the ultimate self-sacrifice.
- It means that God trusts human beings, even to inflict ultimate harm.
- By limiting life, it concentrates our attention on life.
- We learn from the presence of death.

Swinburne rejects a world where there is less suffering as a demand for a 'toy-world' where nothing matters very much. He sees this world as a 'do-it-yourself kit world', which humans can perfect over a long period of time and where we can learn from our mistakes; what appears to us as evil can be occasions for us human beings to develop higher-level virtues. He sees this world, which contains death and innocent suffering, as better than the alternative possible-world types – and better than no world at all.[21]

Peter Vardy previously attacked Swinburne, saying that this is 'an obscene position'. His reaction was shared by the audience at a public debate in which Swinburne suggested that the world containing the Holocaust might be better than one without, because the

---

21 Swinburne discusses these ideas in several different books and articles. To start with, try *Is There a God?*, Oxford: Oxford University Press, 1996.

death camps gave Jews the opportunity to develop virtues such as courage.[22] Richard Dawkins, who was also on the panel, later discussed Swinburne's contribution in *The God Delusion*, referring to it as 'Swinburne's grotesque piece of reasoning' and saying that it is 'damningly typical of the theological mind', a mind which Dawkins argues is callous and out of touch to the point of being immoral.

Swinburne sees human freedom as a precondition of a best-possible-world and sees reproduction and death as necessary means of actualizing that freedom. Without having children, people would be constrained, and without death, limitations would be placed on life. Another critic, Vincent Cosculluela,[23] observed that there are many free choices that people do not have. He asks why God does not trust us and give us the choice over whether or not to surrender our immortality – the old could choose to make way for the young, or people could choose to lay down their life for others. Wouldn't this be a greater sacrifice than a mortal merely accepting death?

Cosculluela also maintains that death undermines justice – it provides a means of escaping one's own failures (for example through suicide) and otherwise means that people are often not brought to justice in this world. For examples, both Fred West and Harold Shipman (who were both obscene killers) committed suicide in prison, and Jimmy Savile died before his abuse of underage girls was uncovered. In a world where humans are immortal there would be no escaping the consequences of one's actions. A world without death would actually be a better world, a world where God trusted human agents more, than a world with death. He argues, therefore, that Swinburne's position is flawed.

Like Swinburne, Norman Kretzmann (1928–98) asked why God would create this world,[24] and like Aquinas, he denied that the main

---

22 http://www.telegraph.co.uk/culture/books/3655792/I-dont-believe-in-Richard-Dawkins.html.

23 Vincent Cosculluela, 'Death and God: The Case of Richard Swinburne', *Religious Studies* 33:3 (1997), pp. 292–302.

24 Norman Kretzmann, 'A Particular Problem of Creation: Why Would God Create This World?', in Scott MacDonald (ed.), *Being and Goodness: The Concept of the Good in Metaphysics and Philosophical Theology*, New York: Cornell University Press, 1991, pp. 229–49.

objective of the universe is to make things easy for human beings. He wrote that 'the degree of perfection in a world depends on the degree to which God's goodness is manifested in it, the degree to which it fully represents God . . . In creating, God undertakes to represent simple, eternal, perfect goodness in a composite, temporal, necessarily imperfect medium . . .',[25] continuing '. . . considered as a representation of God [this world] is as good as possible in the sense that any world better than this one in terms of improved precision of representation would be no better at all in its capacity to represent God to any possible created percipient.'[26] Kretzmann parts company from Aquinas, who denied the idea that God had to create, when he argued that there is a necessity about God's creative act. Unconvinced by the idea that a God who could have not-created would have been better to create this world, Kretzmann quotes the Dionysian Principle: 'Goodness is essentially diffusive of itself . . . The Divine Love did not permit him to remain in himself . . .'.[27]

For Kretzmann, there is a need to create beings who can freely respond to love in relationship; God needs to create human beings in order to fulfil his loving nature. God creates the best possible world with respect to the need to fulfil God's nature and with respect to the necessarily contingent, limited nature of any created thing. The best-possible-world must exist and must include creatures who love, creatures who are finite and mortal, creatures like us. The price, of course, is the possibility of evil and suffering.

Kretzmann's position is reminiscent of, but not quite the same as, that of St Bonaventure. Paul Rout of Heythrop College, University of London, holds that Bonaventure does indeed maintain that goodness and love must be expressed (self-diffusive), but for Bonaventure, God's goodness and love are fully and perfectly expressed in the active relationships between the persons of the Trinity. God, therefore, does not need to create human beings in order to express God's loving nature.

---

25  Ibid., pp. 236–7
26  Ibid., p. 238.
27  Ibid., p. 245.

## A Good God?

Beyond the detail of whether this world is the best, some scholars ask whether God has a moral obligation to create the best possible world at all.

This raises the issue as to whether there is any independent standard of morality against which God can be judged.[28] If there is no such standard, then God is not a moral agent and cannot be subjected to moral praise or blame. Further, if God is wholly simple and cannot change, then the idea that God is free enough to be held morally accountable seems tricky. Remember, when Aquinas held that God was *perfectly good*, he did not mean this in a moral sense.

For Robert Adams (b. 1937), although God could, in principle, be judged morally – suggesting that God is in time and that independent standards exist – God cannot wrong non-existents.[29] God cannot wrong beings who don't and never existed just by not actualizing them. It follows that:

- God does not wrong unicorns or centaurs by not creating them.
- Nor does God wrong the moon-people by not creating them.
- Nor does a woman wrong the 15 children she might have had, if she had never used contraception.

Adams elaborated, using the more controversial example of a woman who takes a drug (*before* becoming pregnant) to have a handicapped baby. She would not have had a baby at all, if the baby was not handicapped. Adams argues that the baby is not wronged by the woman – the baby did not exist when the drug was taken and, what is more, would not have existed at all were it not for the woman's decision. God may well have created beings less free from suffering than they might otherwise have been so as to maximize their need of and love for God – God does not *wrong* anyone by doing this.

---

28  Cf. Peter and Charlotte Vardy, *Ethics Matters*, London: SCM Press, 2012.
29  'Must God Create the Best', *Philosophical Review* 81 (1972), pp. 317–32.

Similarly to Adams, Ian Narveson, in a discussion of the moral consequences of utilitarianism, maintains that there are no moral duties to non-existent persons and hence no duty to increase the total happiness of the human race. There is no duty to increase the number of happy persons but only a duty to increase the happiness of such persons as do exist.

Swinburne agreed, arguing that God would only wrong people if it were better for them not to exist at all than to exist as they do. Hence Swinburne maintained that God has no obligation to create the greatest number of happy beings nor does God wrong anyone by creating beings less perfect than they might have been. God is, therefore, under no obligation to create the best possible universe.

This could be challenged, however. Present generations might well have a responsibility to future generations as yet unborn with regard to the environment. If this is accepted, then it may well be held that we *do* have moral obligations to potentially existent people. If I smoke, drink or fail to eat enough folic acid, knowing that if I get pregnant the baby would be damaged by my behaviour, before I was even in a position to know and change my behaviour, I would be morally wrong. Similarly, if God even knew that God might create human beings, when God started creating the world, God might be held to be morally responsible, if God did not create a world which would limit future human suffering as much as was possible.

This discussion raises significant questions about the concept of God:

- Can God be judged morally – when this suggests the existence of divine freedom and independent standards of goodness? Aquinas would say that this is not possible.
- Can creation be seen to have occurred in time such as God's intentions and design might have developed and changed? What does this suggest for omniscience and omnipotence?
- If God has the freedom to adapt and decide to change God's creation, then does not a need to consider the welfare of possible future creations represent a constraint on present action, limiting God's omnipotence?

## Summary

The problem of evil can present itself as a logical puzzle. Scholars are challenged to reconcile the existence of evil with God's omnipotence and omnibenevolence. They may respond by denying or redefining evil, omnipotence or omnibenevolence, by providing a morally sufficient reason for God to allow evil, such as that this is the best possible world, or by denying that there is technically a problem at all. The developed theodicies of Augustine and Aquinas carefully incorporate all of the possible angles, yet their logical manoeuvrings seem to exacerbate rather than resolve the problem.

In the famous O. J. Simpson trial, expensive lawyers spent weeks developing every possible defence. They chose the jurors with care, questioned every last piece of evidence, grilled every witness, suggested every mitigating circumstance and ended by attacking police procedure and suggesting that the case was technically flawed. O. J. was acquitted, but he looked worse than he might have if he had admitted his guilt, and the whole US Justice system became a laughing stock.

There is a parallel here with the problem of evil. God is on trial for the crime of creating or allowing evil and suffering. Big-name lawyers such as Augustine and Aquinas (and their juniors Swinburne and Adams) produce the possible defences. However, even if they win, the case could be argued to be a Pyrrhic victory. God ends up looking distant and/or callous.

There is, however, a prior question which is not brought out in the literature and which Swinburne and Adams do not sufficiently address and which might, just, salvage the situation. If I ask 'Is this the best possible orange?', you would probably ask me what I mean by 'best'. Are judgements to be made in relation to colour, size, juiciness or longevity? The orange which looks best might not be the tastiest.

In asking 'Is this the best possible world?' people really should be clear about their criteria – 'Is this the best possible world with respect of maximizing human freedom?' or even 'Is this the best possible world with respect of demonstrating God's love and creativity?' The answer to each question is likely to be different.

Critics of best-possible-worlds theodicies assume that the question is 'Is this the best possible world with respect of minimizing human suffering?' This question is likely to elicit a negative response. Nobody who has toured the battlefields of the Second World War, visited Auschwitz or even watched the news could really accept that an omnipotent God could not do something to cut down on the horror. Nevertheless, it is worth at least considering that the question could be wrongly framed.

# 19

# Suffering

No statement, theological or otherwise, should be made that would not be credible in the presence of burning children.

(Victor Greenberg, Auschwitz survivor)[1]

St Augustine and St Thomas Aquinas agreed that evil is a lack of good and has no positive existence. It follows that nothing can be 100 per cent evil; something lacking all positive existence cannot exist. Even the devil, if he existed, even Hitler and Stalin have to be acknowledged to have some goodness in them just in terms of their existence.

This is not how some people experience evil. Throughout history people have been convinced that evil is a definite, malign force in the universe. Augustine spent his youth as a Manichean. Manichaeism was one of the larger gnostic religions in the declining Roman Empire. Based on the third-century writings of Mani, a Persian prophet, Manichaeism taught that the universe was locked in a battle between the forces of good and evil. Like in *Star Wars*, *Harry Potter* or novels like *1984*, followers saw themselves as the underdogs, representatives of the light, always resisting the encroaching darkness, whose ranks of evil forces threaten to crush freedom, love, beauty – indeed the individual.

There is a broad similarity between this sort of popular cosmic dualism and some forms of Christianity, Judaism and Islam. Jesus' teachings about the end of time set the disciples up as facing overwhelming odds, triumphing over adversity through faithfulness. From the third century BCE, Jewish sects in Qumran expected the end of time and saw themselves as a tiny group of enlightened pure

---

1 'Cloud of Smoke, Pillar of Fire?', in Eva Fleischner (ed.), *Auschwitz: Beginning of a New Era?: Reflections on the Holocaust*, New York: Ktav Publishing, 1977, p. 23.

souls preparing to fight and achieve salvation. Muslim writings see the Ummah, the brotherhood of Islam, standing up for goodness and hoping for eternal salvation in the face of corruption.

For many people, therefore, evil is far more than a metaphysical absence – it is a real, positive threat which sometimes engulfs individuals or even whole societies.

Peter Vardy has written about the problem of *institutional evil*, whereby people are caught up in a corrupt system and seem to lose their perspective and their freedom to question what is going on. Arguably this is more of a problem and causes more suffering than individual acts of evil. There seems to be much more than absence of good when greed and hate take hold and become embedded in society. Did the Final Solution arise out of a lack of understanding, a lack of virtues on the part of Hitler, Himmler, Eichmann – and the many thousands of subordinates who carried out their ideas – or was there something diabolical at work?

Philosophers tend to avoid discussions of the problem of positive evil. The God of the philosophers, being omnipotent, is difficult to reconcile with the existence of any real opponent. The devil in Christian and Islamic thought is a dependent, created being – not something with an existence independent of God. Discussions of the reality of evil in people's lives tend to be couched in terms of suffering and the real effects of evil.

Some philosophers respond to the problem of suffering by developing morally sufficient reasons for God to create or allow evil.

## Irenaeus and John Hick

Irenaeus (130–202) argued that humans are made *in the image* of God in the same way that a small child is made in the image of its parents.[2] The child has potential to follow its parents' example and become *like* them, but as yet much of this potential is unrealized.

---

2 Recommended reading: John Hick, *Evil and the God of Love*, London: Collins, 1966.

The parents may be wise and make sensible decisions about when to cross the road in order to reach the other side safely or when to stand up against personal temptation. The child on the other hand has all the potential to make equally good decisions but owing to its lack of experience and untried senses it is likely that, left alone, it will make a bad decision and be hurt. Evil and suffering are the inevitable results of the bad decisions human beings make – because we have not yet realized our potential to become *like unto God*.

Furthermore, as any parent knows, the only way to get children to learn and develop their abilities is to let them gain experience that is full, both positive and negative. In the role of the parent, God creates an environment which is ideal to test and stimulate humans by developing their abilities through a full range of experiences – both positive and negative. Thus the world is created with some natural evil to allow the possibility of humans learning from the experience of dealing with it.

Irenaeus never intended to tackle the classical problem of evil – he simply reflected on the problem of suffering in letters to friends affected by Roman persecutions. Yet this early, fragmentary approach is often seen to provide a more pastorally satisfying theodicy than the fully developed efforts of Augustine and Aquinas.

Irenaeus encouraged believers to put their experiences in context and not see them as obstacles to faith. He saw suffering as an opportunity for growth rather than as a purely negative experience. For Irenacus, something positive will come out of even the most desperate situation. What does not kill us makes us stronger – and what does kill us immediately brings us close to God in heaven.

Further, his suggestion that human beings grow into the likeness of God offers great hope that things will gradually improve. Humanity started off in a childlike state and, through making mistakes and learning from them, has developed. By this token we should expect that as humanity matures, fewer mistakes should be made (though in the adolescent stage these mistakes may become ever more serious) and humans should begin to enjoy a more harmonious adult relationship with their maker.

There are obvious philosophical objections to a theodicy based on Irenaeus' approach. Although God allowing – or even creating – suffering as a learning opportunity might be a morally sufficient defence, it seems rather extreme.

- What responsible parent would allow or create experiences such as incurable childhood cancer, the Rwandan massacres, the Oklahoma tornado or alzheimer's disease as a means of teaching children a lesson? Would such a God be omnibenevolent?
- How do we account for the gross inequality between people's experiences of suffering, including the afflicted lives of some for whom suffering is so extreme that they lose any possibility of growing or learning?
- Would an omnipotent and omniscient God not be able to come up with a better, more efficient means of helping human beings to fulfil their potential?

Despite these philosophical objections, the Protestant reformed epistemologist philosopher John Hick (1922–2012) used Irenaeus' writings as the basis for his own more developed theodicy.

- Like Irenaeus, Hick saw life as a test which gives us the opportunity to come into God's likeness, describing life as a *vale of soul-making*.
- Hick supposed that an *eschatological verification*, a levelling in the afterlife or at the end of time, will make up for the inequality between people's experiences of suffering and between the opportunities offered for growth, vindicating the fairness of God's creation and God's benevolence.

There is no way for God to preserve both freedom and growth without allowing the potential for suffering. Imagine you have a teenage daughter. You want to protect her from the 'dangers' of some boys. You decide to lock her up permanently in her room, which is comfortable, and you provide everything she could want (except internet access as this might also expose her to temptation). Would this be a good way of showing your care? If you really loved her, you have to trust her in the knowledge that she could make mistakes and get hurt.

- Hick argues that human beings are created at an *epistemic distance* from God – they cannot know God directly and are created imperfect with the potential to grow towards God. Like Swinburne, he argued that the virtues need to be hard won and cannot be ready made, even by an omnipotent being.

For Hick, God gave human beings freedom in the knowledge that this could be used either to draw closer to God or to move away. The world is evidentially ambiguous – created *etsi deus nondaretur*, as if there were no God. Equally it can be interpreted as the creative work of God or as the product of chance and scientific process. If God obviously existed, humans could not come to know and love God by free choice. Similarly, Peter Vardy has built on C. S. Lewis' example of King Cophetua in *The Problem of Pain*, suggesting that God cannot present himself directly to human beings, else their love for him will be forced and their freedom undermined.

Perhaps surprisingly for someone from an evangelical, Protestant background, Hick argues that everyone will eventually come into the presence of God, and this entails arguing that progress towards God can continue after death.

For both Irenaeus and Hick, instead of suffering being the regrettable side-effect of the best-possible-world, God might well deliberately create a world where suffering is bound to occur, in order that human beings can grow into the likeness of God.

Neither Hick nor Irenaeus offer very satisfactory explanations of animal suffering.

## Is this Adequate?

While Irenaeus, with or without Hick's developments, might provide a more pastorally satisfying response to the reality of evil and suffering than either Augustine or Aquinas, this approach still risks being shown as inadequate in the face of extreme affliction.

Dostoevsky in his novel *The Brothers Karamazov* sets out a very powerful attack against the possibility of God being omnipotent, omnibenevolent and worthy of worship, through his character Ivan Karamazov.

Ivan and Alyosha are two brothers – Alyosha is a gentle and holy young monk, while Ivan is a worldly-wise young man returning home from the big city. The two brothers have been apart for some time and they get reacquainted. Ivan accepts that God exists, but he rejects God because of the suffering of innocent children. He gives various horrific examples taken from stories in Russian newspapers at the time:

1 A five-year-old girl wets her bed so her mother, in anger, strips her naked, covers her with her own excrement and then locks her outside all night in the privy, where she beats with her tiny fists on the door praying to her 'dear kind God'.

2 A young boy throws a stone and injures one of the legs of the local lord's dogs. The lord notices, has the boy and his parents called to him and sets the boy off running across the fields. He then sets his hounds on him, and they tear the boy to pieces in front of the parents.

3 The Turks invaded southern Russia, and their soldiers took pleasure in getting babies to smile. They would then pick them up, throw them in the air and shoot their eyes out with their pistols – the fun was doing it in front of the babies' mothers.

We can think of similar examples from the recent past, such as children under five being thrown alive into the lime pits of Belsen, before the dead bodies of adults were thrown in on top of them; arms and legs of young children cut off by neighbours in Rwanda, children being gassed in Syria, and many others. Ivan says to Alyosha that *nothing* is worth the suffering of innocent children. Adults have 'eaten the apple', they must take responsibility for their own lives, but 'what have the children to do with it'?[3]

---

3 Fyodor Dostoevsky, *The Brothers Karamazov*, London: Vintage, 1992, p. 286.

Ivan rejects God, even though he accepts that God exists.

Ivan rebels against God, saying that nothing can be worth the price of innocent suffering, and if, therefore, it was necessary for God to have created a world in which suffering took place, then the price was simply too high. Far from creation being good, Ivan maintains, it is fundamentally flawed. He 'returns his ticket' and refuses to play God's game. God created the world. He must take responsibility for what human beings do with their free decisions.

Nevertheless, after Ivan attacked God in the name of humanity, human beings killed more than 70 million of their own during the twentieth century. Ivan judged and condemned God as unjust; he appealed to a standard of justice higher than God and assumed that he, a man, could judge God against it. After Ivan, man replaced God as the highest arbiter of what is right, man became the measure of all things – and this seems to have led indirectly to the Holocaust.

In another story told by Ivan, that of *The Grand Inquisitor*, Ivan maintains that human beings cannot cope with the gift of freedom. Very few can really exercise the high degree of freedom that Jesus assumed, most are simply too weak. The Church deceives people by 'lovingly lightening their burdens' – and does so in the service of Satan, not of God. This rests on the view that Jesus' call is an incredibly demanding one, and few will be prepared to take it seriously and to follow it; most will refuse the call and will settle for lives of comfort and convention instead.

Dostoevsky, therefore, lays down two immensely powerful challenges against religious belief – first that nothing is worth the suffering of innocent children; and second, that the demands of real faith are simply too great for all except a tiny minority.

## Does God Suffer?

The Protestant writer Jürgen Moltmann (b. 1926) attempts a theological response to suffering through the figure of Jesus. He rejects natural theology as traditionally practised and maintains that the only way past the protest of atheism is through a theology of the cross – the suffering God who, on the cross, can cry out 'My God, my God, why have you forsaken me?' He writes: 'In this theology, God and suffering are no longer contradictions, as in theism and atheism, but God's being is in the suffering, and suffering is in God's being itself, because God is love.'[4]

The theology of the cross stems from St Paul, but was developed further by Luther in the Heidelberg Disputation of 1518. Moltmann maintains that on the cross Jesus overcomes suffering:

> suffering is overcome by suffering, and wounds are healed by wounds. For the suffering in suffering is the lack of love, and the wounds in wounds are the abandonment, and the powerlessness in pain is unbelief. And therefore the suffering of abandonment is overcome by the suffering of love, which is not afraid of what is sick and ugly, but accepts it and takes it to itself in order to heal it. Through his own abandonment by God, the crucified Christ brings God to those who are abandoned by God. Through his suffering he brings salvation to those who suffer . . .[5]

The God who is responsible for suffering is also the God who suffers. God's power is shown in love and in weakness when God dies on the cross identifying with all those who suffer.

This answer, however, would not satisfy Ivan. An omniscient God knew that suffering would occur, an omnipotent God could have created without it, or else not created at all. God must be limited in power or God must be uncaring; either way, God is not worthy of worship.

God suffering alongside the sufferers does not take away the suffering or make up for the fact that God failed either to predict problems and not create a better world.

Imagine that a geography teacher organizes a school trip down an old mine. While the class is at the bottom of the shaft, it begins to rain. The tunnel collapses, and the group is trapped in the dark and

---

4  *The Crucified God*, London: SCM Press, 1974, p. 227.
5  Ibid., p. 46.

cold and with slowly rising water. Some of them are badly injured, crying for their mothers. They are all facing horrific deaths. Does the fact that the teacher is in the mine, suffering alongside the innocent victims of her planning, make a lot of difference to the situation? Would she seem worthy of praise and promotion, given that she failed to expect danger in an old mine-shaft and caused a disaster by ploughing on with the trip, regardless of the likely problems? Moltmann's proposed solution to the problem of evil fails to engage with the reality of Ivan Karamazov's challenge.

## Before the Lime-pits . . .

Elie Wiesel, the Holocaust survivor, provides an account of the Holocaust. In his book *Night* are found far worse accounts of suffering than those cited by Ivan Karamazov. For Wiesel, like Ivan, it is the suffering of children that leads him to abandon belief in God.

> Never shall I forget that night, the first night in camp, which has turned my life into one long night, seven times cursed and seven times sealed. Never shall I forget that smoke. Never shall I forget the little faces of the children, whose bodies turned into wreaths of smoke beneath a silent blue sky. Never shall I forget those flames which consumed my faith for ever. Never shall I forget that nocturnal silence which deprived me, for all eternity, of the desire to live. Never shall I forget those moments which murdered my God and my soul and turned my dreams into dust. Never shall I forget these things, even if I am condemned to live as long as God Himself. Never.[6]

Wiesel echoes Ivan's words in a conversation with his father, the first time he saw a lorry-load of dead babies being consigned to the incinerator. 'I could not believe that they could burn people of our age, that humanity would never tolerate it.'

---

6  Elie Wiesel, *Night*, London: Penguin, 2006, Chapter 3.

His father replies: 'Humanity? Humanity is not concerned with us. Today anything is allowed.'[7]

At the Nuremberg trials, a Polish guard described how children were thrown straight into the furnaces without first being gassed. He said: 'They threw them in alive. Their screams could be heard at the camp. We don't know whether they wanted to economize on gas, or if it was because there was not enough room in the gas chambers.'[8] In 2004 Kenneth Surin maintained that no theodicy can meet this test. Any attempted justification of God in the face of this reality is a blasphemy – we must just be silent.[9]

Perhaps attempts to rationalize faith and to understand God's reasons for creating as God did and to defend God are misplaced. Perhaps we lack the perspective to be able to judge God and God's creation, and perhaps all our philosophy is based on arrogance and a misplaced belief that man can be the measure of all things. Yet, if we give up, there are significant consequences.

First, accepting human limitations and resigning ourselves to the impossibility of understanding the mind of God pushes faith towards fideism, being disengaged with reason. It opens people to accepting many other things which do not make sense. Faith might then become, as Dawkins says, anti-intellectual to the point of being dangerous.

Professor Nelson Pike (1930–2010) observed that 'when the existence of God is accepted prior to any rational consideration of the status of evil in the world, the traditional problem of evil reduces to a noncrucial perplexity of relatively minor importance'.[10]

This is certainly how evil is being treated by modern reformed epistemologists. Plantinga seems to ignore the lime-pits while writing

---

7  Ibid., p. 48.

8  Quoted in Fleischner, 'Cloud of Smoke, Pillar of Fire?', p. 9.

9  *Theology and the Problem of Evil*, Eugene, OR: Wipf & Stock Publishers, 2004.

10  Nelson Pike, 'Hume on Evil', in Marilyn McCord Adams and Robert Merrihew Adams (eds), *The Problem of Evil*, Oxford: Oxford University Press, 1990, p. 52.

clever technical articles which aim to invalidate J. L. Mackie's claim that faith is 'irrational'.

The philosophy of religion is neither totally irrelevant nor just a game for clever people. Never forget that evil is not just a puzzle, that what we are discussing is reality itself and that everything we think or say matters absolutely.

Second, giving up our sense that absolute values exist and/or that we can know what they are invalidates faith. What is the point in believing in God unless that belief inspires us to make the world better, not just to achieve a reward for ourselves? In *Mere Christianity*, C. S. Lewis (1898–1963) wrote:

> My argument against God was that the universe seemed so cruel and unjust. But how had I got this idea of just and unjust? A man does not call a line crooked unless he has some idea of a straight line. What was I comparing this universe with when I called it unjust? . . . Of course I could have given up my idea of justice by saying it was nothing but a private idea of my own. But if I did that, then my argument against God collapsed too, for the argument depended on saying the world was really unjust, not simply that it did not happen to please my fancies.[11]

Is justice just a private idea? Once we accept this position then there really is no point in life except to enjoy ourselves for the short time we are alive. The fact that we see order and value in the world is a major reason for belief, and without the belief that these are real we are left in water-world. Grahame Greene wrote in *Brighton Rock*: 'You cannot conceive, nor can I, of the appalling strangeness of the mercy of God.' This is appealing, but it is also playing the mystery card and refusing to engage with reason and philosophy. Also, God can then be accused of being just an arbitrary tyrant-deity like Baal, Marduk or Zeus. Faith needs to question itself and to respond to challenges – otherwise it will become increasingly irrelevant.

---

11  C. S. Lewis, *Mere Christianity*, New York: Touchstone, 1980, pp. 45–6.

*Summary*

As one stands by the lime-pits in Auschwitz or Treblinka, one has to make a decision as a human being as to where one stands. It may be that at this point philosophy and theology fall silent – certainly they stop having answers, though that does not mean they lack meaning and importance.

After the Holocaust, nobody can be ignorant of or ignore the reality of evil and suffering. Those who make crass suggestions about divine justification no longer seem funny like Dr Pangloss, they seem dangerous and immoral.

W. K. Clifford wrote:

If a man, holding a belief which he was taught in childhood or persuaded of afterwards, keeps down and pushes away any doubts which arise about it in his mind, purposely avoids the reading of books and the company of men that call into question or discuss it, and regards as impious those questions which cannot easily be asked without disturbing it, the life of that man is one long sin against mankind.[12]

Philosophy and theology must, for once and for all, renounce the charge of being an academic game. What we are doing in this subject is *not* discussing a 'noncrucial perplexity of relatively minor importance'. We are, or should be, trying to come to grips with truth and reality itself. Traditional theodicies can seem to demonstrate that scholars have lost their way.

---

12  W. K. Clifford, 'The Ethics of Belief', http://www.infidels.org/library/historical/w_k_clifford/ethics_of_belief.html.

# 20

# Life After Death

Belief in a life after death is central to most religions.

- Given that good people rarely get their reward and bad people frequently prosper in this life, without an afterlife there would be no way of defending God's goodness and justice, and the problems of evil and suffering would be an insurmountable obstacle to faith.
- Further, that God can raise people to an eternal life is a final demonstration of God's power. If there is no hereafter, despite millennia of revelations to the contrary, would any God who did exist be worthy of worship?

Nevertheless, the reality of a life after death is impossible to prove and seems ridiculous to many scientists and atheists. As previously discussed, near-death experiences can often be explained physiologically in terms of oxygen deprivation in the brain or similar. Beliefs in or about what happens after death can seem like groundless speculation to many outside of faith communities. They give fuel to the suggestion that faith is just wish-fulfilment or living in denial about the realities of the human condition.

In addition, different religious groups have had different concepts of life after death at different times – and none is without its problems in terms of ensuring justice and demonstrating God's power.

The early Hebrews seem to have had little concept of either individual physical resurrection or an individual spiritual existence after death. For the Hebrews, relations with God were corporate, as a people. The reward for a good life was to live long, have many children and have worked to sustain the people and improve the land – and be remembered by one's descendants. 'When your days are over and you rest with your ancestors, I will raise up your offspring to succeed you, your own flesh and blood, and I will establish his kingdom' (2 Sam. 7.12).

The idea of individuals surviving death was probably first imported by ancient Israel from Egypt. In Egypt the preservation of the physical body was important; the wealthy were mummified and sealed into huge stone pyramids, as close as possible to important temples. Their names and deeds were recorded in inscriptions, so that their descendants would always remember them with respect. Within Judaism, it became the practice to seal bodies into rock-cut tombs or pile a cairn of small stones on top of a grave – the more stone on top of the body and the closer it was buried to the Temple Mount, the more highly respected it was, and this remains the case today. The names of the dead were recorded on plaques inside synagogues, so that they could be remembered aloud at least once a year. In Egypt and later in Judea, the hope was that one day the physical body would be re-animated and go on to have an idealized existence.

By the first century, it was common for Jews to believe in a final judgement, when God would return to the Temple, rout the enemies of God's people, judge the living and the dead and found a new, eternal kingdom. Scholars combed the works of the prophets, searching for clues and portents.

People were not clear what would happen to the dead between the time when they died and the time of judgement. Jesus himself seems to have been unclear – saying 'Truly I say to you, today you will be with me in paradise' (Luke 23.43), while also referring to a final judgement which would take place at the end of time. Though maybe it was just the evangelists, or editors of the Gospels who had different visions of the afterlife?

In modern Christianity, there are three radically different ways of approaching life after death, resulting in confusion for many ordinary believers over what they really have faith in.

1 The idea of the **kingdom of God** which endures for ever under the lordship of the risen Christ.
2 The idea of **heaven and hell** and perhaps purgatory.
3 The idea of the **beatific vision**.

## 1. The Kingdom of God

Some Christians maintain the Jewish belief in a final judgement or *eschaton*. According to the book of Revelation, this will take place after a period of chaos; a final battle on the plains of Megiddo in northern Israel – Armageddon – will lead to the establishment of an ideal state under God's direct governance. The good will enter into the kingdom and the bad will be cast out into nothingness. People who believe in a final judgement usually believe in physical resurrection. 'For this is why Christ died and came to life, that he might be Lord of both the dead and the living' (Rom. 14.9).

As in the book of Ezekiel (37.1–14), God will raise valleys of dry bones, but this presumes that the bones are all present and together. It also raises questions over how those who died in infancy or who died after mutilation will fare. Although Orthodox Jews hope for a physical resurrection, despite these potential problems, and go to extreme lengths to ensure that the whole body of a relative is interred together. Job 19.26 claims that 'after my body has been destroyed, yet in my flesh I will see God', which might suggest a physical re-creation, not just a resurrection.

Paul, originally a Jewish Pharisee, believed in physical resurrection but gradually realized the need for such a transformation – or for the resurrection to be spiritual and not in body – if justice were to be served.[1] He wrote: 'After that, we who are still alive and are left will be caught up together with them in the clouds to meet the Lord in the air. And so we will be with the Lord for ever' (1 Thess. 4.17).

In the case of physical resurrection, re-creation or spiritual resurrection, the existence of something that is us beyond what is normally physical is presumed. Either bones can be re-animated with some sort of identity-essence, or what is resurrected is recreated into a new, maybe idealized body which retains identity after a break in time and space (replica theory) or there is some form of separable soul, containing personal identity and memories, which is resurrected (dualism).

---

1 Walter Gahan, 'The Eschatology of St Paul II', *Irish Church Quarterly* 5:19 (1912), pp. 238–49.

## Replica Theory

Critics have suggested that even if God resurrected the dead into a new body, because there would be a break in continuity there could be no sense that the person who is resurrected is the same person as the one who died. Life after death, therefore, would not really be a personal reward for faith or good works and nor could it make up for unearned suffering in life.

John Locke and Bernard Williams argue that the one sure test of identity is 'spatio-temporal continuity'. The one thing that makes you the same as the embryo in your mother's uterus, the baby you once were, the teenager, the adult and the old person in a hospice is continuity of a single body through space and time. The body may have changed radically but there is continuity through different bodily states.

The reformed epistemologist John Hick observes that this sort of physical continuity is not necessary to acknowledge the continued existence of a person after death. Hick argues that if God could create an identical copy of the person who died, complete with memories, then the claim that they have survived death is meaningful.

## Criticisms of Replica Theory

Critics argue that the replica is not really the same person.

- Imagine you were told that you would die tonight but that a replica would be produced overnight that would have all your memories and thoughts – would you feel relaxed about this?
- Monozygotic identical twins, brought up and educated together, have identical genetics, physical appearances, knowledge and memories – but are undeniably different people.
- If God recreates us in an idealized body (to make up for inequalities in terms of the age and physical conditions of people at death) there is even less sense that the replica would be the same person.
- If God erases the appalling memories some people have of abuse, torture and anguish in life, making their eternal existence more appealing, then there is even less sense of continuity in

personal identity – but if replicas have to live for ever with the memories of Auschwitz, then the idea that life after death is a reward starts to look silly.

- What is to stop a God who can create one replica from creating multiple replicas? Would each of these be the same person? The replica theory really puts strain on our sense of identity and meaning.

As a reformed epistemologist, Hick seeks less to convince us that God does create replicas than to convince us that the idea of surviving death is possible. For reformed epistemologists, faith does not depend on argument, but argument is used to 'defeat the defeaters' and show that faith is coherent.

Peter van Inwagen (b. 1942) argued against Hick's theory, writing:

Suppose a certain monastery claims to have in its possession a manuscript written in Augustine's own hand. And suppose the monks of this monastery further claim that this manuscript was burned by Arians in the year 457. It would immediately occur to me to ask how this manuscript, the one I can touch, could be the very manuscript that was burned in 457. Suppose their answer to this question is that God miraculously recreated Augustine's manuscript in 458. I should respond to this answer as follows: the deed it describes seems quite impossible, even as an accomplishment of omnipotence. God certainly might have created a perfect duplicate of the original manuscript, but it would not be that one; its earliest moment of existence would have been after Augustine's death; it would never have known the impress of his hand; it would not have been a part of the furniture of the world when he was alive; and so on.[2]

The central question is: what makes you the same person you were yesterday or in twenty years' time? If personal identity is based on spatio-temporal continuity, then life after death is impossible if one

---

2 Michael C. Rea, *Oxford Readings in Philosophical Theology: Volume 2: Providence, Scripture and Resurrection*, Oxford: Oxford University Press, 2009, p. 12.

is a monist (that is, if one holds that there is no separate soul) as spatio-temporal continuity is necessarily broken by death – unless one accepts the replica theory, in which case the replica would be the same person as the person who died. However, if identity depends on something else, maybe our memories, minds and physical appearance, then recreation could offer a means of defending the coherence of beliefs in life after death.

## Dualism

Dualism has a long history, although its most significant proponents were probably Plato and Descartes.

For Plato, human beings are made of two substances, neither of which can be reduced to or explained by the other. These substances are body and soul. Consciousness, mind and memory belong to the soul, not to the body. The soul contains *a priori* ideas, information not known from physical experience, including mathematical and logical concepts. On death, the soul separates from the body and goes before the judges and reviews the whole of the life that has just been lived. The judges will then decide in what body the soul should be reincarnated so that it can learn the lessons it failed to live in this life.

In the *Phaedo* Plato records that Socrates, when he was about to take the Hemlock, laughed at Crito's question 'In what fashion are we to bury you?' and said: 'He imagines that I am that dead body he will see in a little while . . . But . . . when I drink the poison I shall no longer remain with you, but shall go off and depart for some happy state of the blessed.'

Descartes, in *Meditations* II and VI, provided the classical argument in support of the dualist position. He wrote:

My essence consists solely in the fact that I am a thinking thing. It is true that I may have (or, to anticipate, that I certainly have) a body that is very closely joined to me. But nevertheless, on the one hand I have a clear and distinct idea of myself, in so far as I am simply a non-extended thinking thing, and on the other hand I have a distinct idea of body, in so far as this is simply an extended non-thinking thing. And accordingly, it is certain that I am really distinct from my body and can exist without it.[3]

Descartes experienced himself as a thinking thing and reasoned that this is what he, and all human beings, must also be. We can think of ourselves without a body but we cannot think of ourselves not thinking; the body can be doubted and the soul cannot. The body and soul cannot be one and the same. Norman Malcolm challenged Descartes' view, writing:

> If it were valid to argue 'I can doubt that my body exists but not that I exist, ergo I am not my body', it would be equally valid to argue 'I can doubt that there exists a being whose essential nature is to think, but I cannot doubt that I exist, ergo I am not a being whose essential nature is to think.' Descartes is hoist with his own petard.[4]

As Brian Davies O. P. put it, the fact that I consider myself to be sober does not mean that I am sober!

Nevertheless, the great advantage of dualism is that the soul is held to be both immortal and unique to human beings. Dualism dominated early Christianity and Islam; Augustine argued that God implanted a soul into every human being, and Islam still maintains this – it is this that makes human beings distinct from animals. The great attraction of dualism when considering life after death is that it overcomes the identity problem, as, while the body will rot or be burnt, the immortal soul survives, and it is this that makes a person what he or she is. However, dualism has been subject to devastating criticisms – not least from Gilbert Ryle.

---

3 VI, 54.

4 'Descartes' proof that his Essence is Thinking', Willis Doney (ed.), *Descartes: A Collection of Critical Essays*, Notre Dame, IN and London: University of Notre Dame Press, pp. 315–33.

## Criticisms of Dualism

Apart from the difficulties in explaining how the soul and body interact or what content can be given to talk of the soul in the light of increasing knowledge about the mind and its dependence on chemical processes in the brain, dualism has been subject to sustained philosophic criticism.

Gilbert Ryle in *The Concept of Mind* described the dualist view as the 'doctrine of the ghost in the machine' and said that it rests on a category mistake.[5] Ryle argues that it is a mistake to regard the soul as a substance – to think of it in these terms means placing the word in a mistaken category.

Imagine showing a foreigner a game of cricket. You show him the fielders: silly-mid-on, square leg, short leg, long leg, extra cover, mid-wicket, the wicket keeper and the bowler. You show him the batsmen and explain their order of play. He then says 'Yes, I have seen all this, but where is the team spirit?' The mistake the visitor makes is to think that 'team spirit' is something other than what he has seen. If a team lacks team spirit, it is not possible to go out and buy some in the way that one would buy another player. Instead, team spirit will only be fostered by the ways the different players work together. For Ryle 'the soul' is not another thing but a function of all the physical processes which make up a person working together.

Peter Chan in *The Mystery of Mind* argues that dualism also faces the problem of unconsciousness.[6] If memory and consciousness reside in the soul and not the brain, why is it that when a person gets tired or the brain is affected by injury or drugs, consciousness and memory are directly affected? If the soul is really separate from the brain, then surely there should be no effect at all? If it is counter-argued that the brain is necessary for the soul to have consciousness and memory, then the independence of the soul seems to be radically undermined. Either consciousness and memory do not reside in the soul (if it exists at all) or else the soul is so dependent on the brain and body that it cannot be independent of it and survive without it.

---

5  Harmondsworth: Penguin, 1990.
6  iUniverse, 2003.

If the existence of a separable soul can be established – or at least seen to be coherent – there is no need for people to wait for a final judgement or kingdom of God in time. If the soul could separate from the body at death, the fate of the body does not matter, and the soul could continue to exist, be rewarded or punished, in another dimension. It could also be reunited with a new body at the end of time (this is the traditional Catholic position) and identity would be maintained through the continuity of the soul.

## 2. Heaven and Hell

Ideas about heaven and hell have changed through the centuries.

Early beliefs focused on a single judgement and a single, eternal reward or punishment. In ancient Israel, there were ideas about a reward in 'Gan Eden' or a punishment in 'Gehinnom' – but this did not address the complex inequalities between people's lives where some endure great suffering and hardship and others live a life of comfort and ease.

There is little to suggest the existence of complex realms of reward or punishment, such as are depicted in medieval paintings and in cathedral windows, in the Bible – yet they remain part of many people's Christian faith because they serve to explain just *how* God's justice can be reconciled with the complexities of everyday life.

Of course, through parables Jesus taught that hell was associated with fire and eternal torment, while heaven was to be close to God and God's angels, perhaps living in a many-roomed palace. Faith and good actions would be rewarded, sin and doubt punished; the sheep would be divided from the goats. There would be a 'great gulf' between heaven and hell and transition from one place to another would not be possible. Even at the time, scholars questioned the logic of Jesus' teachings, setting him trick questions such as if a woman marries seven times, each time being widowed, to whom will she be married at the resurrection? Jesus brushed this pedantry aside and warned people to be ready for judgement, which would arrive suddenly, like a thief in the night.

Throughout the Middle Ages, the Church used Jesus' warnings of eternal punishment as a means of persuading people to be good and support the institution of the Church. Ever more detailed depictions of hell, now including *purgatory*, a place of temporal punishment where lesser crimes would be punished through finite sentences, were carved on buildings, painted on furniture, embroidered on tapestries and recited in poetry. Everyone in purgatory would eventually attain the beatific vision of God, but in the meantime they had to undergo great suffering to atone for their sins.

Dante's *Divine Comedy* contains the archetypal description of the hereafter, with different levels of the inferno reserved for different crimes and Satan frozen in the bottommost pit. It also tried to resolve difficult questions about this sort of afterlife.

- What would happen to good people who lived before Jesus, to good people from different religious traditions, or to unbaptized infants?
- Would every crime lead to eternal damnation – or is there hope that less serious crimes could eventually be paid off, enabling the soul to progress to heaven?

The Church started to teach that different crimes earned different sentences and that sentences might be shortened through penance in this life. Such penances started off as good works, statements of public contrition, pilgrimages – but soon came to include *indulgences*, certificates guaranteeing a certain amount of time off a sentence in purgatory in return for contrition and a financial donation to the Church.[7]

Today, preachers tend to focus on the positive side of Jesus' teaching and the hope and promise of eternal life; they often ignore the negative side. Some modern theologians argue that hell does not exist or is equivalent to annihilation, non-existence. Nevertheless, without the threat of punishment and with the promise of eternal forgiveness and acceptance, the motive for living a good life and taking religion seriously may be reduced.

---

7 It was the sale of indulgences which, rightly or wrongly, aggrieved Protestant reformers like Martin Luther.

Islam also has a clear concept of heaven and hell. In the Qur'an the faithful are promised rewards in very earthly terms: 'They shall recline on jewelled couches face to face, and there shall wait on them immortal youths with bowls and ewers and a cup of purest wine (that will neither pain their heads nor take away their reason); with fruits of their own choice and flesh of fowls that they relish' (Qur'an 56.12–39). Some of the most controversial Islamic traditions promise believers 72 virgins. Muslim philosophers such as al-Ash'ari (d. 935) and al-Ghazali (d. 1111) both discussed the sensual nature of paradise in Islam. Clearly, this implies a bodily resurrection which is somewhat hedonistic.

## Criticism

If heaven is a place in space and time, then this involves having a body which can exist in space and time. If heaven also involves dwelling in the presence of God and the angels, then this implies a God who is in space and time. This is the view held today by most Protestant Christian theologians and also by mainstream Islam. However, there are considerable philosophic problems with this position, as well as considerable advantages. While a God who might have a body and who could change on some level fits in well with the univocal language in most sacred books, if God really is in time and space, then critics will hold that God is limited and too anthropomorphic to be worthy of worship.

Further, given that there is limited scriptural basis for the complex doctrines of heaven and hell, they could be argued to be speculations about what might or might not happen after death rather than a clear proclamation of what does happen.

## 3. The Beatific Vision

The idea of a life after death in time and space suffers from considerable problems – not least the question of boredom. What would the blessed do after 10,000 years in heaven? Conceiving this form of existence (whether bodily or as a disembodied soul) is fraught with difficulties.

A philosophically convincing alternative is available, and this is directly related to the idea of God as being wholly simple, timeless, bodiless and utterly unchanging. Many of the great Islamic philosophers held this view, as did Thomas Aquinas and the mainstream Catholic Christian tradition. If God is beyond time and space, then the idea of God as the Lord of a temporal kingdom of God or a temporal heaven no longer makes sense. The final end for human beings lies in the contemplation of God in the timeless beatific vision. The third-century theologian Cyprian of Carthage wrote: 'How great will your glory and happiness be, to be allowed to see God.'

The destiny of human beings lies in becoming timeless and spaceless and 'seeing God' directly. There can be no question of boredom as there is no longer any time – instead human destiny lies in the beatific vision which is wholly satisfying. Human beings no longer have bodies, but are beyond time and space – just as God is. It is, of course, almost impossible to imagine such a form of existence.

Thomas Aquinas wrote: 'Man is not perfectly happy, so long as something remains for him to desire and seek.'[8] And 'But this kind of perfect happiness cannot be found in any physical pleasure, any amount of worldly power, any degree of temporal fame or honor, or indeed in any finite reality. It can only be found in something that is infinite and perfect – and this is God.'[9] Biblical passages seem to reflect this – for instance:

- 'Blessed are the pure in heart, for they will see God' (Matt. 5.8).
- 'For now we see only a reflection as in a mirror; then we shall see face to face. Now I know in part; then I shall know fully, even as I am fully known' (1 Cor. 13.12).
- 'They will see his face, and his name will be on their foreheads' (Rev. 22.4).
- 'As for me, I will be vindicated and will see your face' (Psalm 17.15).

---

8  *Summa Theologica* 1, 2, q.3, a.8.
9  *Summa Theologica* 1, 2, q.2, a.8.

The Catholic tradition came to develop three main ends for human life:

- The timeless beatific vision of God – this is the final destiny of all those who faithfully believe and follow God.
- Purgatory – a temporal realm of cleansing and punishment where the human being is purified from sin. Everyone who enters purgatory will eventually achieve the beatific vision.
- Hell – a place of eternal exile from God which is temporal and everlasting.

In a personal capacity, Pope John XXII (1316–34) argued that those who are saved do not reach the beatific vision until judgement day. He never proclaimed his belief as doctrine but rather as an opinion. Pope Benedict XII later declared it doctrine that the saved see God and heaven before judgement day.

The Catholic Christian tradition holds that there will be an initial judgement on death, when most people will go to purgatory or to hell (a very few, such as the Virgin Mary, go directly to the beatific vision without needing to pass through purgatory), and then a second, general judgement when those who are living and those who have died will be judged. After this judgement, the soul will be given a new and glorified body and will enter into the beatific vision.


## Criticism

There is a clear problem here. What possible identity could the individual have, if he or she is literally timeless and spaceless? Whatever our identity criteria may be, they seem to be based on bodily identity and/or memory. If there is no memory (because we are timeless) and no body, then what would make whatever survives death the same person as the one who died? One possible answer is to say that the individual lives for ever in the memory of God, but this seems to deny personal immortality.

Also, both Christian and Islamic scriptures and creeds refer to bodily resurrection. Arguing that there is to be no such resurrection necessitates a reinterpretation of texts to allow for such references to the metaphorical. This is what the great Aristotelian Islamic philosophers did – but they were criticized for so doing by al-Ghazali and others, as it means rejecting a literal reading of the Qu'ran. Protestant theologians, in wanting to abide by 'the plain word of scripture', have rejected the idea of the beatific vision and held to a heaven in time and space, which, of course, fits in well with the idea of God in time.

## Science and the Survival of Death . . .

Atheists will almost always be monist materialists – they will utterly reject dualism and will argue that any sense of 'soul', 'mind' or 'consciousness' is just the product of physical processes.

Francis Crick, one of the two discoverers of the DNA double helix, devoted much of his life to explaining consciousness in material terms. He accepted that his material hypothesis was an astonishing claim. Who we are, our loves, joys, sorrows and tears are no more than the mechanical interaction of nerve cells and electrical impulses which, in theory at least, science will one day be able to explain – and yet he maintained that it must be correct. The strongly atheistic philosopher Daniel Dennett argued that all subjective experience is an illusion. He wrote (the emphasis is his):

> I adopt the apparently dogmatic rule that dualism is to be avoided AT ALL COSTS. It is not that I think I can give a knock down proof that dualism, in all its forms, is false or incoherent, but that, given the way that dualism wallows in mystery, ACCEPTANCE OF DUALISM IS GIVING UP.[10]

Despite the strength of most atheists' monist, materialist belief, it is as difficult to prove that a separable soul does not exist as to prove

10  *Consciousness Explained*, London: Penguin, 1991 in Ch. 4.

that it exists. Dualism refuses to die, not least because we all have the sense that what it means to be 'me' is more than and other than the material body which I inhabit.

Science has not even begun to explain the existence of consciousness or how pure matter can give rise to consciousness with all that this means in terms of the richness of human experience. The debate, therefore, between monist materialism and dualism is very much current and central to what it means to be human.

## Dual-aspect Monism

A number of major philosophers have argued that there is one reality (they are thus monists) but there are two aspects to this reality – the material and the spiritual. Baruch Spinoza (1632–77) was one of the most prominent philosophers to hold this position, although he was in advance of his time and was regarded by some within his own Jewish community as an atheist, because he denied the independent reality of God. Other philosophers who can be broadly grouped under this heading include Arthur Schopenhauer (1788–1860) and, more recently, John Polkinghorne (b. 1930). Polkinghorne argues that scientists and theologians both look at the same reality and both seek truth, but they emphasize different aspects. He rejects the materialism of atheists like Richard Dawkins, as they focus on only one aspect of reality, and he sees discussion of the brain, the mind and the soul as all focusing on the same single reality – but a material explanation alone will only provide a partial and incomplete understanding.

## Quantum Reality

Nils Bohr (1885–1962) was one of the greatest physicists of the twentieth century and one of the founders of quantum mechanics. He was one of the first to argue that consciousness may be explainable in terms of the way the brain works at the quantum level; quantum entanglement and superposition theory may be able to explain consciousness and the sense that the self is other than just the body.

The physicists Roger Penrose and Stuart Hameroff worked together to develop the idea that the brain functions as a quantum computer to produce the theory known as Orchestrated Objective Reduction. Penrose's book *The Emperor's New Mind* argued that the brain has the capacity to perform in a way that exceeds any basic, material explanation.[11] A computer is driven simply by algorithms but the brain can do more than this – the term he gave to this was 'processing that was non-computable'. This is an important idea, as if it was the case then human beings are essentially different from computers and the self-consciousness of humans cannot be explained purely in conventional, physical terms.

Penrose and Hammeroff have suggested that out-of-body experiences (and possibly near-death experiences) could be explained by particles in the brain having equivalents outside the body, in the way that quantum particles can exist in two places at once, activity in one place being mirrored in another by an unknown means. Even if this were the case, it would remain open to question whether such entanglement between the body and beyond the body could persist after death and, therefore, whether it provides any fertile ground for explaining claims to life after death.

Henry Staff (b. 1928) in *Mindful Universe: Quantum Mechanics and the Participating Observer*[12] argued that quantum waves collapse when they interact with consciousness, due to conscious brains choosing one among alternative possibilities as a basis for future action. The advent of quantum science opens up new ways of exploring consciousness and, perhaps, may make the old categorization of monism and dualism inadequate. It is also related to the final issue that needs consideration, monist idealism.

## Monist Idealism

Almost all monists are materialists. They believe that human beings are just one substance (therefore they are monists) and that

11  Roger Penrose, *The Emperor's New Mind: Concerning Computer, Minds and the Laws of Physics*, Oxford: Oxford University Press, 1989.
12  New York: Springer, 2011.

substance is matter (therefore they are materialists). There is, however, an alternative which is deeply unfashionable and seems at first
sight to be ridiculous.

The alternative is monist idealism. Supporters of this view maintain that there is one substance but, instead of this substance being
matter, they hold that it is mind or consciousness.

In 480 BCE, Anaxagoras argued that everything was created by,
and depended on, mind. Consciousness or mind held the cosmos
together, and all human beings were thereby depended on or related
to God. On this view, all of reality is mind dependent.

In Chapter 2, we considered the ideas of W. K. Clifford who, surprisingly, was a monist idealist. Clifford was influenced by, among
others, Bishop George Berkeley (1685–1753), who argued that *esse
est percipi* – to exist is to be perceived. For Berkeley, all material
reality depends on consciousness. At first sight, this seems absurd,
but the more we understand about the quantum world the more
plausible it becomes. We now know that the very act of observing
a quantum event changes the event. It is not possible to observe a
quantum event without affecting it. It may be that, at the quantum
level, the immense fields of potential electrons (not real electrons but
potential electrons) are given reality by being observed.

Hildegard of Bingen (1098–1179) was a German abbess who cor-
responded with poets and popes and who had a series of extraordinary visions which she had captured in paint. Hildegard saw the
Holy Spirit as the fire that suffused the whole of the universe and
gave it its energy. If consciousness is, indeed, primary in the universe
rather than matter this theological idea may have new relevance.
It could be that if consciousness is primary, then the whole idea of
what it may mean to be human will need re-evaluation and, with it,
the whole idea of life after death.

In a book of this length, it is not possible to do justice to what
is an emerging line of enquiry and, obviously, it connects closely
to quantum views of reality, but it remains a position that, in the
future, may become much more influential than it is today, and, if so,
it will challenge our most basic understanding of reality and of what
it means to be human. It could, therefore, change the debate about

life after death. If consciousness is primary and not matter and if consciousness could survive death (and this is a very major assumption), then the plausibility of life after death would greatly increase.

## Summary

The idea of life after death is crucial to most religions but it is directly related to the question of human identity and to questions about God's nature. Neither, as we have seen, are easy to answer.

Supporters of a temporal God will hold to a heaven and hell that is also in time and space – an everlasting kingdom of happiness and peace or everlasting torment. Supporters of a wholly simple God will see the final end for human beings in terms of existing within a timeless beatific vision or permanent exile from God. Nevertheless, both approaches suffer from real difficulties.

In philosophical terms, neither approach provides a clear way of understanding how an individual could be rewarded and punished, how God's justice could be enacted beyond this life, while still maintaining a coherent concept of God and respect for scriptural and prophetic revelations.

In religious terms, neither approach is ultimately compatible with all the biblical or Qur'anic references and traditions that have accumulated. Without at least a philosophically and religiously coherent understanding of what life after death entails, it is difficult to defend having faith that such claims to life after death are true. This may, of course, be a function of our lack of understanding rather than any clear statement that life after death is not possible.

There is no direct evidence of the afterlife. Believing in something that cannot be defined on the basis of a lack of clear evidence could be problematic, pushing faith well beyond propositional and even non-propositional interpretations into the realm of fideism. Nevertheless, without life after death the problems of evil and suffering become all the more acute and believers will struggle to maintain faith in God's goodness, justice or power – or belief that their worship and behaviour will make any real difference in the end.

# Conclusion

# God Matters!

Stone walls do not a prison make, nor iron-bars a cage;
Minds innocent and quiet take that for a hermitage.
                    (Richard Lovelace, 'To Althea from Prison')

God matters. Throughout history, billions of people have devoted their lives to God, God is that in which they live and move and have their being, but God is not just a question of anthropological interest. Freud saw the question of God as the most important that any human being could address, although he was a lifelong atheist. The passion of Richard Dawkins shows that even the non-existence of God is significant.

If God exists, there is meaning, purpose and order in the universe, whether or not we understand it. Freedom may be real; we may have the potential to decide how to live and how to die, what sort of person to become. Human lives are significant; the struggles against evil and to uncover the way things are really matter. Death becomes an 'awfully big adventure' (Peter Pan), and our human perspective may not be an eternal prison. We should not get waylaid by language; the question of God is ultimately that of truth, whether there is an ultimate reality beyond how things appear to us.

If God does not exist, then human beings could seem like robot vehicles blindly programmed to preserve the selfish molecules known as genes (to paraphrase Richard Dawkins). Our perception of order, purpose, freedom and meaning might seem like an evolutionary adaptation that once gave us a survival advantage. We can make the best of things by promoting a humane agenda, engaging with truth as we see it rather than subverting or ignoring it, but in the end it might be hard to see how it really matters.

Thomas Nagel wrote that if, in the end 'there is no reason to believe that anything matters, then that does not matter either, and we can approach our absurd lives with irony instead of heroism or despair'.[1] Living in relation to nothingness means that the only choices are whether to postpone death, whether to find our trilobitic state funny or tragic. On the other hand, living in relation to the light might just open up possibilities.

God's existence cannot be proven. Mostly, our eyes are too primitive. The arguments are all flawed. Ten leaky buckets do not necessarily hold water better than one. Yet, God still seems like the best explanation to many intelligent people.

Faith cannot stand or fall by the evidence because the evidence is insufficient. Evidence cannot adequately support belief or conclusively destroy it. Goethe remarked that '[t]he greatest act of faith takes place when a man finally decides that he is not God . . .', but we feel that the greater act of faith is when a man finally decides that he *is* God. Atheism involves a leap of faith as much as theism. While there is an absence of evidence for God, absence of evidence is in no way evidence of absence. When scientific materialism fails to account for the totality of experience we must at least be open to alternative or additional approaches.

Further, drifting through life without thinking is *de facto* atheism, as insupportable and potentially dangerous as any irrational, unchallenged faith might be. Søren Kierkegaard wrote:

By seeing the multitude of people around it, by being busied with all sorts of worldly affairs, by being wise in the ways of the world, such a person forgets himself, in a divine sense forgets his own name, dares not believe in himself, finds being himself too risky, finds it much easier and safer to be like others, to become a copy, a number, alone with the crowd. Now this form of despair goes practically unnoticed in the world.[2]

---

1 'The Absurd', *Journal of Philosophy* 68:20 (1971), pp. 716–27.

2 *The Sickness unto Death*, quoted in *Provocations: Spiritual Writings of Søren Kierkegaard*, Plough Publishing House, 1999, p. 136.

We are all committed to the journey of life. We have to decide how to live. We have no choice. Pascal and James were right; God matters because the decision is forced and truly momentous. The view *sub specie aeternitatis* is fundamentally different from the view from nowhere.

In the end, 'deep in each man is the knowledge that Something knows of his existence. Something knows, and cannot be fled nor hid from . . .',[3] whatever that Something is. Is it better to try to ignore that Mystery, to live as if it certainly does not exist and to lose out on the possibilities it might offer, or to embrace it, however difficult that might be, and be open to meaning and ultimate Truth?

---

3  Cormac McCarthy, *The Crossing*, New York: Alfred A. Knopf, 1994, p. 148.

# Index